50 lessons

Maththatmatters 2

a teacher resource linking math and social justice

by David Stocker

Maththatmatters 2 gets to the very root of what education is about: giving students the tools to better understand their world and facilitate positive social change. David Stocker's groundbreaking work provides educators and students with timely and engaging lesson plans, designed for grades 6-9, using math to teach about social justice in a way that is both accessible and powerful.

....

BTL

UNIFOR
Local567

Founded in 1980 and with provincial offices in British Columbia, Saskatchewan, Manitoba, Ontario, and Nova Scotia, the Ottawa-based Canadian Centre for Policy Alternatives is Canada's leading independent progressive think tank.

The Canadian Centre for Policy Alternatives would like to express sincere and ongoing appreciation to our supporters, and to our network of research associates who so generously give of their time, energy and expertise. Thanks also to the CCPA staff.

Many thanks to the Elementary Teachers' Federation of Ontario — and their longstanding commitment to social justice and public education — whose support helped make this book a reality.

The opinions expressed in Maththatmatters 2 are those of the author, and do not necessarily reflect the views of the CCPA.

Maththatmatters 2

© 2015, 2017, 2019 David Stocker

First published in 2017 by
The Canadian Centre for Policy Alternatives
141 Laurier Ave. West, Suite 1000
Ottawa, ON K1P 5J3
Canada

Between the Lines
401 Richmond Street West
Studio 281
Toronto, Ontario M5V 3A8
Canada
1-800-718-7201
www.btlbooks.com

Library and Archives Canada Cataloguing in Publication

Stocker, David, 1972-, author
    Maththatmatters. 2 : a teacher resource linking math and social justice
/ by David Stocker.

ISBN 978-1-77125-312-3 (softcover)

    1. Mathematics--Study and teaching (Middle school)--Social aspects.
2. Mathematics--Problems, exercises, etc. 3. Social justice--Study and
teaching (Middle school). I. Canadian Centre for Policy Alternatives,
issuing body II. Title. III. Title: Math that matters. 2.

QA135.6.S76 2017   510.71'2   C2016-907850-7

Typesetting and Design: Nancy Reid (nrgrafix.com)
Printed in Canada by RR Donnelly

dedicated to

jazz, kio, storm
and
rogue

o o o

your basic average super star
is singing about justice
and peace
and love
and I am glaring at the radio,
swearing saying
that's just what I was afraid of

~ ANI DIFRANCO

Acknowledgements

I have heard that it's possible to write a book in the span of a year. This collection of lessons has taken me over a decade, in large part because creating a family is no small feat and that is what I have been up to. For those of you who are parents, you may appreciate the fuzziness of mind that goes along with the journey, and likewise my apology to those I fail to mention below. I promise it's not personal.

I have had the good fortune of working with many talented colleagues whom undoubtedly pushed my understanding of issues to greater depths: James Bryers, Janis Cadieux, Colleen Costa, Antonino Giambrone, David Finkelstein, Sue Freypons, Carolyn Jankovskis, Sheena Matheson, Anne McKenna, Hayley Mezei, Michelle Munk, Maria Pasquino, Rico Rodriguez, Christine Saraceno, Nancy Steele, Biljana Svilaric, Shawna Watson, Demitra Zervas as well as dozens of inspiring teacher candidates from York University and OISE. I am grateful to the instructional leaders and professors at universities across Ontario who have graciously invited me in to do workshops on mathematics and social justice: your work gives me hope.

Michelle Munk and Salima Kassam offered many thoughtful revisions to my work and reminded me that the lessons written nine years ago needed updating (apparently the statistics had changed). I appreciate your support. Thanks to Nancy Reid for pulling the pieces into a functional and aesthetic whole, and Minnow Holtz-Carriere for the witty and incisive illustrations that go along with each lesson. Melanie Allison has always been very patient with me, and Erika Shaker has consistently supported my writing and activism: both work at the Canadian Centre for Policy Alternatives. I'm also happy to have the team at Between The Lines working on this book: a lovely, inspiring group of people.

Many thanks to the students at City View past and present for always asking the questions "Why do we have to know this?" and "How will I ever use this in my life?" As frustrating and humbling as that always is, your persistence nevertheless also functions as my encouragement.

Thanks to friends and family: Denise and Lisa, Mom, Dad and Lori, Kevin and Helen, Bob and Valerie, Shelly and Tuval, Jenny and Mark. And especially Emma.

It is difficult to convey the magnitude of my appreciation for my co-conspirator and source of ongoing inspiration, Rogue. It is in the fabric of our lives together that many of the seeds for these lessons appeared. While I may have typed the words, they are ultimately a product of our collaborative efforts and late night discussions over two decades. Our three children, Jazz, Kio and Storm, all activists in their own right, have also enriched my life and have been a source of inspiration. I'm sure they will change the world.

Thanks so much to you all.

Contents: 50 *more* lessons linking math and social justice

Answers: Lessons 1-18

Answers: Lessons 19-36

Answers: Lessons 37-50

Introduction

I like turning over rocks. It's not knowing what's underneath and being surprised by what I discover that motivates me.

Today, my class and I are reading the Upstream/Downstream allegory, as described by Cathy Crowe, a Toronto street nurse. The no-nonsense version is that a community of people living along a riverbank start to notice bodies floating by and, without a shred of time to spare, throw in a rope and pull them out.

Except over the following weeks, the bodies keep coming.

The community responds admirably, with compassion. They train rescue crews, mobilize round-the-clock volunteers, and raise funds to build an on-site hospital. As their success rate goes up, so too their notoriety. Articles and national conferences lead to awards and further funding.

What's missing, of course, is the fact that nobody questions why the bodies are in the river in the first place. What is happening upstream? What are the consequences of devoting all of our efforts entirely to downstream interventions?

The students are turning these rocks over in their heads. "Donations to food banks: upstream or down?" I ask.

"Down," spoken firmly from the back of the room.

"Giving food to someone sitting on the street?" I ask again.

"Down."

"Collections of clothes to give to the Syrian refugees arriving this month?"

"Down."

"Raising money to find a cure for cancer."

"Down. I think. Maybe."

> What's missing, of course, is the fact that nobody questions why the bodies are in the river in the first place. What is happening upstream?

> As social justice has entered the mainstream, the connection to mathematics has followed. People see it in their everyday lives… scratch the surface and you'll be speaking mathematics.

"I'm confused, David. Why did we go out and collect money for women's shelters last week. Is that all for nothing?"

It's an interesting question. Each year, our students raise thousands of dollars for local women's shelters as the culminating task following a couple months of gender studies. The money pays for clothing and food and toys for the children's programs in the shelters.

"People are going to need those shelters in the short term," says one student, "but we've been talking about the construction of masculinity...."

"And femininity," I squeak in.

"...it's like the upstream solutions to violence against women have to be challenging those social constructions. From very early on."

∘ ∘ ∘

A lot has happened in the years since I first wrote **Maththatmatters**. I used to go to conferences where people would look at me strangely for suggesting that math and social justice are intimately connected. Not so anymore. As social justice has entered the mainstream, the connection to mathematics has followed. People see it in their everyday lives, whether it's patterns pertaining to global warming, or the economics of the austerity movement; scratch the surface and you'll be speaking mathematics.

But what has also happened is that social justice work with students has leaned heavily on the downstream solutions. Some people call it "social justice lite", or "social justice cool": the things that we do that we feel pretty good about and that seem to improve people's lives. Who could argue about engaging young students in the excitement and positivity of collecting 10 boxes of food for the local food bank? "Surely something is better than nothing, right?"

Maybe.

But buried in one of the 50 lessons in this book is a mathematical exploration of the iatrogenic effect. 'Pointed Questions' looks at what might happen if people who have cervixes are encouraged to get the HPV vaccination, and then think that they are immune to the human papilloma virus (they are not: there are 200 strains of it). Imagine those people deciding that they no longer needed a Pap test every three years, and instead of the cervical cancer rate going down, it went up.

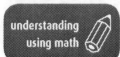

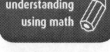

Metaphorically speaking, that's what we need to avoid.

o o o

I went to a talk given by Umair Muhammad, who spoke passionately about the problem with individualist approaches to justice issues, wherein people eat less meat, bike more often, and stop drinking bottled water. Capitalism is delighted by these acts of 'conscious consumerism' and 'lifestyle changes', primarily because they are not a bridge to challenging the roots of injustice, but rather "a distraction". Downstream waters are not only saturated with Sisyphean "activism", but so too have we been convinced that in order to change the world, we must focus on changing ourselves.

I hear the laughter and clinking of wine glasses coming from corporate boardrooms.

The "Call to Action" section of each lesson has therefore concerned me to no end. How do we keep our eye on and meaningfully engage in upstream solutions with youth? Can we learn to collectively fight broader battles and side step the lure of feel-good food drives?

o o o

There are, I suspect, many ways to use **Maththatmatters** lessons with questionable impact. Without knowing the issues of justice that are important to your students, it's hard to imagine that the lessons are necessarily going to mean anything or engage anyone in direct action. Students in Tennessee may indeed face problems similar to young people in Toronto, and probably vastly different ones as well. If it turns out that none of the lessons resonate with the students in front of you, I recommend that you put the book down and mine the classroom for issues that make them passionate or angry.

No lesson is meant to capture the complexity or entirety of the justice topic. They are meant as introductions to a whole world of interesting questions and as such are opportunities to stop along the way when more complex, engaging, or vastly different directions appear from the group. There are days where my lesson develops around a single question from a lesson. And I can rarely anticipate when it will be that way.

The concept of intersectionality has found its way more regularly into discussions about justice, and within lessons it's a good idea to remember that we come to the table with multiple identities and complex layered barriers. It's not good enough to talk, for example, about women's rights. Women have different

In the spirit of upstream solutions, let's also make sure that identity politics inform but don't supplant or cloak the broader challenges to the system.

18

> The connections between lessons are almost more important than the individual lessons themselves.

skin colours, different body parts, different sexualities, different physical abilities, different levels of wealth, and when those complexities and many others come together, we get a more complete picture of what's going on and how to change it. At the same time, and in the spirit of upstream solutions, let's also make sure that identity politics inform but don't supplant or cloak the broader challenges to the system.

Lessons are not designed to stand apart from other lessons. I'd suggest that the connections between lessons are almost more important than the individual lessons themselves. Discussions with students in the second half of the school year inevitably turn out to be far more interesting as learners pull from a much greater range of experiences and ideas. Stop and ask, "How does this relate to what you learned in history last week?" or "Which science unit brought similar questions into this space?"

o o o

I have been turning over rocks for almost 20 years now, and have met a fine group of co-conspirators along the way. Although faced with big challenges that will require complex and creative thinking, I am more hopeful today than at any point in the past that students will be able to make the world kinder and more just. And if mathematics can play a part in that transformation, all the better.

So go ahead.

Turn over some rocks.

DAVID

Lessons Overview: 1-25

Lesson	Page	Number Sense & Numeration	Measurement	Geometry & Spatial Sense	Algebra	Data Management & Probability	Class/Poverty	Gender	Race/Ethnicity	Age/Youth	Ability	Workplace	Big Business	Sexuality	Civics/Community	Intersectionality	Environment
1. Canada: Peacekeeper or Profiteer?	22	✓				✓							✓			✓	
2. Tar-Nished	30	✓	✓		✓	✓			✓				✓				✓
3. Pointed Questions	36	✓			✓	✓	✓			✓			✓	✓		✓	
4. Little Do We Know	41				✓												✓
5. Fear	45	✓				✓		✓	✓				✓				✓
6. All that Glitters	48	✓				✓						✓	✓				✓
7. Exhaust-ed	53	✓	✓	✓		✓				✓						✓	✓
8. Spilled	58		✓		✓												✓
9. Thin	62	✓				✓	✓				✓				✓	✓	
10. Unsettling	65					✓			✓								✓
11. Beyond Left & Right	70			✓			✓						✓		✓		
12. Well Spoke-n	75	✓	✓												✓		✓
13. Jux-tice	78					✓	✓										
14. Bridge Over Troubled Waters	82		✓	✓					✓				✓		✓	✓	✓
15. Exit Strategy	86	✓	✓			✓							✓				✓
16. Cross Roads	91	✓	✓						✓								✓
17. Take A Peak	94				✓								✓				✓
18. Shark Infested Waters	98	✓					✓		✓				✓				
19. Mapping Access	103	✓	✓	✓			✓								✓		✓
20. Unity	106	✓	✓	✓		✓	✓	✓					✓		✓	✓	
21. The (Bottom) Line	109		✓	✓									✓				✓
22. Fare Prices	114	✓			✓		✓								✓		
23. Bitter	117	✓	✓		✓		✓			✓		✓	✓			✓	
24. Washed Up	120	✓	✓	✓			✓					✓	✓			✓	
25. Under Threat	124	✓				✓		✓			✓	✓					

Lesson	Page	Number Sense & Numeration	Measurement	Geometry & Spatial Sense	Algebra	Data Management & Probability	Class/Poverty	Gender	Race/Ethnicity	Age/Youth	Ability	Workplace	Big Business	Sexuality	Civics/Community	Intersectionality	Environment
		Mathematics Strand					Justice Topic										
26. Collapse	130	✓					✓						✓				
27. Where Can They Bee?	134	✓				✓							✓				✓
28. Buffet	137	✓	✓			✓	✓		✓			✓	✓			✓	✓
29. Earthship	143	✓	✓	✓	✓	✓											✓
30. Bay of the Beaver	147	✓	✓	✓	✓				✓				✓				✓
31. Tough Call	151	✓	✓		✓	✓	✓			✓		✓	✓		✓	✓	✓
32. WTF? (What the Frack?)	155	✓	✓		✓	✓							✓				✓
33. David and Goliath	160	✓	✓		✓												✓
34. Trans[form]	163	✓			✓	✓		✓	✓	✓				✓		✓	
35. Missing	168	✓			✓	✓	✓	✓	✓	✓		✓			✓		
36. Up Front	174				✓		✓						✓				✓
37. Mouseprint	177	✓				✓							✓				
38. Tipping Point	180	✓	✓			✓							✓				✓
39. Get Out The Lead	184	✓	✓		✓					✓			✓		✓		✓
40. The Cat in the Coalmine	187	✓			✓	✓			✓	✓		✓	✓			✓	✓
41. Pillaging the Public Purse (P3s)	191	✓			✓	✓						✓	✓			✓	
42. Damned	195		✓	✓					✓						✓		✓
43. Pad-dling Upstream	199	✓	✓		✓	✓		✓		✓			✓				✓
44. Vice Grip	202	✓										✓	✓				✓
45. The Drone of War	206	✓	✓				✓			✓						✓	
46. Layers	210	✓					✓	✓	✓	✓	✓			✓		✓	
47. The Threat of a Good Example	213	✓										✓	✓		✓	✓	
48. Sweet and Dangerous	216	✓	✓		✓		✓		✓							✓	
49. Unplug	219	✓			✓	✓	✓	✓	✓	✓						✓	
50. Paying for It	222	✓			✓	✓	✓	✓				✓					

21

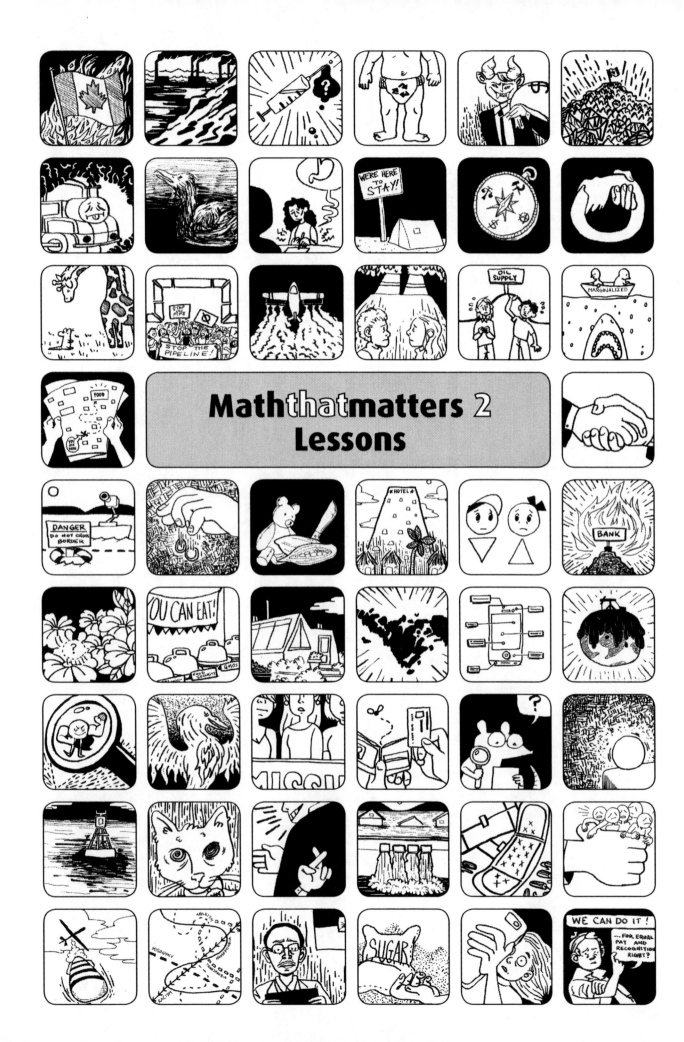

Maththatmatters 2
Lessons

Excel formulas

Canada: Peacekeeper or Profiteer?

"For the powerful, crimes are those that others commit."

~ NOAM CHOMSKY

25

setting the stage

In December of 1997, the Ottawa Treaty opened for signatures at the United Nations. Instigated by Canada, it banned the production, use and trade of anti-personnel landmines. Each year, thousands of civilians worldwide are killed or injured by exploding landmines[1], so it was no surprise, perhaps, that less than a year and a half later the Treaty became international law. One hundred and twenty-two countries signed the document, and Canada was heralded as a peacekeeper.

Historically, landmines were built in World War I to destroy a new war machine: the tank. Soldiers could easily remove anti-tank mines, so landmines were built to protect these anti-tank mines. These anti-personnel weapons were then used to block roads and bridges, water sources, and to terrorize communities.

When you turn 18, and if you are working, mandatory deductions from your paycheques will go to the Canadian government. The Canadian Pension Plan Investment Board (CPPIB) will take that money, invest it, and when you retire, will give it back to you in monthly instalments. This is a social program to make sure that people who are not working have money to live on after retirement.

In 1997, the Liberal government enacted a law to allow the CPPIB to invest money in the stock market. The CPPIB invests your money in corporations that are highly profitable, so that you in turn will retire with more money. Some of the companies that it invests in sell tobacco, alcohol, oil, and... weapons. In fact, $2.5 billion of pension plan money is sitting in the hands of over 100 foreign and Canadian weapons manufacturers. And as you may have guessed by this point, some of those weapons manufacturers make landmines.[2]

What do you think Noam Chomsky is saying in the opening quote? Can you think of any examples that support his idea when you think about powerful people or governments?

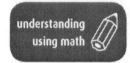

1. Enter the following table into a spreadsheet.

Who is hurt by landmines?[3]				
People killed and injured annually by landmines	Number of Civilians	Number of Combatants	Number of Civilians (Children)	Number of Civilians (Adults)
20,000				

2. Over 80% of those killed or injured by landmines are civilians. Type the following formula into cell B3: "=A3*0.80". Explain in words what the formula is asking the computer to do.

3. What equation would you put in cell C3 to get the number of combatants?

4. One third of those killed or injured by landmines are children. In cell D3 type in the following formula: "=A3*0.3333" and format cell D3 so that there are no decimals. Explain why it doesn't make sense to have a decimal answer.

5. If you assume that all children are civilians, then how many killed or injured are innocent adults? Use a formula in cell E3 to get your answer.

6. Create a pie graph using the data in cells C, D and E to show the breakdown of the people who are hurt or killed by landmines each year. Don't forget a title and have the program show the percentages next to each pie piece on the pie graph. Print out both the pie graph and the chart on the same sheet of paper.

7.a. Enter the following table[4] into a spreadsheet and create a three-dimensional bar graph showing some of the questionable investments made by the CPPIB. Make sure to include a title and x and y axis labels. Print out both the table and the bar graph on the same sheet.

Some Questionable CPP Investments[4]		
Tobacco Stocks	GAP, Walmart, Nike, Nortel	Weapons Manufacturers
$100,000,000	$350,000,000	$2,500,000,000

7.b. Name the groups of people who might be opposed to each of the three categories of investments from the table in 7.a.

7.c. The above table contains data from the CPPIB's 2004 report. Do some investigative research to find out what the most current values are.

8. The following table shows CPPIB investments in corporations that specifically produce landmines (as opposed to weapons in general), from a report put out in 2003.

   a. Create the table in a spreadsheet.

   b. Highlight the investment column and the corporation column and use the sort function to sort from least to greatest investment value.

   c. Highlight the investment values and one blank cell underneath for the total and use the "sum" function key to get the total.

   d. Have the spreadsheet calculate the mean and the median for you in the appropriate cells, using formulas.

   e. Create a bar graph of the data and print it out.

   f. If you wanted to pressure the CPPIB to divest its investments in corporations that produce landmines, where would you put most of your energy into, based on the data in this chart? Explain your answer.

Canadian Pension Plan Investments in Corporations Producing Landmines[5]	
Corporation	Investment
General Electric Company	137,326,000
Raytheon	2,940,000
Texas Instruments (subsidiary Unitrode)	17,059,000
Rockwell (subsidiary Allen-Bradley)	1,176,000
Total:	
Mean:	
Median:	

Bonus: Find the most current investments in these corporations. Are you surprised by the changes?

9. The CPPIB gives two reasons that it does not divest its investments in alcohol, oil, tobacco and weapons. Following each reason, try to give some evidence to either support their position or an example that challenges their position.

a. "The laws that tell the CPPIB what it can or can't do don't allow the CPPIB to use ethical standards in their investment choices."

b. "It is impossible to invest using ethical standards on behalf of 16 million people, because they have such a wide cross-section of personal beliefs, and we'll never get everyone to agree with what is ethical and what is not."

10. Find a definition for the word "hypocrisy" in the dictionary.

a. Give an example of hypocrisy.

b. Do you think that the CPPIB investments in landmine-producing corporations are hypocritical? Why or why not?

11. Explain mathematically (with hypothetical numbers) or by marking up the graph below (or even better, both) how the following could be possible:

a. General Electric's production of landmines is 1% of its entire product line and that's a bigger amount than Raytheon, whose landmine production is 40% of its products.

b. Raytheon produces more landmines than General Electric.

c. It might be easier to pressure for divestment from Rockwell than General Electric.

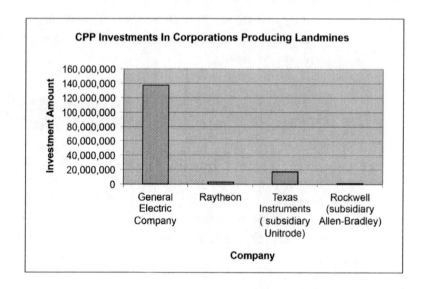

make it better

The CPPIB maintains that because it is a shareholder in some of the corporations that have been criticized, it can use its proxy voting power at annual shareholder meetings to hold them accountable.

Contact the CPPIB and ask them to send a representative to your classroom. Research the Board's investment decisions and proxy voting record prior to the visit.

Explore the work of Control Arms at **http://controlarms.org/**.

Endnotes

1. http://www.the-monitor.org/en-gb/home.aspx
2. Banking on War, *NOW Magazine*, August 12-18, 2004 pp 22-24.
3. www.canadianlandmine.org
4. https://nowtoronto.com/news/banking-on-war/
5. http://www.vivelecanada.ca/article/101709523-cpp-landmine-investments-are-we-breaking-the-global-ban-treaty

Ratios
Proportions

Tar-Nished

"You know you are at the bottom of the ninth when you have to schlep a tonne of sand to get a barrel of oil."

~ JEFF RUBIN, CIBC'S CHIEF ECONOMIST

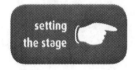
setting the stage

Ten years ago, people called them "tar sands". Now the petroleum industry calls them "oil sands".[1] They make Canada home to the third largest oil reserve in the entire world, with 170 billion barrels of oil trapped in a mechanical mixture of 83% sand, 3% clay, 4% water and 10% bitumen.[2]

Twenty percent of the tar sands are less than 100 metres deep and so in these areas the forests can be clear-cut, the wetlands can be drained, and the rock and soil can be taken off to get at the resource below. Industry calls this "**overburden**".[3] It takes 2,000 kilograms of tar sands to create a single barrel (136 kg) of synthetic crude oil.

The oil is processed and then the idea is to ship it to the Pacific Coast by a proposed pipeline called the Northern Gateway Pipeline. What gets left behind are huge tailings ponds — the remnants of the petroleum processing, including naphthenic acid, which is toxic to the liver and brain of mammals.[4] First Nations communities living downstream from the tar sands have been raising alarm bells about increased rates of cancer, lupus and multiple sclerosis.[5]

While the world is slowly shifting to green alternatives to our energy needs, we need to be asking why the Canadian government is promoting an energy source that creates carbon emissions 3.2 to 4.5 times as much as other Canadian or American sources of energy per barrel.[6]

Why do you think the industry involved in extracting the tar sands would prefer to call them oil sands?

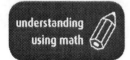

1. One hundred seventy billion barrels of oil sit in the tar sands. One barrel of oil is the equivalent of 0.158987295 m^3. How many cubic meters of oil sit in the tar sands?

2. The Roger's Centre (formerly known as the Skydome) is a baseball stadium in Toronto and is the equivalent of 1.6 million m^3. How many Roger's Centres could be filled with the oil in the tar sands? (Why do you think that the name Skydome, which was picked by the people of Toronto, was changed?)

3. Canada has an estimated total of 175 billion barrels of oil. What percentage is the oil from the tar sands?

4. If it takes 2000 kg of tar sands to produce 1 barrel of oil, find something that you can imagine that is 2000 kg. Using the internet, you might ask how much the average car weighs, or a big animal. Is it close? Do you need to think bigger or smaller?

5. Five hundred and twenty-five thousand barrels of oil are to be shipped to Kitimet on the British Columbia coastline each day.[7] How many kilograms of tar sands would have to be extracted per day to achieve that amount of oil? Find something in the world that has that mass.

6. Eighty percent of British Columbians oppose opening the Northern coast to oil tankers. Why do you think they are opposed to oil tankers?[8] Does that mean that 20% of British Columbians approve of oil tankers? What might their reasons be?

7. Each cubic metre of bitumen that is taken out of the ground creates 3-5 cubic metres of tailings.[9] How many tailings are created by the creation of 525,000 barrels per day?

8. Five scenarios were mapped out estimating the total seepage from all tailing ponds. The results ranged from seven to 36 million litres per day out of the total of 1.8 billion litres per day of tailings that are produced.[10] The report that went out to the public used 11 million litres per day of tailings. Does that reporting seem fair? Why or why not?

9. Assume that it is indeed 11 million litres of tailings leaking from tailings ponds per day.[11] How many litres is that per year? What is a comparable amount of litres that you can imagine?

10. Scientific studies of dangerous substances were measured in the waterways upstream and downstream of the tailings ponds. Upstream of Tar Island Pond One, arsenic was measured at 0.0029 mg/L and downstream, it was measured at 0.0147 mg/L.[12]

31

a. What is the ratio between upstream and downstream arsenic?

b. The safe level of arsenic is 0.005 mg/L. How many times over the safe level is arsenic measured downstream of the tailings pond?

11. Further measurements of the following low molecular weight polyaromatic hydrocarbons (PAHs) were taken upstream and downstream of tailings ponds in the Athabasca River in the summer of 2006.[13] Fill in the effect ratio and the difference columns.

Substance	Nanograms per sample of river sediment		Effect Ratio	Difference
	Upstream	Downstream	Down – Up	Down – Up
C1-Dibenzothiophenes	27.4	197.9		
C3-Dibenzothiophenes	58.3	874.6		
C3-Flourenes	83.2	1007.2		

12. Twenty-six of the 28 PAHs that were compared between downstream and upstream of tailings ponds were found to show increases. What percentage of PAHs showed increases?

13. The following table shows the amount of mercury found in Walleye fish in the Athabaska River over 29 years.[14]

a. What is the percentage increase between 1976 and 2005?

b. The Health Canada guideline for safe levels of mercury is 0.20 mg/kg. How many times more is the 2005 level of mercury in the fish?

c. Why is a dangerous substance in fish important to measure?

Mercury mg/kg	Year
0.32	1976
0.36	1992
0.41	2005

d. A later study found the following results from the tar sands area of the Athabaska River:[15] What do you think accounts for the difference?

Mercury mg/kg	Year
0.35	1984
0.32	2002
0.33	2003
0.28	2005
0.25	2008
0.27	2011

14. Water is taken, for free, from the Athabaska River to use in tar sands projects. In Calgary, roughly 1.3 million people use 185 million cubic metres of water a year. The water taken from the Athabaska River would be double that amount. How much water is that?

15. Why might a drop in the level of water by only a few centimetres in the Athabaska River be harmful?

16. It takes 12 barrels of water to process one barrel of pit-mined oil.[16] What is the algebraic equation for the number of barrels of water required to process a barrel of pit mined oil and how many barrels of water would be required to process 525,000 barrels of oil?

17. Large businesses in the tar sands project are supposed to aim for a 12% carbon emissions target but instead can pay $15 per tonne of carbon into a climate fund. On site costs to capture and store carbon would be $175 to $230 per tonne.[17] How many times more expensive is it to capture carbon on site than to pay the tax, and what is that likely to mean?

18. Every barrel of oil creates 35 kg of CO_2 emissions, so how many kilograms of CO_2 would be produced each day to transport 525,000 barrels to the Pacific coast?[18]

19. Fifty-five kg of CO_2 emissions are created when drilling the 80% of the tar sands that lie below 100 metres.[19] What percentage is that of the emissions for tar sands above 100 metres, and why the increase?

20. The Canadian Association of Petroleum Producers says that the number of barrels extracted from the tar sands per day in 1980 was 0.1 million, in 2014 it was 2.2 million, in 2025 it is expected to be 3.5 million and in 2030 it is expected to be 4 million.

If you were trying to minimize the appearance of oil production growth from the tar sands which of the following graphs would you use?

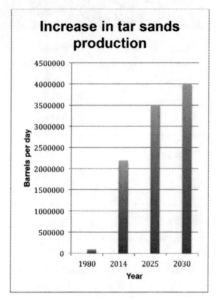

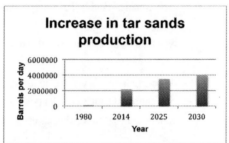

Source: www.capp.ca/~/media/capp/customer-portal/publications/270274.pdf

21. The tar sands industry points to the fact that it will pay $766 billion in taxes in the coming 25 years, which can be used by our government to do great things for Canadians. The BP oil spill in the Gulf of Mexico cost $40 billion to clean up.[20]

    a. What is the average tax collection per year from the tar sands industry?

    b. How does that compare to the costs to clean up a single oil spill?

22. The Canadian Association of Petroleum Producers (CAPP) says that the jobs produced by the tar sands will jump from 75,000 in 2010 to 905,000 in 2035.[21] What questions might you ask about those numbers?

23. Suncor, one of the major businesses in the tar sands made a profit of $3.571 billion in 2010.[22] CAPP says that it has contributed $5.5 million to Aboriginal community programs. What is that amount as a percentage of Suncor's 2010 profits?

Food for thought:

The U.S. Department of Defense uses 340,000 barrels of oil per day, more than the national consumption of oil in Sweden or Switzerland.

make it
better

The First Nations of the Yinke Dene Alliance in British Columbia have a website where you can pledge your support for stopping the Northern Gateway Pipeline at **http://www.holdthewall.ca**.

Watch the short YouTube video about how our tax dollars subsidize the oil, gas and coal industry (**https://www.youtube.com/watch?v=tGUkma2qzhQ**). Then write a letter to your Member of Parliament asking them for clarification.

There are many useful resources at **www.climateactionnetwork.ca**.

Endnotes

1. http://www.reuters.com/article/2010/03/24/us-oilsands-summit-quotes-idUSTRE62L5VA20100324
2. http://www.capp.ca/UpstreamDialogue/OilSands/Pages/default.aspx
3. http://www.greenpeace.org/canada/en/campaigns/Energy/tarsands/Resources/Fact-sheets/Threats-Climate-change/
4. Ibid
5. http://www.greenpeace.org/canada/en/campaigns/Energy/tarsands/Resources/Fact-sheets/Threats-Climate-change/
6. http://www.pembina.org/oil-sands
7. http://www.flickr.com/photos/pembina/sets/72157625482805251/show/
8. Ibid.
9. http://www.greenpeace.org/canada/en/campaigns/Energy/tarsands/Resources/Fact-sheets/Threats-Climate-change/
10. Timoney K. and Peter Lee. Does the Alberta Tar Sands Industry Pollute? The Scientific Evidence. *The Open Conservation Biology Journal*, 2009, 3, p. 72.
11. http://www.greenpeace.org/canada/Global/canada/report/2010/4/Watershed_FS_footnote_rev_5.pdf
12. Timoney K. and Peter Lee. Does the Alberta Tar Sands Industry Pollute? The Scientific Evidence. *The Open Conservation Biology Journal*, 2009, 3, p. 70.
13. Timoney K. and Peter Lee. Does the Alberta Tar Sands Industry Pollute? The Scientific Evidence. *The Open Conservation Biology Journal*, 2009, 3, p. 68.
14. Timoney K. and Peter Lee. Does the Alberta Tar Sands Industry Pollute? The Scientific Evidence. *The Open Conservation Biology Journal*, 2009, 3, p. 69.
15. https://www.ceaa-acee.gc.ca/050/documents_staticpost/59540/82534/Journal_of_Environmental_Monitoring_Article.pdf
16. http://www.greenpeace.org/canada/Global/canada/report/2010/4/Watershed_FS_footnote_rev_5.pdf
17. 10. http://www.pembina.org/oil-sands
18. http://www.greenpeace.org/canada/en/campaigns/Energy/tarsands/Resources/Fact-sheets/Threats-Climate-change/
19. Ibid.
20. http://www.huffingtonpost.com/2010/11/02/bp-oil-spill-costs-hit-40_n_777521.html
21. http://www.capp.ca/UpstreamDialogue/OilSands/Pages/default.aspx
22. http://en.wikipedia.org/wiki/Canadian_petroleum_companies

More %s Excel

Pointed Questions

"Immunization is distinct from other medical practices in that healthy individuals assume largely unknown risks with no goal of improving their present state of health."[1]

setting the stage 👉

The human papilloma virus, or HPV, has people talking these days. There are over a hundred types of the virus, and 15 of them are known to cause cancer of the cervix. HPV is a sexually transmitted infection passed by skin contact with the genitalia. Up until recently, the most widely practiced and extremely effective way to prevent cervical cancer was to get a regular Pap test — named after the Greek doctor George Papanicolaou[2] who discovered the test's worth back in the 1920s. Cells from the cervix (or opening of the uterus) are collected and examined for irregularities that might indicate pre-cancerous or cancerous cells, which if found can be removed. Females in Canada are encouraged to get a Pap test no later than three years after becoming sexually active, or by age 21, and then every two years after that.

Enter the U.S. pharmaceutical giant Merck and Co., Inc.. Their vaccine Gardasil targets two strains of HPV, 16 and 18, responsible for 70% of cervical cancer cases. Mass inoculations of people aged nine to 13 are being recommended in several Canadian provinces. In 2016, it was reported that while only 57% of 13 to 17 year old females had had at least one dose of the HPV vaccine, there had been a 56% drop in HPV prevalence in the four years following the vaccine's introduction.[3]

Important questions remain. Diane Harper, the lead investigator of the clinical trials for Gardasil and Ceravix, is on record saying that until both vaccines can effectively prevent cervical cancer for 15 years, the disease will not be considered to have been prevented. Neither vaccine has.[4] In Canada where the rate of cervical cancer is one of the lowest in the world, does this vaccine strategy make sense?

opening question ?

Eighty percent of people with cervixes will contract the HPV virus by age 50 and most will clear it naturally. But those people who are First Nations, immigrant, disabled, low-income, or who live in remote places have higher rates of cervical cancer — why do you think that this is the case?

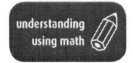

understanding using math

1. The rate of HPV infection in the "developing" and the "developed" world is *roughly* the same, but 83% of cervical cancer occurs in the developing world.[5] What might account for the vast difference between infection and actual cases of cancer?

2. The following chart lists the deaths of females from all cancers in Canada in the year 2015.[6]

Cancer	Number of deaths (in 2015)
Leukemia	1,147
Brain	851
Pancreas	2,294
Bladder	666
Oesophagus	444
Cervix	370
Ovary	1,739
Lung	9,990
Kidney	666
Colorectal	4,255
Melanoma	407
Breast	5,032
Non Hodgkin Lymphoma	1,221
Stomach	770
Body of uterus	1,036
Multiple myeloma	629
Oral	407
All others	4,736
Total:	
Mean:	
Median:	
Percentage of cervical cancer deaths compared to total	

37

a. Input this chart into an Excel file.

b. Sort the list from greatest to least.

c. Use the spreadsheet functions to find the total, the mean, the median and the percentage of deaths caused by cervical cancer compared to the total.

d. Create a fully labelled column graph of all of the types of cancer in 2015. Print it out.

e. Sixty percent of females who die from cervical cancer did not get regular Pap testing or have any Pap testing at all.[7] What number of females did get regular Pap testing and still died?

f. What is the updated percentage of cervical cancer deaths for those who got regular Pap testing and died, as a percentage of the total deaths from cancer?

3. The mortality rate in Canada in the year 2002[8] is listed for four types of cancer. Put the data into a column graph and print it out.

Type of Cancer	Mortality Rate per 100,000
Lung	35
Breast	24
Colorectal	18
Cervical	2

4. The lifetime probability of a female developing cervical cancer in Canada is one in 153.[9] What is that as a percentage?

5. The lifetime probability of a female dying from cervical cancer in Canada is one in 445.[10] What is that as a percentage?

6. Enter the following table into Excel.

Total HPV infections in Canada (2002)[11]	Number of HPV infections that the body naturally clears in 2 years	Number of HPV infections that aren't cleared by the body	Number of people who progress to invasive cervical cancer in 5 years	Number of people who don't progress to cervical cancer in 5 years	Percentage of those who get invasive cervical cancer as compared to total infections
1,350					

a. Ninety-five percent of all HPV infections are cleared by the body in two years.[12] What is the equation that you should put in cell B2 to get 95% of the infections that are cleared.

b. Five percent of HPV infections are not cleared by the body in the first two years.[13] What equation should you put in cell C2 to get the 5% that are not cleared by the body? These can progress to what is called cancer pre-cursors.

c. Twenty percent of people with cancer precursors (specifically called CIN3) will become invasive cervical cancer in five years.[14] What equation would you use in cell D2 to find the number of people who get cervical cancer within five years?

d. What equation would be required in cell E2 to get the number of people who have the HPV virus but *don't* progress to cervical cancer in five years?

e. What equation is required in cell F2 to get the percentage of cases of invasive cervical cancer compared to the total?

f. Use cells B2, D2 and E2 to create a pie graph- label and print it out.

7. Forty percent of the cancer pre-cursors progress to cervical cancer in 30 years. What does this suggest about detection and treatment?

8. An **iatrogenic effect** is where the health care provider, through their treatment, causes an adverse (negative) effect on the patient.

a. The cervical cancer rate in the United States is eight per 100,000. Graph the line for $y=8x$, where x is the number of groups of 100,000 people and y is the number of cases of cervical cancer.

b. What would the line look like if there were an iatrogenic effect?

c. If females who take a HPV vaccine believe that they are immune from cervical cancer and then fail to do regular Pap screen tests, we could see an iatrogenic effect where the number of people with cervical cancer increases. If the rate became 14 per 100,000 instead of eight per 100,000 and we were considering 10 million people in total, what would be the increase in the number of people with cervical cancer?

9. A study done for the BC Cancer Agency looked at the cost to immunize females in British Columbia over the course of 26 years. The number of vaccinations over that time would be 934,000 at a cost of about $400 per vaccination. The costs to treat HPV related diseases over that same time period are estimated at $54,000,000.[15] Which would be more cost effective according to these figures?

Food For Thought:

HPV can be transferred between sexually active males, and the absence of a public health campaign to vaccinate males as well as females has been criticized as homophobic. PEI, Alberta, British Columbia, Nova Scotia and Saskatchewan offer the vaccine to some or all boys. Quebec, Manitoba and Ontario began offering the vaccine to males in September of 2016.[16]

make it better

Use condoms and/or other barrier methods if you are sexually active.

Get a regular Pap test (which means every two years) if you become sexually active.

Before you choose to get the HPV vaccination, be sure to have a conversation about the issues. Brainstorm who would be important people to talk to.

Create a safer sex campaign as a part of your school's health curriculum unit.

Endnotes

1. Diodati, Catherine. Immunization: History, Ethics, Law and Health. Integral Aspects Incorporated, Windsor, Canada, p. 20.

2. Rich, Patrick. New vaccines may have this once-lethal malignancy on the run. Canadian Health. The Canadian Medical Association, www. Candian-health.ca/2_2/18_e.html.

3. http://pediatrics.aappublications.org/content/early/2016/02/19/peds.2015-1968

4. https://en.wikipedia.org/wiki/Diane_Harper#Questioning_the_safety_and_efficacy_of_HPV_vaccines

5. Silversides, Ann. Cost of HPV vaccine is prohibitive in developing world, Nobel winner says. CMAJ December 8, 2009, vol. 181 no. 12.

6. https://www.cancer.ca/~/media/cancer.ca/CW/cancer%20information/cancer%20101/Canadian%20cancer%20statistics/Canadian-Cancer-Statistics-2015-EN.pdf

7. Gulli, Cathy. Our girls are not guinea pigs. Macleans, August 27, 2007.

8. Canadian Cancer Society and National Cancer Institute of Canada. Canadian cancer statistics 2006. Toronto, The Institute, p.97.

9. http://info.cancer.ca/cce-ecc/default.aspx?Lang=E&toc=12&cceid=800

10. http://info.cancer.ca/cce-ecc/default.aspx?Lang=E&toc=12&cceid=800

11. Lexchin, Joel, Neil Arya and Sonal Singh. Gardasil- The New HPV Vaccine: The Right Product, the Right Time? A Commentary. Healthcare Policy, 5(4) 2010; 26:36.

12. Yernan, Diane. An Interview with Dr. Diane M. Harper, HPV Expert. September 2, 2012.

13. Ibid.

14. Ibid.

15. Lexchin, Joel, Neil Arya and Sonal Singh. Gardasil- The New HPV Vaccine: The Right Product, the Right Time? A Commentary. Healthcare Policy, 5(4) 2010; 26:36.

16. http://www.ctvnews.ca/health/ontario-extending-free-hpv-vaccines-to-boys-1.2869481

functions graphing

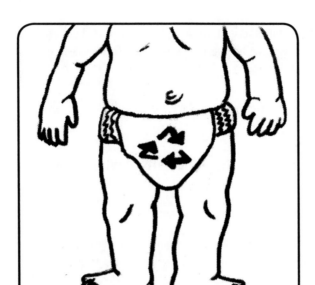

Litttle Do We Know

"It is difficult to get a man to understand something, when his salary depends on his not understanding it."

~ UPTON SINCLAIR

setting the stage

Two interesting and related events took place in the year 1990 that had to do with diapers. The first was that, in honour of the 20th anniversary of Earth Day, 24 states and other local jurisdictions in the United States passed laws to restrict the use of disposable diapers. It had been a full 29 years since the corporation Procter and Gamble had introduced Pampers, the first disposable diaper. But people were raising environmental and health concerns and legislators were taking action.[1]

The second was that a man by the name of Arthur D. Little studied the difference between reusable diapers and disposable diapers. He concluded that reusables took up to six times as much water compared to single-use diapers because they had to be washed over and over again. And that takes a lot of water! Little also said that diaper for diaper, reusables added 10 times more water pollution than making disposables.[2] Throwaway diapers were beginning to sound pretty good.

Strangely though, a year later a new study claimed that compared to reusable diapers, disposables "use 20 times more raw materials, three times more energy, and twice as much water; they generate 60 times more waste".[3] But where did those numbers come from?

One study turned out to be paid for by Procter and Gamble, using their data and data from the disposable diaper companies. The other study came from an independent environmental agency that looked carefully at the existing research.

The public, it seems, had been kept a 'little' in the dark.

Explain, using the above story, what is meant by a conflict of interest.

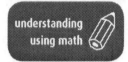

1. Use the graph below to graph the line d = 60r, where r on the horizontal axis represents the amount of waste created per reusable diaper and d represents the amount of waste created by the equivalent number of disposable diapers. Graph the first 15 diapers. Don't forget axis labels and a title.

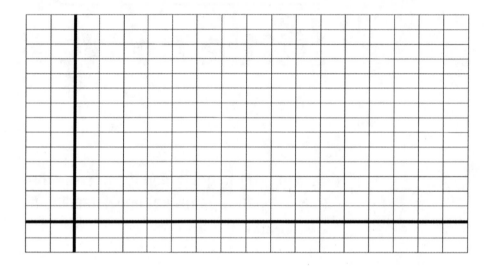

2. **List below** and **graph above** the three other relationships between disposables and reusable diapers that the environmental agency found. Be sure to mark your lines clearly with the algebraic equations.

   Algebraic formula for the amount of raw materials:

   Algebraic formula for the amount of energy:

   Algebraic formula for the amount of water:

3. What are the coefficients of each of the above lines? What is another name for the coefficient?

4. What is the y-intercept for each of the above four lines? What is another name for the y-intercept?

   Let's compare the cost to pay for reusable diapers versus disposable diapers over the course of a baby's journey to being toilet-ready.

There's quite a range of reusable cotton diapers these days, but up front you could pay $500 to outfit yourself with about two-dozen diapers (mixed sizes, with inserts and covers). You might even get a diaper pail included for that amount. That's an upfront cost even before you get started with any diaper changes.

What you won't pay up front is the ongoing charges for your water, your laundry soap, and your electricity to run the washing machine. Estimates vary because it depends on the washing machine, but work with three cents per diaper change.

5. What is the algebraic equation for the amount of money you have, using m for amount of money and n for number of diapers changed? (Remember, you now have a coefficient and a constant, and both are negative to represent that you have to spend the money. Be careful: you also have to remember you're dealing with dollars for one of them, and cents for another.)

Now for the disposables. Again, the costs vary immensely. If you buy in bulk packs they're cheaper. If you have coupons or shop at warehouse stores you may pay less. But let's use 40 cents per diaper, with no upfront costs.

6. What is the algebraic equation for the total cost of your diaper changes, using m for the amount of money you have and n for number of diapers changed? (You only have a coefficient this time, and it's negative.)

7. Let's assume that you do eight diaper changes a day (more at the start, less as the baby gets older) for two years until the baby doesn't need diapers. How many diaper changes is that?

8. Graph the two algebraic equations in questions 5 and 6 above on the same graph below, letting n (on your horizontal axis) reach the number that you calculated in question 7. Label the axis lines and the algebraic lines. Don't forget a title.

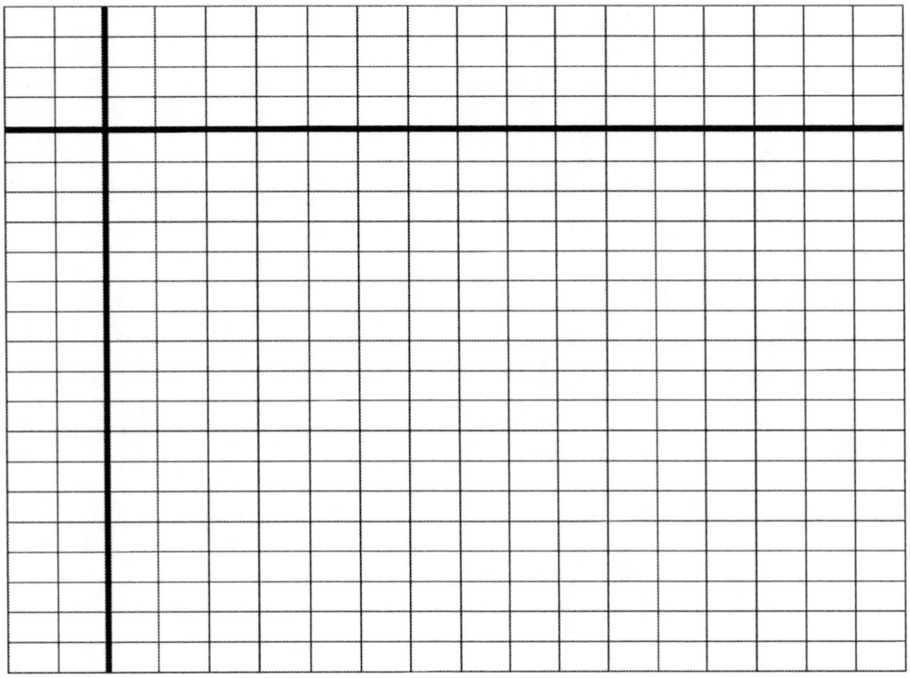

9. At what diaper change do you break even? Use the balance beam method to solve for your answer. Show all of your work.

10. Use your equations in questions 5 and 6 to solve for the total costs for reusable diapers and total costs for disposables over the course of the full 2 years. Which is more and by how much? Show all of your work.

Bonus:
If a family has three children and uses the same set of reusable diapers for all three kids, what is the difference in cost between disposables and reusable diapers by the time all kids are out of diapers?

make it better

Sometimes what is better for your finances is better for the environment too. How many children do the students in your class imagine they will have, collectively? What amount of collective dollar savings does that represent? How many disposable diapers could be diverted from landfill sites?

See if you can find a pattern for reusable diapers online. Try making one! Was it easy to do?

Endnotes

1. O'Mara, Peggy. A Tale of Two Diapers. www.birthlore.com/class/ p.1
2. Ibid. p. 2
3. Ibid, p. 2.

Calculating %
from ratios

Fear

"Keep everyone afraid and they will consume."

~ MARILYN MANSON

setting the stage

Pimples. Wrinkles. Fat. Bad breath. Frizzy hair. Yellow teeth. Body odour. Facial hair. Thin lips. Thick lips. Weird lips. You're *all* wrong, and all of your friends are watching you carefully. Be fearful. Be very fearful. You won't be accepted. You'll be an outcast. Alone.

But wait. There may be a solution. There may be many solutions! Zit cream. Botox. Weight loss plans. Mouth wash. Teeth whiteners. Manly deodorant. To make you manly. Womanly scents. To make you lovely. Microdermabrasion. A dizzying array of products for you to save yourself from being laughed at behind your back. And why stop at your body when there's so much more to fear? Lightning. SARS. Terrorist attacks. Ebola virus. Shark attacks. Brain tumours from cells phones.

Preying on people's insecurities and fears in order to sell products is a piece of what Naomi Klein calls "disaster capitalism".[1] Some of those fears may be sadly warranted when you live in a culture where people are sharply judged on the basis of their appearances. But some of those fears may be in response to events so improbable, that it's worth distinguishing between "likely", "possible", and "exceedingly rare".

What does "if it bleeds, it leads" mean? How might this idea create fears in the general public of events that are very unlikely to ever happen?

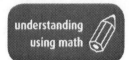

1. In the year 2011 in Canada, there were 242,074 deaths.[2] From the list of some of the causes, what percentage do you believe that they are of the total? Fill in the following table with your guesses.

Cause	Absolute Number[3]	Percentage
Heart diseases and stroke		
Lightning[4]		
Murder		
Cancer		
HIV		
Unintentional accidents including motor vehicle accidents		
Suicide		

2. Compare your responses in question 1 with your calculations of the percentages based on the actual numbers below. If they are different, why do you think they are different?

Cause	Absolute Number	Percentage
Heart diseases and stroke	60,910	
Lightning	10 out of 236,617 (2008)	
Murder	575 out of 236,617 (2008)	
Cancer	72,476	
HIV	407 out of 236,617 (2008)	
Unintentional accidents including motor vehicle accidents	10,716	
Suicide	3,728	

3. If the general public thought that violent crime was a huge problem, who might capitalize on that fear and how?

4. If people believe that certain diseases are very common (for example, measles), who could use the fear of getting those diseases to their advantage? By the way, nobody died of measles in 2008.

5. In Canada, how many people die every hour due to cancer? How many Canadians are murdered each hour on average? Does this surprise you?

6. Who benefits from the public's lack of attention to the root causes of cancer and heart disease?

7. The above table is actually a list of averages, but for some events, the results are gendered. Calculate the percentages for males and females in the following events.

Cause[5]	Number of Males	Percentage of Males	Number of Females	Percentage of Females
Motor vehicle accidents	1,863		765	
Murder	452		123	
Accidental drowing	225		50	
Suicide	2,777		928	

8. Why do you think the above results are gendered?

9. In the chart below, why is it important to list the rate per 100,000 people?

Suicide	Canada	Ontario	Northwest Territories	Nunavut
Absolute values	3,705	1,025	10	22
Males rate per 100,000	16.8	5.7	35.3	109.8
Females rate per 100,000	5.5	5.7	9.5	26.3

10. What factors do you think contribute to the much higher rates of suicide in the north of Canada?

11. The above table only considers suicide of biological male and female people. What do you think the suicide rate might be for intersex people? What rate might you see for people who are transgender? Or not heterosexual? Why is the absence of these categories problematic?

make it better

How do we challenge a culture that has been created to sell products at the expense of you feeling good about yourself?

When the news tells us we should be fearful, how do we respond thoughtfully?

What do you think is the best way to use probabilities to get at the root of problems?

Endnotes

1. Klein, Naomi. The Shock Doctrine.
2. http://www.statcan.gc.ca/pub/82-625-x/2014001/article/11896-eng.htm
3. Mortality, Summary List of Causes 2008, Statistics Canada, 84F0209X
4. http://www.sirc.ca/online_resources/documents/Lightning-relatedinjuriesandfatalitiesinCanada_FINAL-TECHNICAL_1-September-06.pdf
5. Mortality, Summary List of Causes 2008, Statistics Canada, 84F0209X, pp. 12-14.

All That Glitters

"We do not inherit the earth from our ancestors, we borrow it from our children."

~ NATIVE AMERICAN PROVERB

Sometimes in science classes, students study the topic of pure substances and mixtures. Nowhere is the link between pure substances and mixtures more clearly political than in the realm of mining. Gold, for example, is not pulled out of the ground in solid gold bars: six tonnes of rock must be processed in order to end up with one gram of gold (that's like turning a blue whale into half of a penny)!

The chemicals that are used to process the rock and separate out the things that humans have decided are valuable can be extremely toxic. In the case of gold, those processing chemicals are cyanide and mercury. Cyanide is a poison that is toxic to humans (and to wildlife) at 100-300 parts per million.[1] Ore that is treated with cyanide is placed in tailings ponds, and the danger is that a breach of the pond will release cyanide into the environment: this happened in Romania in the year 2000, when 100,000 cubic metres of cyanide-treated wastes were released into the surrounding waters, killing all of the fish and making the water unusable to 2.5 million people.[2]

The expression "all that glitters isn't gold" means that everything that looks precious isn't necessarily so. But sometimes even precious things have dangerous consequences for humans and the planet.

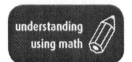

Use the graphic below to briefly identify issues of justice surrounding the mining industry. One has been filled in for you.

The Canada Pension Plan (CPP) is heavily invested in big Canadian mining corporations

Gold Mining

Economic decisions that maximize profit play heavily into the mining industry. The following is a mining simulation to explore some of those decisions. Your teacher will need a couple of packages of chocolate chip cookies — one bag with bigger chocolate chips.

Step One: Selection of the area for mining

You must choose your cookie type. The cookie type represents the potential of the land that you are mining for turning up the valuable minerals that you'd like. The minerals you're after are the chocolate chips within a cookie.

You choose: one regular cookie (land is less controversial, but
(circle one)   potentially has less payoff: fewer chips)   **$5,000**

                    or

                    one exciting cookie (land is more controversial, so
                    there are more barriers to mining it)   **$10,000**

One further decision: if you use some of your money to lobby the government, you may be able to open up the exciting cookie land for less money. If you'd like to lobby government (with no guarantee that it'll pay off) your charge is.....   **$3,000**

If you're going to go ahead and lobby the government, circle any three of the following six numbers, and if on the roll of the die any of those numbers come up, you can purchase the exciting cookie for $5,000.

1   2   3   4   5   6

Total cost for this section: _____

Step Two: Selection of the equipment used for the mining

There are dozens of economic decisions to be made around the equipment and strategy for mineral extraction. Here are some of your choices:

Environmental assessment- what will you do? (Circle one)

1. No environmental assessment   **$0**

2. Minimal environmental assessment and payment to
    enact the recommendations of that assessment   **$10,000**

3. Major environmental assessment and payment to
    enact the recommendations of that assessment   **$20,000**

Two dice will be rolled. Their 36 possible sums are listed.

	1	2	3	4	5	6
1	2	3	4	5	6	7
2	3	4	5	6	7	8
3	4	5	6	7	8	9
4	5	6	7	8	9	10
5	6	7	8	9	10	11
6	7	8	9	10	11	12

If you did no environmental assessment, and a sum of 2, 3, or 4 is rolled, you are taken to court and have to pay $30,000 in damages. What is the probability that a sum of 2, 3, or 4 will appear? What is the probability that a 2, 3, or 4 will not appear?

If you did the minimal environmental assessment, and a sum of 9 appears, then you are fined $10,000. What is the probability that a sum of 9 will appear? What is the probability that a sum of 9 will not appear?

How would the environmental laws in the country with the mine change these probabilities?

Processing:

How will you extract the chocolate chips? You can't touch the cookie with your hands at all: you can only use paper clips or toothpicks. Choose between:

1. More environmentally friendly paper clips ($5,000 each) _____

2. Less environmentally friendly toothpicks ($3,000 each) _____

*Note: if during your mining, your tools break and you want to purchase new ones, you'll need to pay for new ones and adjust the total in this section.

Total cost for this section: _____

Step Three: Cost to remove the chips

Labour charges

Choose:

1. Minimal payment to less protected workers ($4,000/minute) × 5 minutes = _____

2. Higher labour standards including higher wages ($6,000/minute) × 5 minutes = _____

If you chose the minimal payment to workers, you risk your workforce disrupting your operations (for example by going on strike or by slowing down their work). Roll one die. If you get a 1 or a 2 you must wait one minute into the five minutes of mining before you can begin.

*Note: there will be a $1,000 penalty for **every second** of mining beyond the five minute mining period that represents labour costs.

*Note: there will be a $5,000 penalty associated with touching the cookie with your hands at any point, until the go-ahead has been given to eat the cookie at the end.

Total cost for this section: _____

Step Four: Clean up costs

Once you get your cookie, it must be placed on a blank sheet of paper and a line must be traced around the perimeter of the cookie. After the five minute mining operation, you will be charged $1,000 for every crumb left outside of the original outline of the cookie. Your teacher will be the arbiter of the number of crumbs outside of the outline.

Total charge: _____

Caveat: if you roll a 4, 5 or a 6 on a single die, you can just leave your mess and not be prosecuted by the government of the country you're mining in.

Total cost for this section: _____

Step Five: How much did you make?

Each full chocolate chip **or the equivalent** (as determined by your teacher) is worth $8,000.

Total number of chips: _____ multiplied by $8,000 = _____

Add up the total costs from steps one through four: _____

Your profit is your total value of the chips minus the sum of the mining costs:

make it better ✌️   Check out **www.miningwatch.ca** to learn more about Canadian mining companies and their impact in countries around the world.

Endnotes

1. http://www.enviroliteracy.org/article.php/1120.html
2. Ibid.

Coordinate Graphing

Exhaust-ed

"A mighty flame followeth a tiny spark."

~ DANTE

setting the stage

When you hear the words "**Green Agenda**", from the Ontario government you might not think: **diesel trains**. But expansion of the Georgetown rail corridor in Toronto would increase diesel traffic from 50 trains a day to more than 450, running all seven days of the week.[1]

Beyond the rumbling and shaking of heavy diesel trains, there are health impacts from the particulate matter that is carried as far as 200 miles from the tracks. But you don't have to look as far as that: the Georgetown corridor runs through 12 neighbourhoods with a combined 300,000 people, and is next door to 76 schools, 96 daycare centres, and four long-term care facilities.[2] The Ontario Medical Association estimates that poor air quality accounts for 5,800 premature deaths and 16,000 hospitalizations each year in the province.[3]

Electric trains have many advantages. Because they are lighter, they can stop faster, which means that more stops along the route can be opened up for communities to access. Electric trains have no emissions and green sources of energy like wind or solar can increasingly be used to generate the electricity in the first place.

With the Pan Am Games in 2015, there was urgency to have the infrastructure completed in time for the events. Activists have been sounding the alarm on diesel for years, pointing out that in the top 100 cities in the world, only Dhaka in Bangladesh uses diesel to connect to their airport. With electrification simply the best answer for human health, you can see how people are starting to feel…exhausted.

At a public panel on the deadlock between the government and the residents along the Georgetown corridor, professor Christopher Kennedy stated, "No one should be asked to trade public health for public transit."[4] What is Kennedy saying?

1. On the next page, graph the route of the Georgetown rail corridor using the following Cartesian coordinates. Join the points for the rail line and the points for the highway so that you can see the routes. Use the suggested colours to highlight each item.

Rail line to be expanded (red)
(10,-2)
(7, -3)
(5, -2)
(2, 1)
(1,2)
(-1,4)
(-3,6)
(-5,7)
(-10,7)

Proposed Train Stations (blue)
(3,0)
(-1,4)
(-3,6)

Toronto Pearson International Airport (green)
(-10,7)

Union Station- Train and Subway hub (orange)
(10, -2)

Major highway route from downtown to the airport (purple)
(10,-3)
(5,-4)
(3, -3)
(0,-4)
(-6,-4)
(-9,7)

54

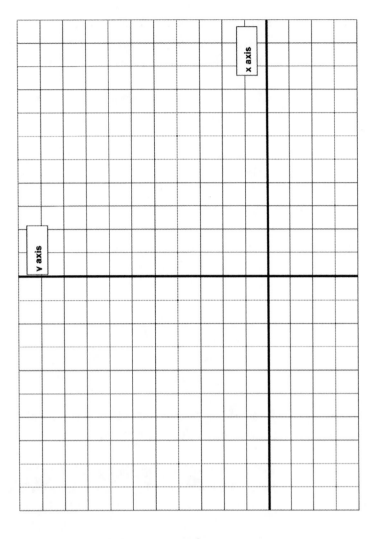

2. What do you notice about the following bar graph?[5]

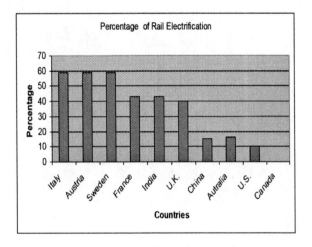

3. Some people have suggested that the rail line be created to run alongside the major highway route from downtown to the airport, instead of through the 12 communities. What is the likely response of the government?

4. Metrolinx, a government agency that coordinates roads and public transport, has estimated the cost of electrification of the Georgetown Corridor at $5 million per kilometre. The distance from Union Station downtown to Brampton is 30 kilometres.[6] What would the total bill be to electrify the line?

5. The current price tag for this line is $875 million. Electrification would add an extra 17% to the bill.[7] What is the added dollar figure?

6. According to a study done by Metrolinx, the costs to operate electric trains are lower than to operate diesel trains. The study concludes that the costs to electrify the route would be recouped from these savings within 10 years. If the cost to electrify the route is $150,000,000, what are the savings each year running electric trains instead of diesel?

7. The government has stated that the best diesel technology, Tier 4 engines, must be used when they are available. But Tier 4 technology would still be the equivalent of running 4,000 trucks through the corridor a day. What is the equivalent number of trucks that would be running through the corridor in a year?

8. Diesel exhaust consists of fine particles that are toxic, and even cancer causing. The U.S. Environmental Protection Agency lists 40 substances in diesel exhaust as hazardous, and 37.5% of those as probable or possible human carcinogens.[8] How many of the 40 hazardous substances are likely carcinogens?

9. The following are the different sizes of particles in diesel exhaust.[9] Fill in the final column. One nanometre is one billionth of a metre.

Particle Type	Diameter	Diameter in metres
Chain agglomerate of soot particles	40 nanometres up to 500 nanometres	
Metallic ash particles from lube oil	10 nanometres up to 20 nanometres	
Hydrocarbon particles	10 nanometres up to 30 nanometres	
Chain agglomerate of soot particles with adsorbed/ condensed layers of hydrocarbon and sulphate and metallic ash	40 nanometres up to 500 nanometres	
Comparison: diameter of human hair	40,000 nanometres	

10. Ultrafine particles are smaller than 100 nanometres and have been found to affect the respiratory and cardiovascular system.[10] Which of the above particles are considered ultrafine particles (UFP)?

11. Nanoparticles are smaller than 50 nanometres and have been found to cause plaque build-up in the arteries.[11] Which from the table above are nanoparticles?

12. How many times bigger is human hair than metallic ash?

13. Why are children and elderly people most at risk from these particles?

14. Write the algebraic formula for the total amount of diesel used, where h is the number of hours the train burns the fuel and t is the total fuel. It takes 75 gallons of diesel per hour.[12]

15. If the collective total hours that these trains run per day is 58.3, use your formula in question 14 to find the total fuel being burned by these trains per day.

16. If 22.38 pounds of carbon dioxide are produced per gallon of diesel burned, how many pounds of carbon dioxide are produced by these trains per day. Why is this important?

make it better

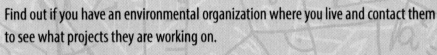

Find out if you have an environmental organization where you live and contact them to see what projects they are working on.

Look at the innovative strategy that the Toronto Environmental Alliance is piloting, using volunteers who track air quality: it's called INHALE. The video can be viewed at **http://www.torontoenvironment.org/give2inhale**.

57

Endnotes

1. www.cleantraincoalition.ca
2. Ibid.
3. Professional Engineers Ontario, West Toronto Chapter. Toward a clean train policy: diesel versus electric. June 2010, *The Journal of Policy Engagement* Volume 2/Number 3 p. 2.
4. Andrew Cash. Dumb Like Diesel. *NOW Magazine*, March 24-31, 2010.Volume 29 No 30
5. Professional Engineers Ontario, West Toronto Chapter. Toward a clean train policy: diesel versus electric. June 2010, *The Journal of Policy Engagement* Volume 2/Number 3 p. 18.
6. www.cleantraincoalition.ca *The Better Move*, p. 3
7. Ibid., p. 3
8. Professional Engineers Ontario, West Toronto Chapter. Toward a clean train policy: diesel versus electric. June 2010, *The Journal of Policy Engagement* Volume 2/Number 3 p. 19.
9. Khalek, Imad. The Particulars of Diesel Particle Emissions. *Technology Today*, Spring 2006, p.3.
10. Professional Engineers Ontario, West Toronto Chapter. Toward a clean train policy: diesel versus electric. June 2010, *The Journal of Policy Engagement* Volume 2/Number 3 p. 20.
11. Ibid. p. 20.
12. http://www.cleantrain.ca

Spilled

"It's not a matter of what if, but when."

~ DR. RIKI OTT

setting the stage

March 23rd, 1989. Third mate Gregory Cousins and Able Seaman Robert Kagan are left in charge of the wheel house of the oil tanker Exxon Valdez, travelling through Prince William Sound on its way from Alaska to California. At 12:04 am on March 24th, the Valdez strikes Bligh Reef, spilling a fifth of its cargo, or about 200 million litres of oil into the region. Hundreds of thousands of animals died instantly; sea otters, fish, harbour seals, bald eagles and orcas.

Exxon was taken to court, and the judge fined the company $287 million for actual damages, and $5 billion in punitive damages. Five billion dollars is equivalent to a single year of profits for Exxon. This amount was later reduced by higher court decisions.

There were many causes of the spill; the partial failure of the Coast Guard, the partial failure of the ship's Captain, and the fact that Cousins and Kagan were put on shift without enough sleep. Alcohol may have played a role as well. Greenpeace put out an ad after the spill with a picture of the Captain and the tag line:

"It wasn't his driving that caused the Exxon Valdez oil spill, it was yours".

opening question ?

What does Greenpeace mean when they say that it wasn't the captain's driving that caused the problem, it was yours?

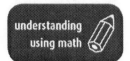

understanding using math

1. Below is what's called a "t chart". Look closely and you'll see the bolded "t".

Remember that $A = \pi r^2$. Fill in the area for each of the fifteen distances from the oil tanker. Imagine that the oil is spilling outwards from the boat- the radius gets bigger and so does the area of the circle.

Graph the radius versus the area of the oil spill. Radius is on the x axis and area is on the y axis.

Title: _____

When the radius is...	The area is ...
r	A
10 m	
20 m	
30 m	
40 m	
50 m	
60 m	
70 m	
80 m	
90 m	
100 m	
110 m	
120 m	
130 m	
140 m	
150 m	

59

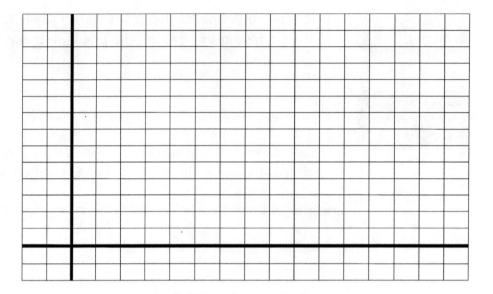

2. Is the growth of the area of oil around the oil tanker linear or exponential?

3. If a rapid environmental response team can enclose a maximum of 18,000 m² of oil by surrounding it with booms, what is the radius at that point (in other words, how far can the oil get from the boat before it can't be surrounded).

4. At that point, what distance of booms will be needed to encircle the oil?

5. If two rapid response teams working synergistically can enclose 23,000 m² of oil by surrounding it with booms, what is the radius at that point (in other words, how far can the oil get from the boat before it can't be surrounded)?

6. At that point, what distance of booms will be needed to encircle the oil? In other words, what is the circumference of the oil circle at that point?

7. If oil spills outwards from the boat at a rate of 0.5 metres per minute, how long will it take to reach the radius from question #5? Does that seem long enough to respond to the disaster?

8. Is the rate that the oil spills outwards from the boat likely to remain a constant 0.5 metres per minute? Why or why not?

9. Studies later showed that only about 14% of the oil was ever cleaned up.[2] What is 14% of 200 million litres of oil?

10. One barrel of oil is 159 litres. How many barrel-equivalents of oil were spilled?

11. In another spill in the Gulf of Mexico, a fine was proposed of $4,300 per barrel of oil spilled.[3] How much of a fine would those responsible for the Exxon Valdez have to pay at that rate?

12. If a fine was composed of a baseline fee of $100,000 plus $4,300 per barrel of oil spilled, what would the algebraic equation be for the total fine amount?

make it better

From Greenpeace's 10 ways to reduce your oil consumption, you might try biking to school, purchasing items without plastic including bottled water, re-using containers, and eating food that hasn't been grown with pesticides and fertilizers, which are made with oil.[3]

Consider how these solutions, which focus on individual responses to injustice may get in the way of upstream solutions to these problems (which address the root causes).

Endnotes

1. http://arcticcircle.uconn.edu/SEEJ/Alaska/miller2.htm
2. http://www.nola.com/business/index.ssf/2015/02/11_memorable_quotes_from_the_b.html#1
3. http://www.greenpeace.org/international/en/news/Blogs/climate/10-simple-ways-to-use-less-oil/blog/12883/

Thin

"The more corrupt the state, the more numerous the laws."
~TACITUS

In March 2005, the Ontario Coalition Against Poverty stumbled across a little-known law stating that people receiving welfare could apply for a Special Diet Allowance, up to $250 per month. Within months, the direct action group had medical practitioners signing the required form, and was helping people living in poverty to understand their rights with respect to receiving the allowance. There was even a Special Diet sign-up clinic on the lawn at Queen's Park, where over 1,000 people signed up.[1]

As the number of people claiming the benefit soared from 5,300 in 2002 to 31,000 in 2007 the provincial government made it increasingly difficult to get the funds, introducing more forms, and forms that required applicants to disclose confidential medical information.[2]

In March 2010 the provincial Liberals delivered their budget. The Finance Minister announced that the Special Diet Allowance would be eliminated and the Ministry of Health would introduce a new nutritional supplement program.[3] Critics of the Special Diet Allowance have often suggested that poor people have been taking advantage of the system. But like the amount of food people living in poverty receive, some people feel that the government's excuses are a bit... thin.

opening question ?

A group of activists fighting against violence against women vocally opposed cuts to the Special Diet Allowance. So did the Ontario AIDS Network. What reasons do you think they might have given?

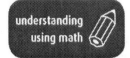

understanding using math

1. The number of people in Ontario living on social assistance rose 1.44% from 442,599 in January of 2015 to January of 2016.[4] How many people were on social assistance in Ontario in January 2016?

2. The probability of qualifying for Employment Insurance if you lose your job is 3/10. The remaining people will require welfare.[5] How many people would have to stand up in your classroom to represent the number of people who, if they lost their job, would end up on welfare?

3. In Ontario, the welfare payment for a single mother with two school-aged kids is $1,184 per month. It is supposed to be allotted as follows: $582 for housing and $602 for everything else.

   a. Create a pie graph showing the two allotments.

   b. The average rent for a two-bedroom apartment in Toronto is $1,052 a month. How much is then actually left for food and everything else? Create a second pie graph with the updated rent information. How do the two graphs compare?

4. An applicant with heart disease generally qualifies for an additional $10 a month with the Special Diet Allowance. If you have diabetes, you can claim an additional $42 a month. And if you had AIDS you could get the entire $250 a month.[6] What are those as yearly totals?

   a. Heart disease: _____ per year

   b. Diabetes: _____ per year

   c. AIDS: _____ per year

   d. How do you think those supplements compare to the costs associated with those diseases?

5. Cuts were made to welfare in 1995 by the Conservative government in power. Since that time, the welfare rates have been reduced in real terms by about 40% .

   a. What is $800 reduced by 40%?[7] Put this number in the blank box in the table below.

   b. How does that work? How can the same $800 monthly cheque be worth 40% less?

	1995	2010
If the welfare cheque was:	$800 per month	Still $800
And was worth:	$800 per month	

6. Ontario Social Assistance is broken down into two main programs. The first is called Ontario Works, which provides employment and financial assistance on a temporary basis as people re-enter the workforce.

63

The second is called the Ontario Disability Support Program, which is designed to provide income support to people with disabilities. Parents of children with disabilities can qualify for benefits under the Assistance for Children with Severe Disabilities program.

Look at the summaries of these two programs for September 2014 and answer the following questions. The summary can be found at :

http://www.mcss.gov.on.ca/documents/en/mcss/social/reports/OW_EN_2014-09.pdf and
http://www.mcss.gov.on.ca/documents/en/mcss/social/reports/ODSP_EN_2014-09.pdf

    a. How many cases are there in total for the Ontario Works program?

    b. How many beneficiaries are there in total for the Ontario Works program?

    c. Why are the two numbers in (a) and (b) different?

    d. How many people can fit in the SkyDome?

    e. How many times could we fill the SkyDome with the beneficiaries of Ontario Works?

    f. What trend do you see, if any, of the Ontario Works Beneficiaries over the past 12 months?

    g. What possible explanation could there be for this trend?

    h. How many beneficiaries are there under the Ontario Disability Support Program in total for all family structures?

    i. How much of an increase is your answer to (h) from August 2014?

64

make it better

Research "Fight For 15" Campaigns that are trying to raise the minimum wage to $15 per hour. What position does your province or territory have with respect to minimum wage?

Endnotes

1. Bonnar, John. Timeline: Ontario Eliminates Special Diet Allowance for Social Assistance Recipients. http://rabble.ca/blogs/bloggers/johnbon/2010/03/timeline-ontario-eliminates-special-diet-allowance-social-assistance- March 28, 2010
2. Ibid.
3. Ibid.
4. http://www.statcan.gc.ca/tables-tableaux/sum-som/l01/cst01/demo02a-eng.htm
5. Ibid.
6. Goar, Carol. Poverty is a medical condition. The Toronto Star, December 15, 2006.
7. http://update.ocap.ca/node/843
8. White, Ben. Israeli *Apartheid A Beginner's Guide*. Pluto Press. London, & New York

Unsettling

"You are not entitled to your opinion. You are entitled to your *informed* opinion. No one is entitled to be ignorant."

~ HARLAN ELLISON

65

setting the stage

There's a knock at the front door. No sooner have you turned the doorknob than a crowd of strangers bursts on in, suitcases in hand. "Where shall we set up our rooms?" they ask, but more to each other than to you — whom they eye with some displeasure.

By the time the first crowd is sitting down at your dinner table, enjoying the contents of your refrigerator, several more waves of strangers have arrived. You're starting to feel a little ill, but are unsure if it's the fact that the newcomers have now emptied your home of coffee and chocolate, or that maybe they've brought bacterial and viral visitors along with them.

In any case, they seem here to stay.

Settler colonialism is a unique form of colonialism in which the incoming settlers intend to stay, set up structures within the territory that allow them to dominate, and then eliminate indigenous populations in a way that precludes any challenge to the settlers' rule.[1] There are many examples of settler colonial states past and present, including Canada.

Canada's Indigenous populations face many challenges as a direct result of settler colonialism. Because of the complexity of the issues and the general lack of awareness about discrimination, inequity and racism that they face, education is key to building public support. Enter the 'infographic'.

Infographics are "graphic visual representations of information, data or knowledge. These graphics present complex information quickly and clearly."[2] Some activists have turned to infographics as a way to reach large audiences effectively. This lesson is a chance to try your hand at it.

Who are **Idle No More**? What do they say about the Treaties?

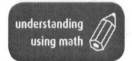

1. The following infographic is courtesy of the Canadian Centre for Policy Alternatives.[3] It compares the rate of child poverty on First Nations reserves and the rates of child poverty on average across the country.

a. Do you think the infographic is effective at conveying the data about child poverty in First Nations communities? Why or why not?

b. What recommendations do you have for making the infographic more powerful?

2. Choose any one of the following issues related to the conflict between a historical or current settler colonial state and the indigenous inhabitants and create your own infographic. Remember that your infographic is trying to convey important information in a clear way, using facts that can be verified. Feel free to explore other issues as well.

Housing:

What quantity and quality of housing is accessible to indigenous inhabitants? When housing needs repair and replacement, what happens?

Transportation:

Are indigenous inhabitants able to move about freely? What kinds of transportation do they have access to? Are there restrictions to movement?

Education:

Is access to education equivalent amongst all people in the country? Is the quality of the education equivalent? Are there differences in elementary, secondary and/or post secondary opportunities?

Access to natural resources:

Do all people have access to and/or decision-making power over natural resources within the territory?

Poverty/income:

What differences are there in levels of poverty, income levels and employment levels? Do all people have the same job security?

o o o

Here are some examples of settler colonial states, past and present, which you might want to explore. Feel free to explore other historical and contemporary settler colonial states as well.

Canada:

The history of Canada is one of land seizure from the original inhabitants, appropriation of resources, the removal of Indigenous children from their families and the use of residential schools to eliminate Indigenous languages and cultures. These residential schools were places of physical, sexual and emotional abuse for many children.[4] The Sixties Scoop saw upwards of 20,000 Indigenous children taken and fostered or adopted by primarily white families.[5] Now 51% of status First Nations children live in poverty.

United States:

The "Five Civilized Tribes" (Cherokee, Creek, Choctaw, Chickasaw and Seminole) is but one of many examples of indigenous populations on Turtle Island that were targeted by settlers: houses burnt down, population removal/displacement, and shifting collective tribally 'owned' lands to individual settlers. Captain Richard Pratt would make the famous statement "Kill the Indian...and save the man."[6] Manifest destiny was the idea that settlers were fated to expand westwards to control all of America from coast to coast.[7]

Australia:

In 1787, over 1,000 settlers from Britain, many of them convicts, were taken to Australia to build roads, farm, and establish colonies. This was followed by waves of other settlers, who came for free land. Indigenous peoples, following animist beliefs, were faced with Christianity, devastating diseases like smallpox, measles and influenza, and an incoming population with no interest in negotiating land treaties. Aboriginal resistance was early, and ongoing.[8] In the past 60 years, Aboriginal children were taken from their homes, and the life expectancy of the population is now 25% lower than the general population.[9]

South Africa:

Early Dutch settlers set up farms at the tip of the African continent, starting in 1652, to supply ships sailing east with the Dutch East India Company. Indigenous Khoikhoi were pushed out by force.[10] The colony grew and migrated further and further inland.[11] Later, when the British took over and new settlers arrived, the Dutch migrated inland yet again. Much later, starting in 1948, laws that created a racially segregated society (today referred to as "Apartheid") forced African people into reserves (or "Bantustans").[12]

Food for thought:

Former Prime Minister Stephen Harper commented that Canada has "no history of colonialism".

make it better

Create an infographic gallery and invite people to a display of the work that you've done.

Acknowledge that the land we go to school and live on is the site of traditional territory, ceded or unceded.

Print out and reflect on the study *Shameful Neglect: Indigenous Child Poverty in Canada* by David Macdonald and Daniel Wilson. How can this study help to inform policymakers?

In 2012, the United Nations made a call to return public lands to Indigenous peoples.

Stand with First Nations peoples when they fight to oppose pipelines.

Check out Visualizing Palestine's infographics and research how similar debates about occupation and settler states are playing out in Palestine and beyond.

Endnotes

1. https://globalsocialtheory.org/concepts/settler-colonialism/
2. Newsom and Haynes (2004). Public Relations Writing: Form and Style, p. 236.
3. https://www.policyalternatives.ca/publications/facts-infographics/infographics-shameful-neglect#sthash.H8QMBumP.dpuf
4. http://www.thecanadianencyclopedia.ca/en/article/residential-schools/
5. https://en.wikipedia.org/wiki/Sixties_Scoop
6. http://www.tandfonline.com/doi/full/10.1080/14623520601056240
7. https://en.wikipedia.org/wiki/Manifest_destiny
8. https://en.wikipedia.org/wiki/History_of_Australia_(1788–1850)
9. http://www.tandfonline.com/doi/full/10.1080/14623520601056240
10. https://en.wikipedia.org/wiki/History_of_South_Africa#Early_European_exploration_and_settlement
11. https://en.wikipedia.org/wiki/Dutch_Cape_Colony
12. https://en.wikipedia.org/wiki/History_of_South_Africa#Early_European_exploration_and_settlement

Beyond Left & Right

"You can't be neutral on a moving train."

~ HOWARD ZINN

For a long time, people have thought about politics by describing a line: those on the **left** are interested in sharing wealth, are critical of privatization, and generally stand up for the rights of workers. You might hear the terms **communism** or **socialism** associated with the left.

On the right of the political spectrum, you have people who believe that social inequality is "inevitable, natural, normal or desirable"[1], arising out of tradition or competition in a market economy. People or businesses compete with one another and the strongest survive. You might hear the word conservatism associated with the right.

But there are groups that think that a single axis is too simple to capture the spectrum of political beliefs. **Political Compass** is one such group that has designed a two dimensional grid, using economic beliefs along the traditional left-right x axis, and social beliefs along the vertical y axis, ranging from authoritarian at the top (strong governmental control and authority, or even dictatorship) to libertarian at the bottom (the belief that people's freedom should be maximized).

As a simple example of how the two-axis model is important, consider groups that want to share wealth but are run by dictators (like Stalin), who would find themselves in the top left hand quadrant of the grid, compared to people who want to share wealth but are more interested in people working together cooperatively without being directed by the state. Gandhi and the Dalai Lama would find themselves in the bottom left quadrant.

Can you think of any reasons why it might be important to understand where different political groups are on the political spectrum? What are they?

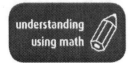

1. Below is a list of popular figures. You may know of some of them. Use the information in the introduction to try and guess which quadrant, and even which coordinates (x, y) you would find them at on the political compass.

   Using a coloured marker, graph the points on the next page.

Name	Which coordinates (x,y) would describe this person or group's politics?
Barack Obama	
Mitt Romney	
Hugo Chavez	
Mahatma Gandhi	
Hitler	
Stalin	
Milton Friedman	
Nelson Mandela	
Canada's Conservative Party 2011	
Canada's Liberal Party 2011	
Canada's NDP Party 2011	
Canada's Green Party 2011	
Canada's Bloc Party 2011	

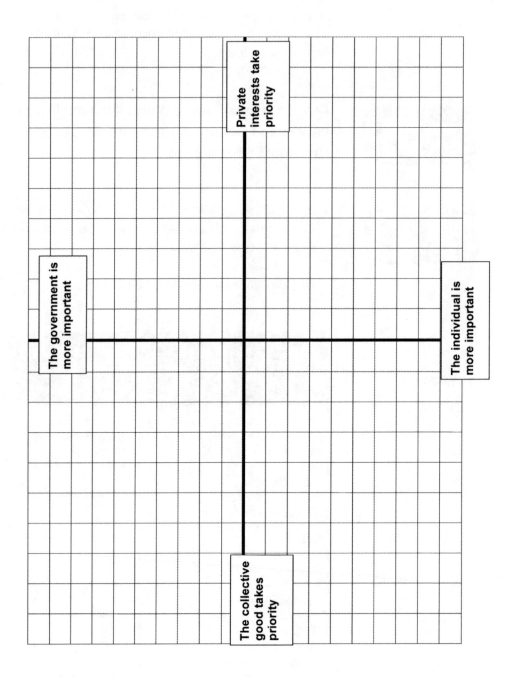

2. Now with a different coloured marker graph the coordinates that Political Compass.org roughly has figured out.[2]

Name	Which coordinates (x,y) would describe this person or group's politics?
Barack Obama	(6, 6)
Mitt Romney	(7, 6.5)
Hugo Chavez	(-4.5, 6)
Mahatma Gandhi	(-6, -4)
Hitler	(2, 9.5)
Stalin	(-9, 9)
Milton Friedman	(8, -2)
Nelson Mandela	(-2, -3)
Canada's Conservative Party 2011	(7, 6)
Canada's Liberal Party 2011	(3, 3)
Canada's NDP Party 2011	(-1, -1.5)
Canada's Green Party 2011	(0, 0.5)
Canada's Bloc Party 2011	(-1.5, -1)

3. Using Wikipedia, research and list below which political parties the following media sources endorse (most often). Plot them in a third colour on the graph.

Media source	Which Canadian political party do they often endorse?
The National Post	
The Toronto Star	
The Globe and Mail	
Rabble.ca	

4. The Linchpin is an anarchist online media source. What quadrant would it be found in? (See below for a reminder of the quadrant labels.)

5. The Marxist-Leninist is a revolutionary communist website. What quadrant would it be found in?

Reminder:

II	I
III	IV

Gauge your own political beliefs by taking the political compass questionnaire on-line at **politicalcompass.org**.

Cut out the following boxes below and with a partner, try to place them on the political compass in the correct spot. Compare your answers with other groups in the class.

Discuss.

Libertarian Conservatism	Communitarianism	Social Democracy	Democratic Socialism	Mutualism
Anarcho-Capitalism	Conservative Republicanism	Classic Liberalism	Activism	Modern Liberalism/ Centrism
Syndicalism	Minarchist Socialism	International Communism	Democratic Capitalism	National Socialism
Anarcho Collectivism	Conservative Fundamentalism	Individualist Anarchism	Authoritarianism	Anarcho Communism
Socialist Anarchism	Progressivism	Libertarian Socialism	Statism	Libertarianism
Social Nationalism	Right Libertarianism	Fascism/Ultra Nationalism	National Communism	

Endnotes

1. http://en.wikipedia.org/wiki/Right-wing_politics
2. http://www.politicalcompass.org/analysis2
3. http://www.candidatex.us/wp-content/uploads/2014/03/political-compass-zones.jpg

circles
radius
area

Well Spoke-n

"If you are not willing to risk the unusual, you will have to settle for the ordinary."

~ JIM ROHN

setting the stage

Sometimes when you live a certain experience, it's hard to imagine that there might be a different way to live. Surrounded each day with a regular pattern, doing much the same things in much the same way, it can be difficult to break out of your own ideas, to remember that *we don't know what we don't know*.

Intentional communities are created by people who have thought carefully about the way in which they would like to live. The spaces they create might emphasize the environment (like **ecovillages**), particular religious views, housing for students, or places where people want to work cooperatively together for the benefit of everyone in the community, like **communes**.[1]

Highly cooperative groups have even re-imagined physical space so that it is in line with their philosophical views of the world. For example, urban planners have created communities of concentric circles where the common buildings and services are in the centre circle, the housing is in the next ring, and farmland is in the final ring. The cooperative farming community of Lahalal in northern Israel is an example of one such design. Some indigenous groups, like the Bororo and the Kraho in Brazil, also use circular community designs.[2]

opening question ?

Can you think of any benefits to living in an intentional community? How about drawbacks?

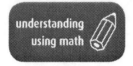
understanding using math

Ariel View of the Community (not to scale)

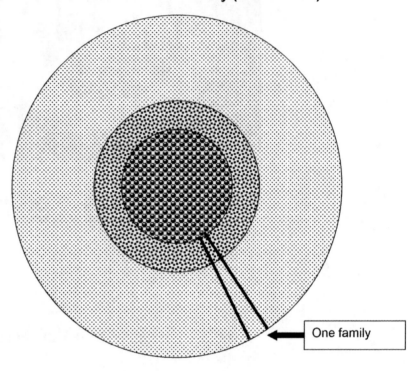

One family

Legend:

 Communal Buildings

 Homes

 Farmland

1. You are a municipal planner designing an intentional communal agricultural community. In the centre of the community you want to put buildings and facilities that will be important to the members of your community. List six buildings that you think would be important in the centre circle.

2. The radius of the central hub is 400 metres. If you can walk 100 metres in 1.5 minutes, how long would it take you to walk from one side of the community's centre to the other?

3. How much land area is used by the centre circle? Show your work, including the formula.

4. What is the circumference of the inner circle? Show your work.

5. If each home that fronts onto the central circle has to be 15 metres wide, and there are eight roads (like spokes of a wheel) that lead out from the centre circle each with a width of six metres, how many homes can fit around the hub? Show all of your work clearly.

6. If the depth of the land allocated to housing is 50 metres, what is the area of land allocated to housing in this community (include the area of the eight roads that run through the housing section)? Show your work.

7. Remember that at the inner edge of the housing section the properties had 15 metres of frontage. The outer edge of the housing section will still need to accommodate the eight roads, but the individual properties at that point will be wider. What is the length of the outer boundary of each housing section?

8. If it is determined that the farmland needed to support this many families is 1,500,000 square metres, what will the depth of the farmland section need to be?

9. What is the radius of the entire community?

make it better

Explore the huge range of intentional communities, and compare their similarities and differences. Are there any that seem appealing to you? What would you want to know before you lived in one?

Endnotes

1. http://www.ic.org/
2. Munduruku, Daniel. Tales of the Amazon: How the Munduruku Indians Live. Groundwood Books, Toronto, 1996, p. 34.

Lesson 13

Jux-tice

"Creativity is that marvelous capacity to grasp mutually distinct realities and draw a spark from their juxtaposition."

~ MAX ERNST

setting the stage

Sometimes, it's just about seeing things in a new light. The cost to end world hunger has been estimated by the United Nations at a massive $19 billion more per year than what's already being spent. Just for some perspective, 19 billion seconds is about 600 years ago. That's back when the world was recovering from losing 100,000,000 people from the Black Death.

But wait just a minute. The estimated spending on toys worldwide is about $122 billion per year. Hmmm. Suddenly, $19 billion is looking a bit more reasonable. Even achievable. Of course, nobody trying to solve world hunger believes that we'll just take all of our spending on toys and put it towards food, or even that throwing a bunch of cash at our problems will make it all better. But keeping some perspective can be a powerful way to motivate people.

The estimated cost to end the HIV epidemic is about $6 billion a year. Not many people or their governments have $6 billion lying around. And yet, people in the United States spend about $110 billion on fast food each year. Perhaps the problem of AIDS is less intractable than we believe.

The act of putting two things side by side in order to compare or contrast them is called juxtaposition. Effective use of juxtaposition may cause us to wince, but more importantly, invite us to discuss the message being communicated.

Search for the Cordaid ad campaign online and pull up the images. As a class, discuss the significance of the pictures and the use of numbers in this campaign. How effective do you think the campaign was, and why?

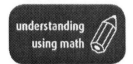

understanding using math

1. The End Poverty by 2015 Millennium Campaign has estimated the cost to end world illiteracy as approximately $10 billion per year. The estimated spending on fast food in the United States alone is $110 billion per year.[1]

Here is how a student graphed the data using a spreadsheet.

   a. What point do you think that the student is making?

   b. What is the significance of the title (look carefully)?

   c. Which do you think makes the point more powerfully, the pie graph or the bar graph below? Why?

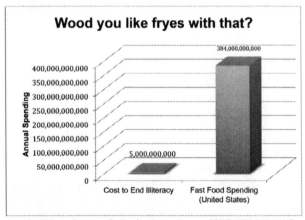

Source: https://www.reference.com/food/much-money-americans-spend-fast-food-597cd336a3c818fb

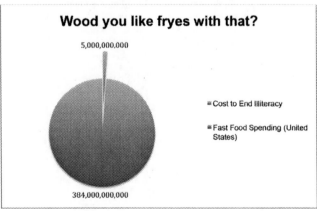

Source: www.borgenproject.org

2. Create your own juxtaposition using a spreadsheet program.

a. If you find the number of bikes produced this year in the world and juxtaposition it with the number of cars produced each day, why is that an unfair comparison? What two things could you do to make it more fair?

b. Go to Worldometers: Real time world statistics at www.worldometers.info/ to get some ideas. After each of their statistics they list their source. Why is that important?

c. Make sure your own juxtaposition has a witty title (perhaps a double entendre) and the graph is well proportioned on the page. Print it out and hand it in.

You may want to use other statistics that you find on the Internet or in books. Here are some ideas that may help you search:

Spending on perfume	Spending on pet food
Spending on video games	Spending on fossil fuels
Spending on candy	Spending on cosmetics
Spending on advertising	Spending on war
Spending on hunger	Spending on homelessness
Spending on HIV/AIDS	Spending on education
Spending on health care	Spending on health and nutrition
Spending on reproductive health	Spending on clean water and sanitation
Spending on ending illiteracy	Spending on green initiatives

3. Create a new juxtaposition using your city's most recent budget. Here is how the property tax is spent if you live in Toronto and have a house with an assessed value of $447,090 (which is the median value of a home in Toronto).[2] Don't forget a witty title!

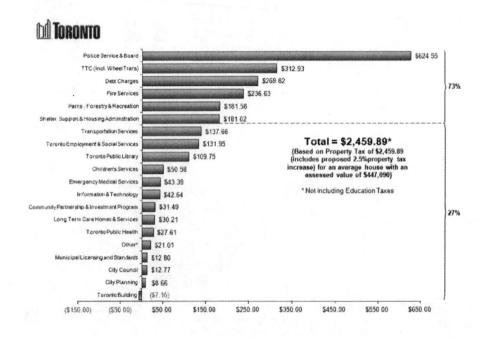

make it better

Produce a gallery of the class assignments. Collectively decide to support one or more of the issues highlighted in your assignments, and collect donations from the visitors to your gallery. Remember to keep in mind upstream solutions aimed at the roots of the problem when you make donations.

Endnotes

1. Forbes.com
2. http://www.toronto.ca/budget2012/2012_budget_summary/howtax.htm

Bridge Over Troubled Waters*

"We are not opposed to development. But we are opposed to stupidity and placing our homelands at terrible risk in order to satisfy the insatiable greed of the international oil industry. We do not accept the Prime Minister's claim that this project is in Canada's national interest, and it is certainly not nation building, but rather, planet destroying."

~ GERALD AMOS, FORMER CHIEF COUNCILLOR, HAISLA FIRST NATIONS

setting the stage 👉

The Northern Gateway Pipeline is quite a proposal: two pipelines between Bruderheim, Alberta, and Kitimat, British Columbia. The crude oil taken from the tar sands would travel westbound to a marine terminal on the coast, then move in huge tankers to Asian markets and California. The eastbound pipe would transport natural gas condensate, which is used to make the crude oil less viscous and easier to transport. Both are trips of 1,177 kilometres, crossing First Nations territories and many lakes and rivers. More than 100 First Nations Bands in B.C. have signed a declaration opposing the project.[1]

Enbridge, the company that wants to build the pipeline, says that this project is not just about oil: they say that it provides opportunities to build relationships with Aboriginal peoples (by offering them a 10% share in the project), employment, procurement and access to Enbridge's stewardship programs. [2]

The National Energy Board was responsible for a joint review panel to hear citizens' concerns about the project. More than 5,000 British Columbians along the pipeline route were allowed 10 minutes each to speak to the panel in 2012 and 2013. There was a resounding "no": no to putting the ocean economy at risk of an oil spill, no to putting communities at risk, and no to violating Aboriginal treaty rights. The panel compiled a report for the federal government, which concluded that 209 conditions had to be met before the pipeline could proceed. [3]

In 2014, Justin Trudeau said that if he were elected Prime Minister the Northern Gateway would not happen. Trudeau is now in office: was that promise just a pipe dream?

On Enbridge's website, there is a short animated video of the route of the pipeline, meant to be "broadly representational". Look carefully at the waterway leading into Kitimat at second 45. Now go to the website www.sumofus.org/campaigns/enbridge/?sub=fb to look at a real map of the Douglas Channel leading into Kitimat. Discuss the differences.

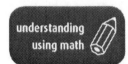

1. Mark the graph's x and y axes on the next page.

2. Plot these points on the map of BC and Alberta, and connect the points where indicated.

    a. **Path of Pipeline** (connect the dots)—mark the line in RED. When names of towns/cities/communities are listed along the route, make a BLACK DOT.

1.	(15, 0)	Bruderheim
2.	13, -1)	Morinville
3.	(10, -1)	Mayerthorpe
4.	9, 0)	Whitecourt
5.	(7, 1)	Fox Creek
6.	(1, 2)	
7.	(-2, 1)	
8.	(-5,0)	Bear Lake
9.	-8, 0)	Fort St. James
10.	(-12, -1)	Burns Lake
11.	(-17, 0)	
12.	-18, -1)	Kitimat

83

b. **Rivers or other bodies of water** that are crossed by the proposed pipeline- mark the pipeline with a BLUE X.

(9,0) – Athabasca River   (3, 2) – Smoky River

(-2, 1) – Peace River   (-4, 1) – Williston Lake

(-8, 0) – Stuart River/Stuart Lake   (-10, -1) – Babine Lake

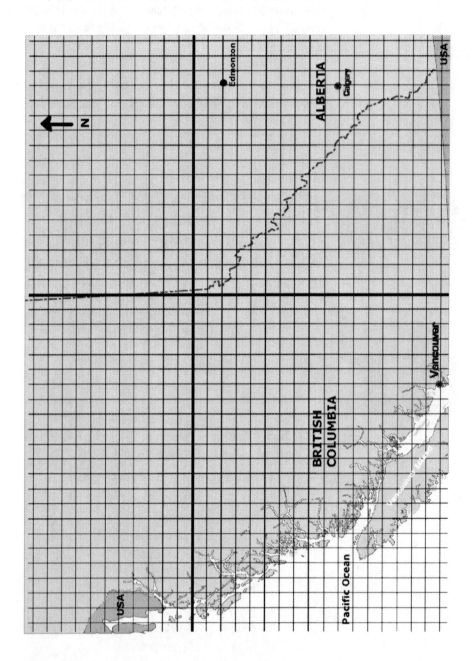

c. **First Nations Lands, and Provincial Parks.** The pipeline would pass through or near many First Nations lands, and provincial parks/wildlife protections areas. Some of the most closely affected areas are listed on the next page. Plot the approximate boundaries of each in a different colour.

Haisla Nation: (yellow)	Wet'suwet'en Nation (orange)	Dakelh Nation (purple) – west borders Wet'suwet'en lands	Monkman Provincial Park (green)
(-17, 0)	(-17, 0)	(-15, -2)	(-1, 0)
(-18, 1)	(-15, -2)	(-12, -5)	(-2, 1)
(-19, 1)	(-11, -2)	(-5, -7)	(-3, 0)
(-19, -2)	(-8, 0)	(1, -5)	(-1, 0)
(-17, -4)	(-11, 1)	(3, -3)	
(-16, -4)	(-12, 2)	(-2, 3)	
(-16, -1)	(-13, 4)	(-5, 1)	
(-17, 0)	(-14, 5)	(-12, 8)	
	(-16, 3)	(-14, 5)	
	(-15, 2)		
	(-17, 0)		

3. Enbridge has a history of oil spills: 800 in the last 10 years. How often is that on average?

4. There are 1,000 square kilometres deleted from the Douglas Channel leading into Kitimat . What is something that is the equivalent of 1,000 square kilometres?

5. The map you have been plotting points on was adapted from the Enbridge Northern Gateway website. If you have ever seen an actual map of British Columbia, what is most obviously missing from this map? Why do you think these features were omitted from the map?

6. A competing pipeline project to move crude oil from the tar sands, the Keystone XL Pipeline, has been rejected (for now). Do you think the delay of and opposition to the Keystone pipeline will make the Enbridge Northern Gateway pipeline project more likely to proceed? Less likely to proceed? Why?

85

Food For Thought:

Enbridge is responsible for the largest onshore oil spill in the history of the United States, in August of 2010.

make it better

Follow the 18 legal challenges to the Northern Gateway Pipeline, after its approval by the federal government. They began in October of 2015.

The website www.pipeupagainstenbridge.ca has a "Be Heard" section with some ideas for taking action. One possibility is to hold a fundraiser for the legal fees associated with the court challenges. **Pull-together.ca** has some resources.

Endnotes

1. www.wikipedia.org/wiki/Enbridge_Northern_Gateway_Pipelines
2. www.northerngateway.ca/economic-opportunity/benefits-for-aboriginals/
3. http://gatewaypanel.review-examen.gc.ca/clf-nsi/dcmnt/dcsnsttmnt-eng.html
4. www.sumofus.org/campaigns/enbridge/?sub=fb
5. Ibid.
6. http://www.pipeupagainstenbridge.ca/timeline

* With much appreciation to Shannon Taylor for her hard work on this lesson.

Exit Strategy

"Some are born great, some achieve greatness, and some hire public relations officers."

~ DANIEL J. BOORSTIN

setting the stage

Oil spills are a disaster for living things. They are also a public relations disaster for the big corporations that cause the spills. When the Exxon Valdez oil tanker spilled between 41,000 and 119,000 m³ of crude oil along 2,100 km of Alaskan coastline in 1989,[1] billions of dollars of damage payments were at stake.

Exxon had developed a chemical dispersant called Corexit (an **emulsifier**), which when sprayed on the spill atomizes the oil into tiny **micelles**. A micelle is a microscopic sphere that traps the oil and allows it to sink from the surface of the water down into the water column.[2] Oil that would naturally rise and be available for containment and collection suddenly becomes invisible.

Nalco Holding Company makes Corexit. They say that the micelles are **biodegradable** and because they sink, they "reduce exposure to birds, fish and sea animals." They go on to say that Corexit products "do not **bioaccumulate**, are not human **carcinogens**, do not degrade into endocrine disruptors, and are not reproductive toxins."[3]

But marine toxicologist Riki Ott disagrees. She points to a chemical in Corexit called 2-butoxy ethanol that is known to cause respiratory, nervous system, liver, kidney and blood disorders, and to the fact that 6,722 health claims were made against Exxon by clean-up workers following the Valdez spill.[4]

When billions of dollars in profits are on the line, it's good to have an exit strategy.

opening question ?

understanding using math

Hot water spraying of the shorelines was conducted by clean-up crews in Alaska. Can you think of two possible consequences?

1. In the very early stages of an oil spill from a tanker, the oil might approximate the shape of a circle. Here is a circle not to scale, obviously, with a radius of 100 metres. Calculate the area.

2. If a dispersant were used on this spill which dropped atomized oil straight down 60 metres into the water column, what shape would that look like? Name and sketch the shape.

3. What would the volume of that oily water column be?

4 a. Estimate the area of the oil slick on the next page given a scale of 1 cm^2 = 585 km^2.

b. If dispersant is used on this entire oil slick and creates droplets that fall 80 metres, what is the volume of the affected water?

c. The effectiveness of Corexit 9527 in Alaska has been estimated at 5 - 10%, which is the "amount of oil the dispersant puts into the water column compared to the amount of oil that remains on the surface."[4] If the Valdez lost an average of 500,000 barrels of oil, how many barrels ended up below the surface (list the range)?

87

Oil Slick Aerial View

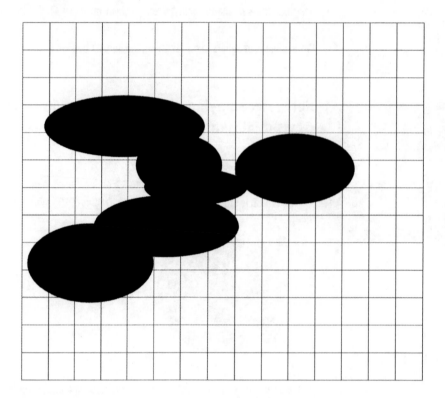

5. When scientists want to test soil samples for contamination, they are often pulled out in a cylindrical shape, like the graphic below right, and sent to a lab.

   a. If the radius of this cylinder is 5 cm, and the height is 20 cm, what is the volume of the soil sample?

   b. A LC50 is what is known as a "lethal concentration 50%", or in other words, the least amount of substance that will kill 50% of the animals they are testing it on. Which would be more toxic: a lower LC50 or a higher LC50?

   c. For oil, there's quite a range, but one estimate says 4000 parts per million as the LC50 for local fish. If the lab report comes back saying there's 8 cm^3 of crude oil in the soil sample from the cylinder above, is the soil toxic to the fish?

6. The micelles look something like the graphic below. The diameter could be 10 micrometres (a micrometre is one millionth of a metre). What would the volume of this micelle be?

7. The distance the oil travelled from the spill site is listed in the table below.[6] Graph the days versus the distance.

Day	Total Distance from spill site (mi)
4	37
7	90
11	140
14	180
19	250
40	360
56	470

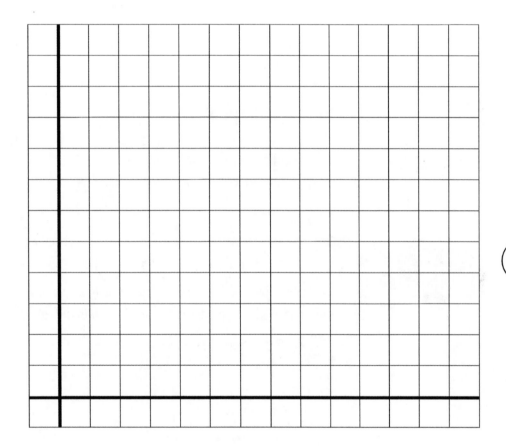

8.a. Workers cleaning up the shoreline were exposed to oil in the mist that was created from spraying the beach with hot water. If the exposure level was supposed to be 0.32 ppm but the workers experienced 128 ppm, how many times higher was their exposure than the safe level?

b. Ten years after the spill, only three of the Valdez's 26 ships were double hulled[7] (safer than single hull ships). What percentage of the ships were double hulled?

9. On April 20, 2010, the United States had its biggest oil spill ever, in the Gulf of Mexico. Five million barrels of oil were released into the ocean when the Deepwater Horizon Oil Rig failed. Seven million litres of Correxit were used to protect the shoreline, and to break the oil into tiny pieces so that it could be biodegraded by bacteria.[8]

   a. Explain mathematically why smaller pieces of oil should experience biodegradation more quickly.

   b. The University of Georgia tested ocean water with oil alone, and oil with dispersant. Marenobacter and Colwellia both are found in ocean water: the former degrades oil, the latter degrades dispersants.[9] What do you notice? Is this an argument for or against using Correxit?

	Oil alone	Oil with dispersant
Marenobacter (oil eating bacteria)	Creates a bloom – increases from 1% to 40%	Reduction of Marenobacter
Colwellia (dispersant eating bacteria)	Increase in Colwellia	

Food For Thought:

It was the largely African American fisher population that lost their livelihoods in the destruction from the Deepwater Horizon spill. The story is told in *Vanishing Pearls: The Oystermen of Pointe a la Hache*.

make it better

Consider your own participation in the oil industry, including the use of plastics. What choices can you make to give the oil companies less money?

What limitations are there to this consumer-based approach to solving this problem? Name one upstream solution to the problems with the oil industry.

Endnotes

1. http;//en.wikipedia.org/wiki/Exxon_Valdex_oil_spill
2. The Big Fix, Josh and Rebecca Tickell, Green Planet Productions, 2012.
3. www.nalco.com/applications/corexit-technology.htim
4. www.rikiott.com/
5. www.pwsrcac.or/docs/d0002700.pdf, A Review of Literature Related to Oil Spill Dispersants Especially Relevant to Alaska, Merv Fingas, March 2002.
6. www.rikott.com/
7. http://arcticcircle.uconn.edu/SEEJ/Alaska/miller2.htm
8. CBC Radio, Quirks and Quarks, Saturday Nov. 14, 2015.
9. CBC Radio, Quirks and Quarks, Saturday Nov. 14, 2015.

circles
volume of
cylinder

Cross Roads

"Water and air, the two essential fluids on which all life depends, have become global garbage cans."

~ JACQUES-YVES COUSTEAU

setting the stage

It's called Chemical Valley for a reason. The factories began arriving in the 1950s and today there are 62 large industrial facilities that surround the First Nations Aamjiwnaag reserve in Sarnia, Ontario.[1] Imperial Oil, Shell Canada, Ontario Power Generation, coal fired power plants and a slew of others collectively pour greenhouse gases, respiratory toxicants, reproductive and developmental toxicants and endocrine disruptors up into the sky.[2]

A group called Ecojustice is mounting a court challenge against the Ontario Ministry of the Environment on behalf of two local residents who argue that their Charter Rights have been violated. Ecojustice points to a survey of 411 residents that show high rates of asthma, high blood pressure, severe and chronic headaches, ADHD, skin rashes, kidney problems and even miscarriages and still births.

You may have heard of the idea of a watershed, which is how water travels through a geographic space. We can think about our air in a similar way. An airshed is a boundary within the atmosphere that we can use to think about air quality and how emissions from factories and vehicles affect that space, and ultimately, us.

opening question

Watch the public service announcement about Chemical Valley by Matt Steadman at **https://vimeo.com/28558848**. What point do you think it is making? Do you think that the point is effectively made?

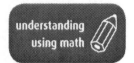

understanding using math

1. You are living in an area that has many factories. The emissions from the factories affect local air quality. Use a compass to draw a circle around your house (which is the square in the middle) that encompasses 80% of the factories (which are the Xs).

Scale

0 km   5 km

2. Using the scale, calculate the radius of the circle that you created.

3. Calculate the area of land (the circle) where people living are most at risk of asthma due to increased exposure to the factory emissions.

4. Consider the airspace up 2 km to be important to test for polycyclic aromatic hydrocarbons. What volume of airspace sits on top of the circle?

5. A major highway travels through community "W" on the map below. A study is conducted to check the air quality in the immediate area. They want to test a radius of 1.5 kilometres from the highway at the point marked.

   a. Using the scale below, draw the circle with radius 1.5 kilometres from the point indicated on the highway.

   b. What is the area of the test site?

   c. If the air above is tested to a height of 800 metres, what volume of air is being tested?

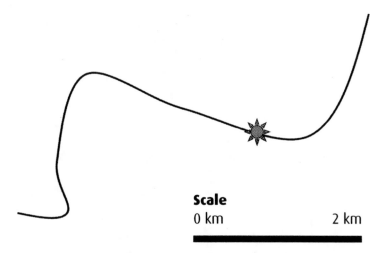

Scale

0 km   2 km

6. A train carrying toxic chemicals has de-railed. Three cylindrical tankers each with a radius of 3.5 metres and a length of 15 metres have broken open. The liquid has spilled out, and the vapours mean that people within a 5 km radius must evacuate.

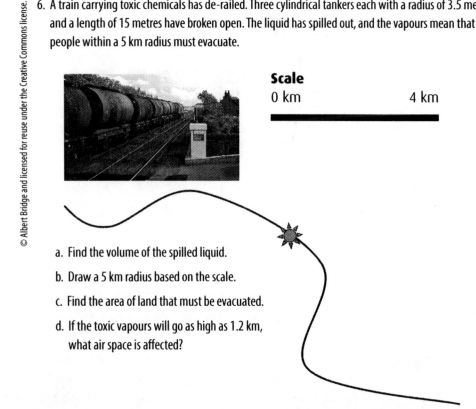

Scale

0 km   4 km

a. Find the volume of the spilled liquid.

b. Draw a 5 km radius based on the scale.

c. Find the area of land that must be evacuated.

d. If the toxic vapours will go as high as 1.2 km, what air space is affected?

93

make it better

On July 6, 2013, 47 people in Lac Mégantic, Quebec, died when a train derailed. Call your Member of Parliament and ask what timelines are in place to ensure that older DOT-111 rail cars (which have poor linings, shields and vents)[3] are removed from our rail lines.

Endnotes

1. www.ecojustice.ca

2. Ibid.

3. http://www.theglobeandmail.com/report-on-business/industry-news/energy-and-resources/irving-scuttles-rail-car-model-at-centre-of-lac-megantic-derailment/article16922759/

Take a Peak

"We are only as blind as we want to be."

~ MAYA ANGELOU

setting the stage

What do the following have in common: toothpaste, contact lenses, credit cards, golf balls, polystyrene cups, and plastic bags? They were all made using oil.[1]

Oil's history is a short 150 years, the first 50 of which saw it as a source of heat and light only. But with the introduction of the automobile in the early 1900s, the use of oil to fuel World War I, and the emergence of plastics in the 1920s, the stage was set for the explosive increase in oil use.[2] Now, 96% of the transportation sector is run off of oil, and fertilizers and asphalt also depend on it.

The world has an estimated 1.2 trillion barrels of oil that can be recovered using technologies that we currently possess. We also know that about 83 million barrels of oil were produced a day globally in 2005. It was 97 million barrels per day in 2015. People think that that might increase to 123 million barrels per day by 2030. But at some point, it will peak and then production of oil will fall. While some sources say we have already hit peak oil, others think it may be a few decades away. After peak oil, production becomes more difficult and expensive because the remaining oil is harder to reach and takes more refining.[3]

The most important questions have to do with the consequences of peak oil: will they create a global crisis? Or huge environmental benefits?

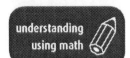

What environmental benefits can you think of that might come about when the production of oil peaks and then begins to fall?

1. The formula that describes the rate of extraction of oil in a particular country is given by $y = -x^2 + 8x$ where y represents **the amount of oil production per day in millions of barrels**, and x represents **time in ten year increments**. Fill in the t-chart on the right and then plot oil production versus time.

Title: _____

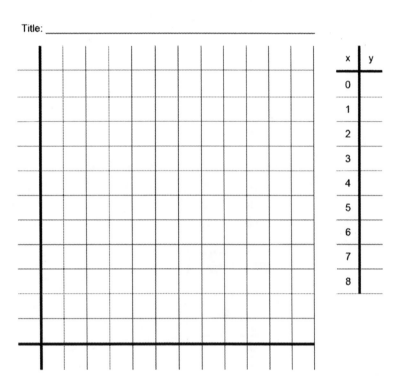

x	y
0	
1	
2	
3	
4	
5	
6	
7	
8	

2. How many years after the beginning of oil production does it peak in this country? (Remember that x is the number of 10 year increments)

3. If demand for oil turns out to be linear and is given by the equation $y = 2x$, how many years will it take for demand to match oil production? First generate points using the t-chart and then plot the points on the graph in question one. Then use the space on the right to solve algebraically for where the two lines cross.

x	y
0	
1	
2	
3	
4	
5	
6	
7	

What is the meaning of the point of intersection?
How will it affect the price of oil before and after?

95

4. If demand for oil turns out to be exponential and is given by the equation $y = x^2$, how many years will it take for demand to match oil production? First generate points using the t-chart and then plot the points on the graph in question one. Then use the space on the right to solve algebraically for where the two lines cross.

x	y
0	
1	
2	
3	
4	
5	
6	
7	

5.a. Let's pretend that the pressures on the oil industry continue to increase and cause less and less oil to be used within the energy sector. If the drop in use of oil is given by the equation $y = 100 \times (0.5)^x$, use your calculator to fill in the following t-chart and then graph the data. Remember that x represents the number of decades and y represents the oil use as a percentage of current use.

x	y
0	
1	
2	
3	
4	
5	
6	
7	
8	

5.b. This kind of graph is an example of exponential decay. Why do you think the term exponential decay is used?

5.c. After how many years does oil use fall below 20% of the current use of oil?

5.d. In order to get a faster drop off of oil use, which part of the equation would have to change, and in what way?

6.a. If the amount of oil use dropped linearly, described by the equation $y = -8x + 100$, how long would it take to drop below 20% of today's use?

6.b. Fill in the following t-chart and then graph the equation.

6.c. Which do you think is more likely: a linear or an exponential drop in oil use? Explain your reasoning.

x	y
0	
1	
2	
3	
4	
5	
6	
7	
8	
9	
10	

7. The following map was created by Emilfaro using GunnMap (http://gunn.co.nz/map/) and shows proven oil reserves. Which countries have the highest proven oil reserves?

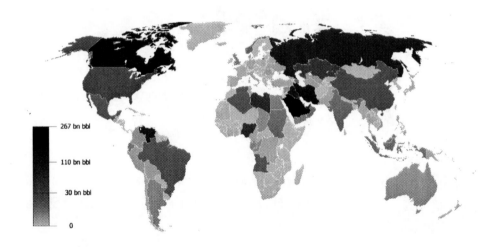

8. Why might a country or corporation understate its oil reserves? Why might a country or corporation overstate its oil reserves? What risks might a country with a lot of oil reserves face?

make it better

Support Indigenous communities when they oppose oil pipelines. Look into the Standing Rock Sioux in North Dakota, and explore the decision made about the Kinder Morgan Trans Mountain Pipeline in British Columbia.

Endnotes

1. http://www.davidsuzuki.org/issues/climate-change/science/energy/oil/
2. Ibid.
3. http://www.arlingtoninstitute.org/wbp/peak-oil/161#

$
%change
APR

Shark Infested Waters

"'I want an Oompa-Loompa!' screamed Veruca."

~ ROALD DAHL

Do you want quick cash? Do you have a bank account, a regular paycheck and are you 18 years old? If so, you can get up to $1,500 instantly. Sound too good to be true? That's your clue that it probably is…

Payday loan companies offer short term, high interest loans at over 1,300 locations across Canada.[1] One measure of the cost of a loan is the annual percentage rate (**APR**). According to the Criminal Code of Canada, it's illegal for any lender to charge more than 60% interest per year, but these businesses sneak in other fees in addition to the interest that effectively push the APR well over 60%.

If you have a lot of money and assets, you can go to a bank and take out a **low interest** line of credit. But for the two million Canadians a year who depend on payday loan centres, their high interest payments feed a $2 billion a year industry.

There are, in fact, other options to payday loans, and so you should always think carefully before you swim with the sharks.

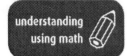

What reasons do you think payday loan centres might give to justify the high levels of interest that they charge on short-term loans?

1. If a payday loan centre charges $31 on every $100, what single number could you multiply $100 by to get the total payback cost of $131?

2. Use your answer from question #1 to calculate your total payback on a loan of $280. What is the loan fee (also called the interest)?

3. The equation to calculate the APR on the above loan is as follows:

   APR = ((Loan fee ÷ Loan amount) × 365 days/year) ÷ Number of days of the loan × 100

   Use the loan amount of $280 and the loan fee that you calculated in question 2, and consider that the loan is for two weeks. What is the APR?

4. Calculate the APR for each of the following sources of money:

Type of credit	Loan (or $)	Loan fee	# of days of the loan	APR
Bank Loan	$200,000	$6,000	365	
ATM Machine	$100	$1.00	1	
Credit card	$350	$9.00	30	
Payday loan (Ontario)	$100	$21	14	
Payday loan (Nova Scotia)	$100	$31	14	
Payday loan (Online)	$100	$33	14	

Remember:

   APR = ((Loan fee ÷ Loan amount) × 365 days/year) ÷ Number of days of the loan × 100

5. Fill in the payday loan sheet. **All entries that are loans or fees or charges should be entered as negative numbers.** All shaded boxes require values.

   Parameters: Your first loan is $500, and you agree to pay it back in two weeks. Because this is your first loan at this business, they charge you a $10 set up fee.

   The finance fee (the interest) is 20% (put in the actual dollar value).

   At the end of the first two weeks you ask to roll over the loan (which means not pay it back but instead continue it for two more weeks) and so are charged a second finance fee at the start of week three (still 20%; put in the actual dollar value).

At the end of the fourth week you write a check to pay off the original loan and the two finance fees, but your check "bounces" (that means that there's not enough money in your bank account). The payday loan center charges you $20 and the bank charges you a NSF ("not sufficient funds") fee of $45.

In desperation at the beginning of week five you take out a second loan at a payday loan center down the street, for $200 with a finance fee of 25%. The first payday loan centre rolls over your original loan for another finance fee (still 20%).

At the end of week six, when you pay back all loans, the first payday loan centre charges you a processing fee of $8.

Week	Original Loan	Set up fee	Finance Fee	Payday loan default charge	Bank overdraft fee (NSF)	Second Loan	Finance Fee	Processing Fee
1								
2								
3								
4								
5								
6								

6. Write an **addition** sentence for the total of your two loans only (no charges or fees). Remember that loans are written as negative numbers.

7. Write an **addition** sentence for the total of all loans and all fees and charges (again, all negative numbers).

8. Write a **subtraction** sentence to find the difference between what you paid in total and what you paid on loans. This represents all added interest and fees.

9. What did the interest and fees turn out to be as a percentage of the loans?

10. The following are questions about the map on the next page and the legend on this page.

   a. What does it mean that the median household income and number of payday loan centres in Los Angeles are **correlated**?

   b. You might hear a **classist** argument that "those people can't manage their money and they got themselves into it." Provide TWO **systemic** (i.e. not personal, but rather societal) reasons why some people with lower median household incomes may need a payday loan.

Median Household Income in Los Angeles and Location of Payday Loan Centres:²

Payday loan centre: ●

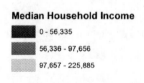

Median Household Income

■ 0 - 56,335

■ 56,336 - 97,656

□ 97,657 - 225,885

Median Household Income in Los Angeles and Location of Payday Loan Centres:[3]

10.c. In the following graph , what median household income matches the highest probability for payday loan centres?[4]

10.d. Explain why the probability is not highest at the lowest median household income levels.

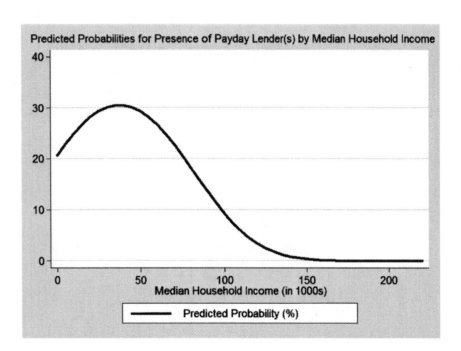

Arrange a class visit to a local payday loan centre. Prepare some questions in advance, and ask the manager if they would respond to your questions.

The Canadian Union of Postal Workers and the Canadian Postmasters and Assistants Association have suggested a solution to payday loan centres: use post offices to provide easily accessible short-term loans. According to CUPW's website, more than 60 countries in the world use these types of banks. Read more about the postal banking campaign here:

http://www.cupw.ca/en/campaign/postal-banking/about-our-campaign

Endnotes

1. Payday Loans: Short-term money at a hefty price. CBC News Online, October 4, 2006.
2. Courtesy of Wade Roberts, 2016
3. Courtesy of Wade Roberts, 2016
4. Courtesy of Wade Roberts, 2016.

Pythagorean Theorem

Mapping Access

"If every U.S. citizen ate just one meal a week (any meal) composed of locally and organically raised meats and produce we would reduce our country's oil consumption by over 1.1 million barrels of oil every week."

~ BARBARA KINGSOLVER

setting the stage

Food security has become a growing issue in the past few years. It has to do with the amount of healthy food in a community and each person's access to it. When a community does not have easy access to affordable, healthy food it is called a "**food desert**".[1]

When some of these neighborhoods were first designed, average incomes were higher and transportation by car was commonplace. Ensuring that grocery stores were in easy-to-reach locations was not a high priority. But as incomes have stagnated and declined and people have shifted to public transit, more and more people find themselves without food security.[2]

Access can be examined more broadly too. People's quality of life depends on access to public services like community centers, public libraries, and green spaces for recreation. Health impacts, like obesity, have an impact on the health of our communities.

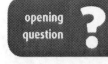

opening question ?

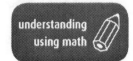

understanding using math

What is it about convenience stores and fast food outlets that would be troubling if people could not access a grocery store in their immediate area?

1. On the next page, fill in the reasonable distance column of the table (in other words, what is a reasonable distance to have to travel to get to this service). Remember to look at the scale on the map, and assume that you do not have a car. You're walking, biking, or taking public transit.

2. Using the Pythagorean Theorem, calculate the direct distance between your residence and the feature that you are looking at. If there is more than one of the feature (for example, there are two libraries), calculate all of the distances and then find the average distance for the final column.

3. Take a compass and draw a 500 metre radius around each of the four food stores.

   a. Carefully shade in the circles. Notice which areas of the map are not covered by any of the circles.

   b. What is the area of each of the four circles in square metres?

4. Pretend that you are a city planner and you have money to create new public transit to make access to services easier. Extend the current public transit line as best you can, to get as much coverage of the map as possible. The cost is $120 million per kilometre for light rail transit, and you have $1,250,000,000 in your budget.

104

1 block length (or width) is equivalent to 100 m

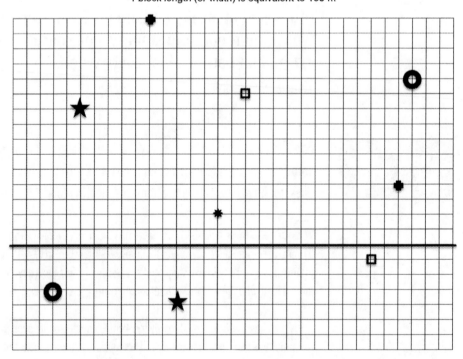

Legend:

Feature	Symbol	Reasonable Distance	Distances		Average Distance
Your residence	✳				
High end grocery stores	◻				
Affordable grocery stores	◉				
Libraries	◆				
Community centers	★				
Public transit line	▬▬▬				

5. Subway lines cost more than light rail transit or streetcars. If you had the same budget but wanted to put in subway lines, it would cost $300,000,000 per kilometre. Use a red marker and extend the current public transit line using subways.

   a. Do you see a significant difference in 'reach' between light rail and subways?

   b. What reasons do you think proponents of subways might give to justify the additional costs?

make it better

Do Something.org has some facts about food deserts in the United States and a link to a Department of Agriculture map showing food deserts. It can be found at **https://www.dosomething.org/facts/11-facts-about-food-deserts**.

Check out a food desert map of Saskatoon at **http://reurbanist.com/wp-content/uploads/2011/11/Saskatoon-food-deserts.jpg** and try creating your own map for your region.

Connect with Food Secure Canada, a group of people and institutions committed to zero hunger, a sustainable food system and healthy and safe food. They argue that Canada needs a national food policy. For upstream solutions, look at their Policy and Advocacy resources, including "A People's Food Policy for Canada".

105

Endnote

1. http://martinprosperity.org/2010/06/15/food-deserts-and-priority-neighbourhoods-in-toronto/
2. ibid.

%
average

Unity

"We are only as strong as we are united, as weak as we are divided."

~ J K ROWLING

setting the stage

Decades ago, in the 1970s, a man by the name of Mohammad Yunus who lived in Bangladesh and worked as a professor of economics began to lend money to women who were poor. Yunis would create the Grameen Bank in 1983, to provide small loans (called micro-credit) to people who lived in poverty and did not have access to the big banks. Big banks typically serve people who already have money.[1] More than 20 years later, Yunus would win the Nobel Peace Prize for his work.

Kiva is a web-based microfinance institution set up by Matt Flannery and Jessica Jackley in 2005.[2] Although micro-finance does not lift everyone out of poverty, it has allowed families to send more children to school, increase nutrition and living conditions and generally move from a focus on survival to a focus on planning for the future. A focus on women has led to an improvement in the status of women, giving them more power in decision making, and control over their own assets, including housing and land.

As one tool in a larger tool kit, microfinance must be seen as a strategy alongside better education, more effective infrastructure and fair laws.

Kiva, which means "unity" in Swahili, has made over 600,000 loans through more than one million lenders. Today about 160,000,000 people are able to use micro-finance in developing countries though thousands of microfinance institutions in 70 countries.

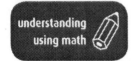

Watch the "How Kiva Works" video on the Kiva website. What questions do you have about the animated short?

1. On its website, Kiva lists some statistics for the week (below).

   a. Extrapolate them to guessitmate yearly totals.

   b. Speculate as to why Kiva picked these particular statistics to share.

4,716	Borrowers funded this week
3,808	New lenders this week
13,820	Lenders made a loan this week
$1,747,150	Amount loaned this week

2. The repayment rate is listed on the website as 98.54% to date. What do you think leads to the very high rate?

3. It has been suggested that sometimes microfinance institutions may themselves pay to cover defaulted loans rather than pass them back to Kiva. Why do you think that they might do that?

4. As of October 2015, Kiva has loaned a total of $763,077,250 to 1,342,681 lenders since its inception.[3] What is the average loan amount?

5. In 2012, $1 million was lent to Kiva, which turned around and gave people $25 each to make a loan for free. How many people were able to make a free loan, and why do you think Kiva did this?

6. In many developing countries, patriarchy limits women's power and so microcredit can address the fact that family resources tend to go to males in the family. "As of April 1, 2012, 80.46% of Kiva loans have been made to women entrepreneurs."[4] If this figure was current as of October 2015, how many loans have gone to women entrepreneurs? Discuss how patriarchy limits women's power.

7. Many people wonder how effective their contributions are to any organization. A website called Charity Navigator gives organizations ratings based on their financial score and their accountability and transparency score. Here is Kiva's rating:

107

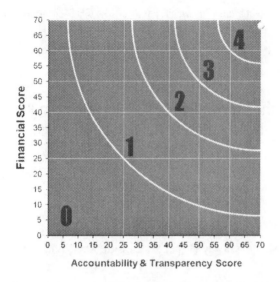

Financial Score vs. Accountability & Transparency Score

a. What are the two individual scores and what are they out of?

b. Would this give you confidence in loaning with Kiva? What else might you like to know before you made a decision?

8. In 2012, Charity Navigator moved to create a three dimensional evaluation of charities in which scores were based on financials, accountability and transparency, and results and were weighted 33%, 17% and 50% respectively.[5] What do you think of the weightings? Would you change them? Why or why not?

Draw a three dimensional proportionally accurate box of a charity that was scored 30 out of 33, 10 out of 17 and 45 out of 50 on the three scales. Show both the full box and the rated charity within the full box.

9. Some people like to know how much of their money goes directly to the services it provides, and how much goes to the administration of the organization. Charity Navigator lists Kiva's use of funds as follows:

Program:	81.7%
Administration	13.3%
Fundraising	5.0%

Make a pie graph of this data and discuss.

make it better

Go to **www.kiva.org** and look at the projects around the world that are in need of loans. If you have the financial capacity to do so, make a loan. Consider a Kiva card as a gift for someone the next time you are searching for gift ideas.

Endnote

1. www.kiva.org
2. http://en.wikipedia.org/wiki/Kiva_(organization)
3. http://en.wikipedia.org/wiki/Kiva_(organization)
4. Ibid.
5. www.slideshare.net/CharityNav/crowdsourcing-transparency-and-results-based-charity-rating

The (Bottom) Line

"Wars are never fought for altruistic reasons."

~ ARUNDHATI ROY

setting the stage

June, 2000. Canadian oil company CGX's operations off of the north coast of South America were met by the Surinamese military forces. Guyana, who had granted access of "its waters" to CGX, responded sharply.[1]

Guyana and Suriname share a common land border, marked by the Corentyne River, which drains into the Atlantic Ocean. In 1936, a boundary commission made up of the United Kingdom, The Netherlands and Brazil decided to clarify the border line out in the ocean and decided that it would begin from a point on the western bank of the Corentyne River called Point 61. The ocean territorial line was to run 10 degrees east of north "to the limit of the territorial sea". But that was 1936.[2]

In 1957, the United Kingdom (Guyana's colonial ruler) decided to change the boundary, following the N10E line to the three mile limit from the coast and then change direction to N33E. Within a year, it began granting oil exploration licenses N32E from Point 61. Suriname granted a concession that had as its western limit N10E.[3]

Almost all countries in the world took part in the United Nations Convention on the Law of the Sea, designed to guide all sea and ocean disputes between countries. The common practice of this convention is to use an ocean boundary which is equidistant between the two conflicting country's shorelines.

When drawing the line affects your bottom line, you may need some help to avoid gunboat diplomacy.

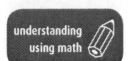

Why do you think that countries care so much about their offshore boundaries?

1. Locate Guyana and Suriname on the following map.

    a. At which latitude and longitude is the capital city of Guyana, Georgetown?

    b. At which latitude and longitude is the capital of Suriname, Paramaribo?

    c. Which ocean borders both Guyana and Suriname?

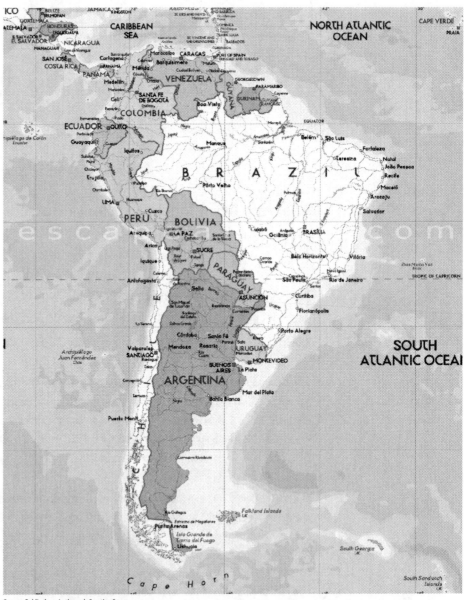

Source: Public domain through Creative Commons:
https://commons.wikimedia.org/wiki/File:%22Political_South_America%22_CIA_World_Factbook.svg#filelinks

2. There is a section of land between the Corentyne River and the New River that both Guyana and Suriname claimed as their own.[4] Use the simplified map below for the following questions (remember this is on shore):

    a. Without using a protractor, calculate the missing angle in the disputed, New River Triangle.

    b. Using the scale, determine the area of the disputed territory.

    c. Why do you think each country had an interest in that particular triangle of land?

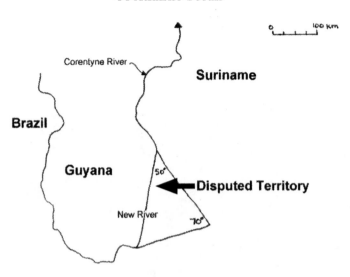

3. According to international law, the first 19 km offshore from a country's coastline belongs to that country exclusively.[5] Use the scale on the map below to draw the 19 km boundary and shade it in.

4. After 19 km, the next 302.5 km also belong to that country with respect to any resources that fall within that zone, but vessels from other countries are allowed to navigate these waters.[6] Use the scale on the map to draw the next zone.

Suriname and Guyana Boundary Dispute

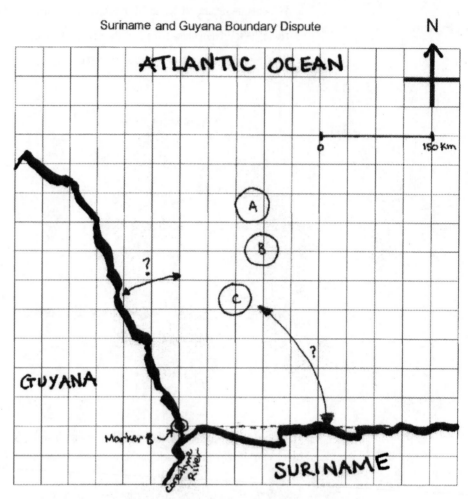

Enlarged views of potential ocean oil reserves

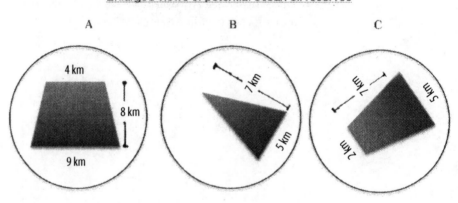

A

B

C

5. From the point labelled Marker B on the west shore of the Corentyne River, draw a line 10 degrees east of north out into the Atlantic Ocean. This is Suriname's claim, based on the 1936 agreement.

6. From Marker B, draw a line that is 34 degrees east of north out into the Atlantic Ocean. This is Guyana's claim, based on the United Nations Law of the Sea Convention.

7. Using the scale on the map, figure out roughly the area of disputed ocean between the two claim lines.

8. Fill in all of the missing angles on the map.

9. The Law of the Sea Convention uses a line that is equidistant from each country's shorelines. How many degrees would be allotted to each country based on the equidistant line?

10. Why do you think that Guyana wants the equidistant line to be the boundary?

11. Oil exploration has taken place within the disputed zone. Use the fictional oil reserve sites labelled A, B and C on the map and enlarged for easier reference to calculate the area of each potential oil reserve. Make sure to show your formula and answer with correct units.

    Area A: Formula: Area:

    Area B: Formula: Area:

    Area C: Formula: Area:

12. The final decision of the dispute in 2007 awarded 33,152 km² of coastal waters to Guyana and 17,871 km² to Suriname.[7] What percentage of the disputed waters did each country receive?

 make it better

Several high profile land disputes have occurred in Canada between the Canadian government and First Nations communities. Choose one such land dispute and research it in detail: what were the circumstances of the conflict, how did the conflict progress, and was there an adequate and fair resolution? Be sure to discuss the issue of colonialism and the idea of Canada as a settler state.

Endnotes

1. http://www.guyana.org/guysur/introduction.html
2. Arbitral Tribunal Constituted Pursuant to Article 287, and in accordance with annex VII, of the United Nations Convention on the Law of the Sea, The Hague, 17 September 2007, p. 29.
3. http://www.pca-cpa.org/upload/files/Guyana-Suriname%20Award.pdf, p. 30.
4. http://www.gammathetaupsilon.org/the-geographical-bulletin/2000s/volume44-1/article6.pdf
5. http://www.offshore-mag.com/articles/2007/09/suriname-guyana-offshore-border-dispute-settled.html
6. Ibid.
7. Ibid.

Fare Prices

"Alone we can do so little; together we can do so much."

~ HELEN KELLER

Imagine a big city where there are subways, buses, streetcars and other forms of public transit. The more people that you can get travelling together, the less energy and oil you will use. As a result, the amount of air pollution drops.

If you fund the system properly and ensure that the cost to ride the vehicles isn't overly expensive, you address issues of poverty by encouraging mobility amongst people who cannot afford cars. In the United States, some studies found that 21% of respondents would not make a trip if transit was not available.[1]

Some places around the world have even moved to free transit, where no fares are charged.[2] Funding is covered either by the government, or by the institution running the service (for example a university campus that offers free transit to its students).

If you were in charge of transit within your community, what would it look like? Who would pay for it? How would it take into account the requirements of people who most need it?

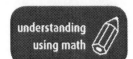

What reasons might a city or community give for zero-fare transit? Can you see any possible downsides?

1. City A has a funding shortfall for their transit system of $14,000 a day. On the following graph paper, draw the line $y = 14$. Label your y-axis "Revenue/ Shortfall in thousands of dollars".

2. Let's pretend that the equation that represents the income that the city collects from fares is $y = -x^2 + 9x$, where x represents "the number of five cent increases to the current bus fare price". What shape is this line?

3. Why does increasing the fares initially increase the revenue?

4. Why will overall revenues peak and then begin to fall? What happens in the real world that would cause a decline in overall revenue after a certain number of five cent fare increases?

5. Fill in the following t – chart for the equation $y = -x^2 + 9x$:

When x is...	...y is equal to...
0	
1	
2	
3	
4	
5	
6	
7	
8	
9	

6. Graph the points from the above t -chart on the same graph paper as you graphed the first line.

7. Visually, where do the two lines intersect (at which points)?

8. Solve mathematically for where the two lines cross. Did you get the same answer as in question 7?

9. How many five cent increases are required for the city to break even?

10. How many five cent increases are required before revenue peaks?

11. What dollar value does revenue peak at?

Number of Five Cent Fare Increases vs. Revenue

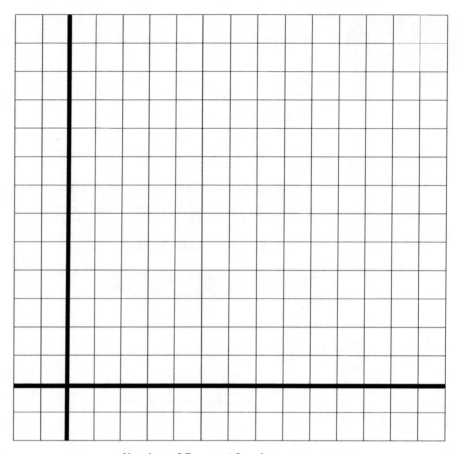

Number of five cent fare increases

make it better

Find out if your city or town has free transit for children or seniors. What ages does this free transit apply to? Are there special accommodations for people within particular income brackets? If your city or town doesn't have free transit for children or seniors or people living in poverty, can you use other cities or towns in Canada that do as a precedent in talking about this issue with your municipal politicians?

Endnotes

1. http://www.fhwa.dot.gov/policy/2002cpr/pdf/ch14.pdf
2. http://en.wikipedia.org/wiki/Free_public_transport

0/0/fractions visual represed.

Bitter

"Our lives begin to end the day we become silent about things that matter."

~ MARTIN LUTHER KING, JR.

setting the stage

You have come to this cocoa plantation in the Ivory Coast from far away. Hidden in your jacket is a video camera, because what you are looking for is illegal, and people are unlikely to treat you kindly if they know what you are doing.

Looking up you see dozens of cocoa pods hanging from the trees, and within them are the beans that will be bought up from some of the largest chocolate companies in the world: Hershey's, Mars and Nestlé. In fact, both Ghana and the Ivory Coast supply three quarters of the world's cocoa![1]

The problem is that children from surrounding countries like Burkina Faso, Mali and Togo work on these farms, and do not always get paid. Some do not get to go to school. They are exposed to the pesticides used on the trees. For all intents and purposes, they are slaves. And although the chocolate industry signed the Harkin-Engel Protocol in 2001 promising to end child slavery within the industry by 2005, continuing reports of abuses remain.[2]

As you turn the corner, you come upon a group of young kids, perhaps 12 years old. They are using machetes to cut open a pile of cocoa pods.

Is this where our chocolate comes from? Does it have to be this way?

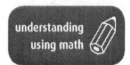

Why do you think the government of the Ivory Coast might not monitor its borders carefully enough to prevent children from being brought into the country to work on the plantations?

1. Ghana and the Ivory Coast supply 75% of the world's cocoa.[3]

   a. Draw three different pictures showing what 75% looks like.

   b. What is the decimal form for 75%?

2. The Ivory Coast supplies 43% of the world's cocoa.[4]

   a. Draw a picture showing what 43% looks like.

   b. What is the decimal form for 43%?

3. There are 600,000 cocoa farms in the Ivory Coast. They are responsible for one third of the country's economy.[5]

   a. Draw three different pictures showing what one third looks like.

   b. What is the decimal form for one third?

4. Three million tons of chocolate are eaten every year in the world. Half is consumed in Europe.[6]

   a. Write the number three million.

   b. What is half of 3 million?

   c. What is the decimal form for half?

   d. How can you use the decimal form to find half of three million?

5. The chocolate companies spend six million Euros per year in aid within the countries that supply them with cocoa. Nestlé made 12 billion Euros in profit in 2009.[7] What is six million as a percentage of 12 billion?

6. The cocoa farmers receive one Euro for every kilogram of beans that they sell. One kilogram of beans will make 40 chocolate bars, which could be sold for a total of about 30 Euros. What is the ratio between the amount that the farmer gets and the amount that the chocolate is sold for?

7. In the movie *The Dark Side of Chocolate*, a plantation owner in the Ivory Coast is caught on film saying that a child can be purchased to work on the plantation for 230 Euros. There are 1.5 Canadian dollars in one Euro. What is the cost in Canadian dollars that is being paid for these slaves?

8. Some of these children are forced to work 80 to 100 hours per week.[8] If a typical full time workweek is 40 hours, calculate what 90 hours is as a percentage of 40.

9. ChocoSol is a chocolate company in Toronto, Canada that sells direct trade chocolate from the southern part of Mexico.

    a. Use the internet to find out what direct trade means.

    b. Use the internet to find out how far Oaxaca, Mexico is from Toronto, Canada.

    c. ChocoSol brings in a single shipment of cocoa per year, by shipping it in a boat up the Atlantic Coast to Nova Scotia and then sending it by train to Toronto. Why is your answer in (b) likely too low?

    d. Why would ChocoSol send the beans a farther distance?

10. ChocoSol can generate a single batch of chocolate from beans in about eight hours.

    a. How many batches could be made in a week?

    b. How many batches could be made in a year?

    c. Why do you think ChocoSol only brings in one shipment of beans per year?

make it better ✌

If you are going to buy chocolate and you can afford it, buy Fair Trade products or search for direct trade chocolate businesses.

Choose not to eat chocolate if you are unsure where it is coming from.

Watch the trailer for *Tony's Chocolonely*, about Teun van de Keuken who, knowing that a portion of the chocolate that we eat is made by child slavery, attempted to get himself arrested for eating it.

119

Endnotes

1. http://www.foodispower.org/slavery-chocolate/
2. http://johnrobbins.info/blog/is-there-slavery-in-your-chocolate/
3. http://www.foodispower.org/slavery-chocolate/
4. Ibid.
5. Ibid.
6. The Dark Side of Chocolate (2010)
7. Ibid.
8. http://www.huffingtonpost.com/amanda-gregory/chocolate-and-child-slave_b_4181089.html

translations
dilations
rotations

Washed Up

"It's not just that the 'aid' isn't aiding, it is that it is hurting."

~ KUMARI, SRI LANKAN ACTIVIST

setting
the stage

You are a fisher. You make your living by heading out into the ocean in your small fishing vessel each day, from a tiny shack that sits on the beach. You and your community have done this for many generations, even in spite of the resistance that you get from the big hotel owners nearby who want the beach cleared for tourists to use. Recently, a mysterious fire swept through the fishing huts, burning many of them down. You all rebuilt.

On December 26, 2004, a massive tsunami swept the shores of your country, killing 35,000 people. As communities reeled in shock, the world responded by sending $13 billion in aid: historically unprecedented. But things have not gone as planned: the Sri Lankan government refused to let fishers back to the beach, making food rations contingent on relocating inland to camps. Although they said it was for your safety, the big hotels were now being allowed full access to the waterfront.[1]

Redevelopment projects to make the area an upscale resort village are getting the money that was supposed to help the victims of the tsunami. People have started to accuse officials of taking money for themselves and their families. And an undemocratically established "Task Force to Rebuild the Nation" is rapidly setting plans in motion. Strangely, five of the 10 member group are business executives with direct ties to the largest resorts in the country.[2]

Naomi Klein, in her book *The Shock Doctrine*, calls this "disaster capitalism".

One of the tsunami survivors, named Renuka, said "If you have something for me, put it in my hand." What do you think she means?

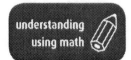

Use the Cartesian coordinates and the graph paper on the next page to plot the following (fictional) items. Each block is 25 metres by 25 metres. The x-axis is the longer axis and the ocean side is on the right.

1. (IN BLUE) Draw the shoreline of Arugam Bay in Sri Lanka. Connect the points as you go. The water is on the right side of the page and the land is to the left of the shoreline.

2. (IN RED) Water naturally rises and falls with the tide. The high water mark is the line beyond which the water does not go. Use the coordinates listed on the attached page to draw in the high water line.

3. (IN BLACK) After the tsunami hit, the government made regulations preventing the small fishers from re-building their fishing shacks on the beaches. They had to be at least 200 metres back from the high water mark. They said it was for their safety. Strangely enough, the hotels were allowed to rebuild along the beach. Draw in the government line, 200 metres back from the high water line.

4. (IN PENCIL) The hotels were small before the tsunami. Because they were destroyed or damaged, they were rebuilt. Many of them moved closer to the water on the nice sandy beaches, to attract more tourists. Draw in the five old hotels using the coordinates on the next page.

5. (IN GREEN) These are the transformations to each of the five hotels.

   a. Hotel A built two new hotels. The first was a translation of the original building in the direction (1, -5). It was the exact same size and orientation. Draw in the first new building. The second new building was a 90 degree rotation of the original building clockwise around point (-20,-3). It was the exact same size as well, but the 90-degree rotation allowed the tourists to watch the setting sun. Draw in the second building.

   b. Hotel B's view was now blocked by Hotel A's new buildings, which had moved closer to the water. So it moved its building closer as well in a translation of (1, -4) AND then dilated the building from the bottom left corner, by a factor of 2. Draw the final building.

   c. Hotel C wanted to move closer to the water, but rotate the building 90 degrees counter clockwise to catch the rising sun in the morning. The rotation is around point (-3,0). After the designs were submitted, the new position was found to be on inadequate soil and so it was translated from that spot (2,1) and dilated from the bottom left corner by a factor of 3. Draw the final building.

   d. Hotel D moved closer to the water with a translation of (0,-3).

   e. Hotel E rotated its building 90 degrees counter clockwise around the point (18,-2) and then dilated from point (18,-2) by a factor of 1.5. Draw the final building.

6. (IN BLACK) The refugee camps were set up behind the government lines in rocky terrain. Draw in the camps using the coordinates and find the area of the two camps using the formula for trapezoids and the scale on the page.

7. If there are 2,250 people in Camp One and 1,850 in Camp Two, what is the number of people per square metre in each camp? Which camp is more crowded?

8. A refugee camp needs to provide 30 m^2 per person.[3] Have these camps met this standard?

9. The world raised 13 billion in aid in a mere six months. If you can count a single number aloud in one second, how long would it take you to count to 13 billion? Don't put your final answer in seconds (what would be a more appropriate unit of measurement?)

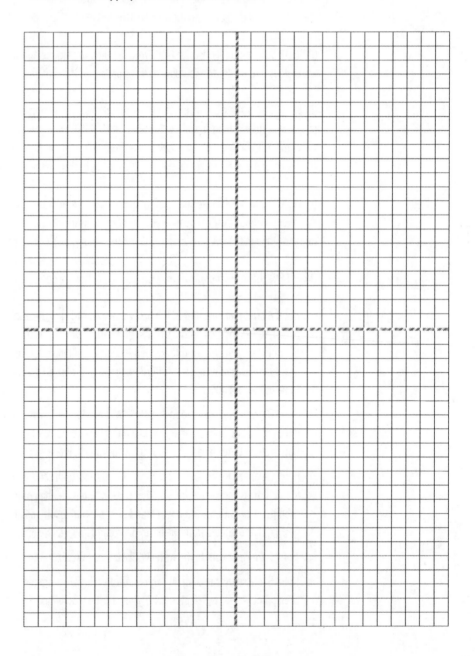

Shoreline (in blue)	High Water Mark (in red)	Hotel A (in pencil)	Hotel B (in pencil)	Hotel C (in pencil)	Hotel D (in pencil)	Hotel E (in pencil)
(21, -11)	(21, -8)	(-20, 1)	(-14, 0)	(-6, 0)	(6, 2)	(18, 0)
(20, -9)	(19, -5)	(-20, 4)	(-14, 2)	(-6, 2)	(6, 5)	(19, 0)
(16, -7)	(16, -3)	(-18, 4)	(-12, 2)	(-3, 2)	(8, 5)	(19, 2)
(15, -4)	(14, -1)	(-18, 3)	(-12, 0)	(-3, 0)	(11, 4)	(21, 2)
(12, -4)	(12, -2)	(-19, 3)	(-14, 0)	(-6, 0)	(11, 2)	(21, -2)
(10, -6)	(9, -2)	(-19, 2)			(6, 2)	(18, -2)
(6, -6)	(7, -4)	(-18, 2)				(18, 0)
(4, -4)	(4, -2)	(-18, 1)				
(2, -4)	(-1, -3)	(-20, 1)				
(0, -6)	(-4, -2)					
(-4, -6)	(-6, -2)					
(-6, -8)	(-8, -5)					
(-9, -8)	(-10, -4)					
(-12, -6)	(-12, -4)					
(-14, -6)	(-12, -5)					
(-17, -10)	(-15, -6)					
(-21, -10)	(-16, -6)					
	(-18, -5)					
	(-21, -5)					

Refugee Camp 1	Refugee Camp 2
(-1, 9)	(7, 9)
(-4, 12)	(7, 12)
(-12, 12)	(17, 12)
(-13, 9)	(19, 9)
(-1, 9)	(7, 9)

make it better

When disasters happen around the world and you want to respond by contributing, do your research. Who is getting the support? How do you know? What systems are in place to make sure that the people who need it most are getting what they need?

Endnotes

1. Klein, Naomi. The Shock Doctrine. Alfred Knopf Canada. 2007.
2. Ibid.
3. http://www.webpal.org/SAFE/aaareconstruction/immediate/refugee_camp.htm

data analysis

Under Threat

124

"The scalp serves as no barrier at all to the psychologically draining or boosting effects of pervasive cultural beliefs."

~ CORDELIA FINE

setting the stage

It was in the 1990s when Mattel's Teen Talk Barbie doll sweetly said "Math class is tough!" and "Let's go shopping!". But gender stereotypes about what girls and boys can and can't do remain firmly entrenched and reinforced by some current day researchers who claim that there is a significant, genetically-based and fixed divide between the sexes.

Playing up tiny differences and claiming that "boys are better at math" and "girls are better verbally" may sell magazines but the research tells a different story. Take math: not long ago, boys did outperform girls by quite large numbers. *The Study of Mathematically Precocious Youth* test results from the early 1980s showed that highly 'gifted' boys outnumbered 'gifted' girls by a ratio of 13:1. If this difference was due to biology, you'd expect it to remain stable, except that by 2005 the ratio had dropped to 2.8 to 1.[1] Hmm.

You'd also expect that differences between boys and girls would be consistent across the globe, but if you look at the Program for International Student Assessment (PISA) exam, given to 15 year olds from 40 nations, you'll see that the girls in Iceland and Thailand outperformed the boys.[2] Hmm, again.

What researchers do know is that when there is a "real time threat of being judged and treated poorly in settings where a negative stereotype about one's group applies", this **stereotype threat** has real impacts on performance.[3] Turns out it's not so much about whether you are a boy or a girl: it's the cultural context that you live in.

If you are in a situation like an exam where you are under stereotype threat, and your focus is on trying not to fail, what words would characterize your behavior on a test? What about if your focus was instead on seeking success?

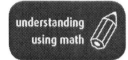

1. The following are two bell curves which demonstrate the range in height between males and females.[4]

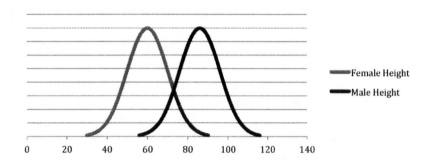

Female Height
Male Height

0   20   40   60   80   100   120   140

a. Is it true or false to say that all males are taller than all females?

b. Is it true or false to say that most males are taller than most females?

2. In statistics, a **difference value** (or **d value** for short) is found by subtracting the mean value for females on a test from the mean value for males on the same test and then dividing the result by the standard deviation of both groups (which measures how wide the curves are). Difference values of 0.8 are considered large, 0.5 is considered medium and 0.2 is considered small.

a. What is the mean female height from the graph above?

b. What is the mean male height from the graph above?

c. If the standard deviation for both groups is 11.54, what is the d value for height?

d. Would that d value be considered large, medium or small?

3. There are 124 extensively studied psychological traits that have been compared between men and women, including all kinds of academic skills. Ninety-six of the 124 show d values less than 0.35.[5] What percentage is that equivalent to?

The following bell curves show what a d value of 0.35 looks like.

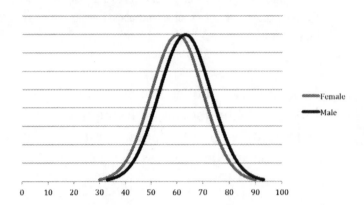

a. Is it true to say that there are many females that outperform males on this particular test?

b. Is it true to say that there are many males that outperform females on this particular test?

c. Is it true to say that there are almost equivalent numbers of males and females at both ends of the curve (high performing and low performing)?

4. One of the reasons that differences are played up in the media is due to the "file drawer effect". Because differences are interesting, they get published. Those studies that show no differences are filed away, never to be seen. What would a pie graph look like that displayed the following data:

No sex based differences found: 58

Sex based differences found: 2

Based on the file drawer effect, which studies would be reported by the media?

5. In many different types of tests comparing males and females, the results for the males tend to be more variable. It has led to something called the Male Variability Hypothesis, which suggests that because the results on many tests are more variable for males than females, there are many more high performing males than females. People go on to say that this is evidence that males outperforming females must be innate (genetically hardwired). It looks like this:

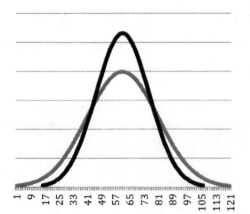

a. Mark the line that represents the males, and the one that represents the females.

b. Are the mean values for each group the same or different? What are they?

c. Is it true to say there are more males that do **less well** on this test than females?

d. Is it true to say that there are more males that do better on this test than females?

e. If you learned that in the top 5% scores on an international math test there was greater variability in the female test takers, what would that say about the Male Variability Hypothesis? (They were, in the Netherlands, Germany and Lithuania.)[5]

f. If the ratio at the upper end shifted over time, as you learned in the introduction to this lesson, from a ratio of 13 to 1 to 2.8 to 1, how would the above bell curves change?

6. One of the ways to prevent stereotype threat is to be surrounded with role models of your same sex. Graph the following data[6] in three pie graphs and comment on the implications of fewer and fewer women at higher levels of mathematics (full professors would be the higher levels in the chart below).

	Math Ph.Ds.	Math assistant professors	Math full professors
Male %	73	80	95
Female %	27	20	5

7. In the journal *American Psychologist*, research was presented by psychologists Claude Steele and Joshua Aaronson. Men and women taking a test were either told beforehand that boys do better on this test, or they were told nothing at all. The following column chart approximates the finding:[7]

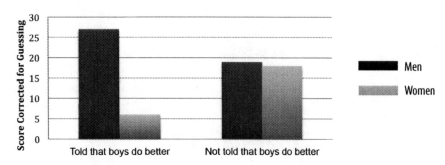

Mean Score on a Difficult Math Test

a. Describe the findings.

b. What recommendations should be made to teachers or others administering tests, based on this research?

8. The International Mathematical Olympiad is a competition of very exceptional math students working on six person teams from about 95 countries. The following is the percentage of females on those teams from different countries from the years 1989 to 2008:

Country	Females/Total[8]	%	Gender Gap Index[9]
Canada	13/120		18
USSR	15/120		45
United Kingdom	13/120		11
Romania	7/120		47
China	4/114		73
Japan	2/114		91
Iran	3/120		118
India	4/119		114
Israel	3/118		36
Korea	9/120		97
France	4/120		51
USA	5/120		31
Germany	8/120		7
Saudi Arabia			124
Pakistan			126
Sweden			1
Norway			2
Finland			3

a. Fill in the middle column (the percentages) for the first 13 countries, which were all in the top 30 ranked countries in the IMO in 2007.

b. Graph the percentage of females on the team versus the gender gap index for 2007. What pattern do you see?

c. Draw in the best-fit line for the data.

d. Based on the pattern, what percentage of females might you expect on teams that came from the bottom five countries on the table above?

9. Using data on male and female students from 10 states in the United States, representing more than seven million young people, researchers in 2008 looked at data on mathematics performance.

Grade	d value
2	0.06
3	0.04
4	-0.01
5	-0.01
6	-0.01
7	-0.02
8	-0.02
9	-0.01
10	0.04
11	0.06

a. Based on what you know about d values, what is the relative difference in mathematics performance between males and females above?

b. What is the difference between the positive and negative numbers?

 make it better

Educate people about the research on sex differences, showing that the historical beliefs about innate differences are false. How does knowing this affect your performance?

Endnotes

1. Fine, Cordelia. Delusions of Gender. W. W. Norton and Company. New York. 2010, p. 181.
2. Eliot, Lise. Pink Brain Blue Brain. Houghton Mifflin Harcourt. Boston. 2009, p. 208.
3. Fine, Cordelia. Delusions of Gender. W. W. Norton and Company. New York. 2010, p. 30.
4. Eliot, Lise. Pink Brain Blue Brain. Houghton Mifflin Harcourt. Boston. 2009, p. 12.
5. Eliot, Lise. Pink Brain Blue Brain. Houghton Mifflin Harcourt. Boston. 2009, p. 13.
6. Fine, Cordelia. Delusions of Gender. W. W. Norton and Company. New York. 2010, p. 181.
7. Eliot, Lise. Pink Brain Blue Brain. Houghton Mifflin Harcourt. Boston. 2009, p. 211.
8. Rivers, Caryl and Rosalind Barnett. The Truth About Girls and Boys. Columbia University Press, New York, 2011, p.67.
9. Hyde, Janet and Jandet Mertz. Gender, Culture, and Mathematics Performance. www.pnas.org/cgi/doi/10.1073/pnas.0901265106
10. http://www3.weforum.org/docs/WEF_GenderGap_Report_2007.pdf
11. Hyde, Janet and Jandet Mertz. Gender, Culture, and Mathematics Performance. www.pnas.org/cgi/doi/10.1073/pnas.0901265106

Collapse

(130)

"Too large a proportion of recent 'mathematical' economics are mere concoctions, as imprecise as the initial assumptions they rest on, which allow the author to lose sight of the complexities and interdependencies of the real world in a maze of pretentious and unhelpful symbols."

~ JOHN MAYNARD KEYNES

setting the stage

Sub-prime mortgages. Collateralized debt obligations. Frozen credit markets. Credit default swaps. It's all enough to make your eyes glaze over and encourage you to throw up your hands in despair. How is it possible to understand complicated banking and investment? And more importantly, why should we even care?

In 2008 and 2009 there was a financial crisis of a scale not seen since the Great Depression in the 1930s. It had worldwide impacts, with businesses failing, people losing their houses and their jobs — especially in the United States — and finally, banks being bailed out with hundreds of billions of dollars from the government.[1]

A part of the problem was created when people were given loans to buy houses even though it was likely that they would be unable to pay back their loans ("sub-prime mortgages"). Although lenders (like banks) suspected that this was the case due to the low credit rating of the borrowers, they were able to pass along these mortgages — and their risks — by selling them to investment bankers. In economic theory, this is called a **moral hazard**: banks were not cautious about their lending because some other group took on the risk.[2]

This lesson is about trying to piece together one very complicated, but important puzzle.

Watch *The Crisis of Credit Visualized* on Youtube (it's just over 11 minutes) and discuss with the class. What questions do you have?

In order to understand how the credit crisis happened, it's important to follow the money. Try to map the following 'rounds' on the classroom blackboard so that you can see the developing pattern.

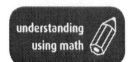

Round one: The first loop

1. Divide the class into three groups: **potential home buyers**, **mortgage brokers** and **lending institutions**.

2. **Potential home buyers**: choose a home to buy by putting an amount of money on a slip of paper that represents the purchase price of a house that you'd like to buy (for example, $350,000). Below that, put what you earn in your job (your yearly salary). Do you know the average salary of a person in your country? Now deliver your slip of paper to a mortgage broker.

3. **Mortgage brokers**: on the back of the slip of paper that you just received, calculate 0.75% of the loan the potential home-buyer is seeking. This is the amount you will get paid if you can successfully find a lending institution that will give this loan. It is called a **commission**. Mortgage brokers, read the purchase price of the home and the amount of your commission to the rest of the class. Explain how you calculated 0.75%.

4. **Lending institutions**: some of you represent banks. You're willing to loan money but want to know that it will be successfully paid back to you. You're eager to loan money because you can charge interest on that money. But you don't want the potential homebuyers to "**default**", or be unable to pay their loan back. If you charge 3.5% interest per annum, calculate the amount of interest you will collect each year from one of the home buyers.

Why are homebuyers willing to pay interest to a lending institution?

Why might lending institutions sometimes decide not to give loans to people?

Round two: Connecting investors with homeowners

1. In order to understand how investment banks can make a lot of money using mortgages, it's important to understand the concept of **leverage**.

   a. If you buy a car for $10,000 and then turn around and sell it to someone else for $11,000, what is the amount of profit you make (the amount and the percentage)?

   b. If instead, you used that $10,000 as collateral to borrow $990,000 more, how much money do you now have (include your collateral)? You'll pay interest on this loan at 1%.

   c. How many cars, selling for $10,000, can you now buy?

   d. If you turn around and sell those cars for $11,000 each, what percentage profit have you made? Is it different than part (a)?

   e. If you then pay back the $990,000 and $10,000 interest on that loan, what is the dollar value of your profit?

   f. Summarize the concept of leverage verbally.

2. Using the concept of leverage, **investment banks** borrow a lot of money and then call up lending institutions that hold mortgages. They offer to buy those mortgages.

   a. Why do the original lending institutions want to sell the mortgages they hold to an investment bank?

   b. When the homeowner is making monthly payments on their mortgage, who is then getting that money?

3. The investment banks then create what are called **collateralized debt obligations** (CDOs), where they put mortgages into three categories: safe, moderately risky, and risky (likely to default). As money comes in each month from the homeowner, these CDOs are paid in a cascading manner: first, the safe are paid off, then the moderately risky and then the risky. They then sell these CDOs to investors. Which category of risk do you think will give investors the greatest rate of return? Why? The least rate of return? Why?

Round three: Where it all starts to unravel

1. If the investors are making 10% profit on risky CDOs, 7% on moderately risky CDOs and 4% on safe CDOs, and they can only get 2% on regular investments, what will investors want to do?

2. If the investor asks the investment banker for more CDOs, and the investment banker calls the lender for more mortgages, and the lender calls the mortgage broker to round up more mortgages . . . but there aren't people trying to get mortgages, what will lenders and mortgage brokers do?

3. Why won't lenders mind too much if a homebuyer defaults on their loan?

4. Define the term "sub-prime loan".

Round four: The collapse

1. Keep in mind that as mortgages are sold from lender to investment banker to investor, at the point at which they are sold, the risk is now gone from the seller: in other words, once the investment banker buys mortgages from lenders, the lender makes a commission and is no longer responsible for any risk that may come from defaults on the loans. That risk is now assumed by the investment banker (who will package up the mortgages into CDOs and sell them to investors, off-loading their responsibility for risk).

2. Let's say that the investment banker is holding many mortgages. What will happen if homeowners default on their mortgage?

3. What happens to the housing market if there are many houses for sale at the same time? What are the houses worth? Can houses be sold easily?

4. If investment banks are holding on to mortgages that are losing value and houses that can't be sold, what will they be unable to do? What happens as a result?

make it better

The Federal Finance Minister (Bill Morneau, Liberal member of Parliament as of 2015) has the capacity to set mortgage lending rules, including limiting the borrowing period on loans, setting the amount that people can borrow from refinancing a mortgage that they already have, and deciding whether the government will insure lines of credit based on home equity. Invite in a banking professional to explain what these rules mean and ask how they can prevent sub-prime mortgages.

Endnotes

1. http://en.wikipedia.org/wiki/Financial_crisis_of_2007–08#Emergency_and_short-term_responses
2. http://en.wikipedia.org/wiki/Moral_hazard
3. www.theguardian.com/environment/2014/jan

trendlines/data percentages

Where Can They Bee?

"Whatever affects one directly, affects all indirectly: this is the interrelated structure of reality."

~ MARTIN LUTHER KING, JR.

setting the stage

Bees are disappearing. While a consensus on what exactly is causing honeybee losses is still taking shape, what we do know is that if humans want to grow fruits and nuts and berries, we depend on bees as pollinators. Entomologist Dennis van Engelstorp at the University of Maryland writes, "One in every three bites [of food consumed in the United States] is directly or indirectly pollinated by bees."

Beekeepers routinely lose their colonies from natural causes and accept an annual loss rate of 15% as reasonable. But documentation since 2006 shows annual honeybee losses ranging from 22 to 36%. Multiple things seem to be happening: flower-rich habitats are disappearing, disease and parasites are taking a toll, and pesticides and fungicides are now taking center stage as the European Union moves to ban the use of three pesticides known as neonicotinoids.[1]

Imidacloprid is a neonicotinoid, and exposure to it seems to cause bees to bring back less pollen to the hive, less often. Navigation also seems to be impacted by neonicotinoids.[2] Low exposure levels also damage the bees' immune systems, giving disease the upper hand.[3]

You'd think that with our food system on the line, a ban on chemicals that may be partially causing the problem would make a lot of sense. But massive chemical companies like Syngenta and Bayer are ready to take the battle to court because they stand to lose billions of dollars.[4] It's a showdown that's got everyone, well, buzzing.

opening question ?

Find a definition for "the precautionary principle" and see if you can explain how it relates to this particular issue.

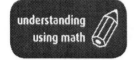
understanding using math

1. A bee colony is usually made up of between 20,000 and 60,000 bees. What is the average number of bees in a colony?

2. In the documentary *Queen of the Sun*, a claim is made that five million bee colonies in the United States have died. Use your answer from question one to calculate how many bees have died.

3. An average bee colony can collect 100 pounds of pollen in a season, which is fed to the young larvae.[4] Nests with bees exposed to imidacloprid end up with 57% less pollen.[5] How many pounds do those nests do without?

4. Multiple factors in bee losses are likely an issue, but it is possible for individual factors to add up to more impact than the sum of the parts. This phenomenon is called **synergy**. Indicate which combinations of factors demonstrate synergy.

Factor:	A	B	C	D	E	F	Total impact
Individual impact:	2	5	1	Not included	Not included	3	11
Individual impact:	2	5	Not included	4	2	Not included	17
Individual impact:	2	5	1	4	2	3	24

If you are trying to understand the interactive effects of hundreds of different chemicals being sprayed on crops, what is the implication of the above table?

5. What is the percentage increase in colony loss in the United States between 2011 and 2012 based on the chart on the next page?

6. Draw in a trend line for the chart on the next page. What does your trend line tell you?

7. If you only graph the last two years, what happens to the trend line?

135

8. Draw a line across the columns to show the 15% loss that is the acceptable range.

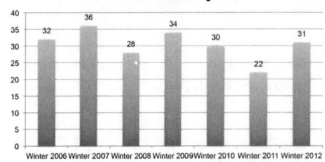

% Total Bee Colony Loss

Source: https://beeinformed.org/2016/05/10/nations-beekeepers-lost-44-percent-of-bees-in-2015-16/

9. A LD_{50} (lethal dose, 50%) means the level of a toxicant that kills 50% of the organism exposed to the toxicant. LD50s can be measured in parts per million (ppm), or even parts per billion (ppb). If a pesticide with a LD50 of 2.1 ppm is being measured in a number of hives, which hives below are at most risk?

Hive	Level of pesticide (ppm)
1	0.9
2	2.105
3	1.8
4	1.6
5	1.98

10. If there are an average of seven pesticides in some pollen samples, how would that change the answer you gave in question 8?

11. It has been estimated that pollination by bees contributes $14 billion to the food system.[7] If you can count one number per second, how long would it take you to count from one to 14 billion?

make it better

The movie *Queen of the Sun* posts 10 suggestions to help bees, on its website **http://www.queenofthesun.com/get-involved/10-things-you-can-do-to-help-bees/**

Three of their suggestions are: plant flowers that are friendly to bees in your garden or planter box, don't put chemicals and pesticides on your lawn, and buy local raw honey.

Endnotes

1. www.theguardian.com/environment/2014/jan/29/bees-pollen-pesticides-ban%20
2. Ibid.
3. www.theguardian.com/environment/2013/sep/04/bees-buzzfeeds-pesticides-ban-congress
4. Ibid.
5. http://www.honeybeesuite.com/pollen-collection/
6. www.theguardian.com/environment/2014/jan/29/bees-pollen-pesticides-ban%20
7. Mullin, Christopher, M. Frazier, J. Frazier, S. Ashcraft, R. Simonds, D. vanEngelsdorp, J. Pettis. High Levels of Miticides and Agrochemicals in North American Apiaries: Implications for Honey Bee Health. March 19, 2010.

Buffet

"You are what you eat eats too."

~ MICHAEL POLLEN

setting the stage

In his book, *In Defense of Food: An Eater's Manifesto*, author Michael Pollen suggests that you shouldn't eat anything that your great grandmother wouldn't recognize as food.[1] This is because our food landscape has been altered so radically over the past several generations, that our food today contains so many additives that it's not so much food as it is chemical soup. As well, a large portion of our diet, in the form of processed foods, contains much more sugar and fat and much less water, fiber and micronutrients.[2]

The world of food politics is vast. There's the carbon footprint of our foods as they are transported to nearby stores from thousands of kilometres away, the fair trade and direct trade movements, and genetically modified organisms. We can consider the amount of water and oil it takes to produce our foods, the aggressive marketing techniques used by multinational corporations and lobby groups, and the build-up of toxic materials in our food system. The list goes on and on.

What you are likely to find though, is that the issues are largely connected. In reading about food security issues for example, you'll almost inevitably be faced with the topic of the rights of agricultural workers, the hundred-mile diet, and the tension between conventional and organic foods. What you're also likely to find is that there are dozens of small decisions that we make daily (consciously or not) that serve as pathways to political action related to food. That's hopeful, because it means that you have more direct input that you may have imagined.

When it comes to food, it's a buffet of issues. Join the discussion table!

As a class, try to identify five more issues related to food politics. Which ones do you think most affect your local community?

1. Eating locally can reduce the amount of greenhouse gases your food contributes to the atmosphere. Carbon dioxide is one such greenhouse gas and is produced in the transport of food from the farm to your table. Here is the formula to calculate CO_2 emissions for your food:[3]

$$\frac{\text{Weight of produce (kg)} \times \text{Distance travelled (km)} \times \text{Emissions factor (g)}}{1{,}000{,}000}$$

The emissions factor is given as follows for different methods of transport:

Mode of transport	CO_2 emissions (grams per tonne-kilometre)
Air	370
Truck	160
Boat	33

a. By what factor is boat transport better than air transport, in terms of carbon dioxide emissions? What disadvantages of shipping food by boat can you think of?

b. A family of six is eating a turkey, and the adults are having wine for Thanksgiving. They live in Toronto. Calculate the CO_2 emissions for the family if they eat from local sources or from more distant sources, using the table below[4] and the formula above.

Distant Food Sources			Local Food Sources		
Food	Distance	Transport	Food	Distance	Transport
Turkey (9.42 kg)	3,562 km from Edmonton	Truck	Turkey (9.42 kg)	117 km from Ontario	Truck
Wine (1.15 kg)	6,016 km from France	Air	Wine (1.15 kg)	142 km from Ontario	Truck

c. What is the CO_2 emission for each family member?

d. It takes 0.18 kg of CO_2 to fill a green garbage bag. Calculate the green garbage bag equivalent of each meal above.

e. What CO_2 emissions sources are missing if you only include transport from the farm to your table? List as many as you can think of. (Experts suggest that the CO_2 emitted from food transport may only account for 10 to 15% of the energy used in the full food life cycle.)[5]

f. What drawbacks may there be to eating food that is grown locally?

g. If you live in Canada, explain how buying food locally might mean buying food from the United States.

2. Although historically humans have eaten up to 80,000 different edible species and about 3,000 regularly, only four species now account for the majority of calories that we eat today. Packaged food products rely heavily on corn, soy, wheat and rice.

a. Create a pie graph of the average calories we consume per day[6] using the chart below (fill in the blank cell too):

Food type	Calories per day
Corn	554
Soy	257
Wheat	768
Rice	91
All others	
Total:	2000

b. What food represents the largest calorie intake per day, as a percentage? What is that percentage?

c. Can you think of reasons why a diet that has historically included a much broader diversity of species might be healthier than a diet that relies on far fewer food items?

3. For one day, collect the number of servings of fruits and vegetables eaten by each member of the classroom. The recommended number of servings is five to 10 a day. What percentage of the students in your class eat five a day? Eight a day? Ten a day? What are the barriers to eating fruits and vegetables?

4. In the United States, $250 billion dollars a year are spent on diet related health care costs.[7] As a class, decide on a measurement in your classroom that will represent a dollar bill (for example, a metre stick, or 10 centimetres or a foot). Based on your reference point, figure out the distance of $250 billion dollars and find a location that is that same distance from your school.

5. One kilogram of rice requires 3,400 litres of water to produce. One hundred and fifty grams of beef requires 2,300 litres of water to produce.[8] Compare the water use of these two foods per kilogram. Why does the production of meat require more water than non- meat food sources?

6. Biomagnification is where toxins in the environment can concentrate in greater quantities as they travel up the food chain. Small toxicity levels at the lowest levels of the food chain may become exponentially greater by the time we as humans eat the omnivores and carnivores at the top (if we do!).

   a. Why would the animals at the top of the food chain have greater levels of toxin in them?

   b. Calculate the biomagnification factors between trophic levels using the following diagram and table below:

Trophic Levels of a Food Chain[9]

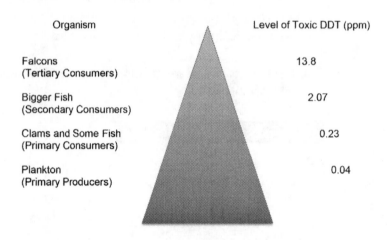

Organism	Level of Toxic DDT (ppm)
Falcons (Tertiary Consumers)	13.8
Bigger Fish (Secondary Consumers)	2.07
Clams and Some Fish (Primary Consumers)	0.23
Plankton (Primary Producers)	0.04

Factor of Difference Between Trophic Levels

	Primary Producers	Primary Consumers	Secondary Consumers	Tertiary Consumers
Primary Producers	1			
Primary Consumers		1		
Secondary Consumers			1	
Tertiary Consumers				1

   c. Graph the first row of data from the above table on a piece of graph paper with the x-axis representing the four trophic levels and the y-axis representing the factor of difference between the primary producers and the other trophic levels. Is this a linear or an exponential pattern of growth?

   d. Why is biomagnification of toxins one justification for a vegetarian diet?

7. A lobby group is an organization that represents the interests of a particular industry, and works to promote their interests by pressuring government officials to adopt policies that are favourable to the industry (for example, lower regulations, fewer laws, less taxes).

a. Lobbying on behalf of the agribusiness industry is graphed below. What is the general trend in spending on lobbying?

b. What year did spending peak, and at what level?

c. This industry is represented by 1,151 lobbyists. In 2010, they spent $121,360,788 on lobbying. How much is that per lobbyist?

d. Using Excel, create a pie graph of the breakdown of that spending using the table below.

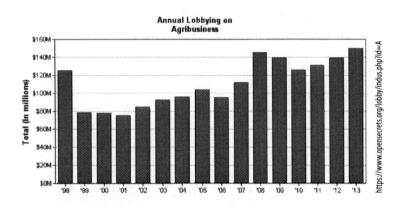

Campaign Contributions from this sector

Industry	Total spending
Agricultural Services/Products	$34,671,733
Food Processing & Sales	$27,831,366
Crop Production & Basic Processing	$19,788,427
Tobacco	$19,615,381
Forestry & Forest Products	$14,126,081
Dairy	$5,662,885
Livestock	$2,639,255
Misc. Agriculture	$777,779
Poultry & Eggs	$672,610

Food for thought:

If a family of four could reduce their meat intake by one steak meal a week, it would be the equivalent of taking their car off of the road for about three months.[10]

make it better

Small ideas can grow rapidly. In Toronto, if you have fruit trees on your property that you are unable to harvest yourself, you can register with a group of volunteers called **Not Far from the Tree**. They arrange to pick the fruit from your trees: one third of the harvest goes to the tree owner, one third goes to the volunteers, and one third goes to local food banks, shelters and community kitchens. As they say, it's a "win-win-win situation"![11]

See if you can find community action groups in your neighbourhood and get involved!

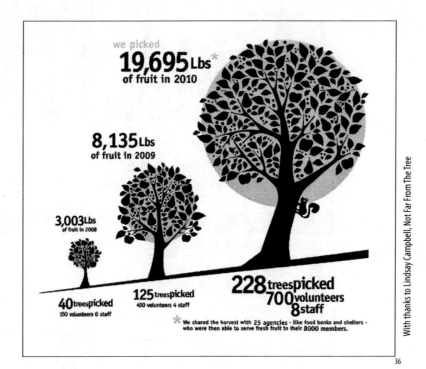

we picked
19,695 Lbs *
of fruit in 2010

8,135 Lbs
of fruit in 2009

3,003 Lbs
of fruit in 2008

40 trees picked
150 volunteers 0 staff

125 trees picked
450 volunteers 4 staff

228 trees picked
700 volunteers
8 staff

* We shared the harvest with 25 agencies – like food banks and shelters – who were then able to serve fresh fruit to their 8000 members.

With thanks to Lindsay Campbell, Not Far From The Tree

36

Endnotes

1. Pollen, Michael. In Defense of Food, An Eater's Manifesto. The Penguin Press, New York, 2008, p. 148.
2. Ibid. p. 150.
3. Farley, Catherine and Stuart Laidlaw. Time to talk turkey. Toronto Star, A18. December 18, 2005.
4. Ibid.
5. Roberts, Wayne. Myth of the 100 Mile Diet. NOW Magazine, p. 17, August 20 – 26, Issue 1439, Vol. 28, No. 51.
6. Pollen, Michael. In Defense of Food, An Eater's Manifesto. The Penguin Press, New York, 2008, p. 148.
7. Ibid, p. 135-136.
8 Royal Ontario Museum, Water Exhibit, August 20, 2011.
9. http://users.rcn.com/jkimball.ma.ultranet/BiologyPages/D/DDTandTrophicLevels.html
10. http://www.opensecrets.org/lobby/indusclient.php?id=A07&year=2010
11. Jacobson, Michael. Meat and Heat. Centre for Science in the Public Interest. Nutrition Action Health Letter. September, 2011.
12. www.notfarfromthetree.org
13. www.notfarfromthetree.org

Earthship

"The most powerful thing Earthships do is force people to think differently about how we live."

~ JORDAN LEJUWAAN

What if you could make a sustainable home out of recycled materials that required little or no fossil fuels in order to function? What if you could collect water off of your roof and use it for your daily needs? What if you could build to reduce your impact on the planet, still have heat, light, hot water, sewage treatment, electricity…AND save money at the same time? You can: it's called an Earthship, and there are already more than 1,000 of them around the world.[1]

Inventor Michael Reynolds began building Earthships in the United States in the 1970s. The main walls are made of used tires, packed with earth, clay, sand or rock. The sun enters through typical glass windows and hits these very dense walls, which then store the heat energy. Insulation on the outside of the walls prevents heat from escaping. When it's hot outside, simply draw the shades and let the coolness of the Earth bring the temperature down.

Earthships can be either on or off of the city's electricity grid, meaning that they can harvest their own electricity from the wind (with turbines) and the sun (with photovoltaic panels) or connect to a pre-existing energy source. Some homes make enough energy to feed it back into the energy grid! Reynolds calls it biotecture. Some just call it 'the way of the future'.

Watch an online segment of the film *Garbage Warrior*, which features Michael Reynolds and his Earthships. Discuss what you see as a class. What questions do you have?

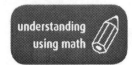

1. Look carefully at the following graphic of an Earthship.

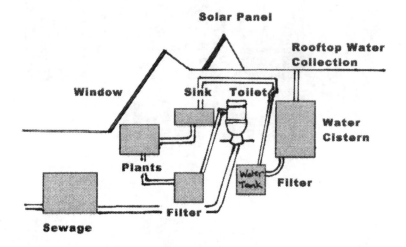

a. What direction must the windows on the left side of the building be facing? Why?

b. How many times does it look like the water from the roof is re-used for different purposes? Can you tell what they are?

2. In an Earthship, water can be caught off of a potable roof and funnelled into a cistern. In this way, aquifers and the water table are not depleted. In 2009, the average number of litres used per person per day in Canada was 274.[2] The average amount of precipitation in Canada is 537mm (which would vary greatly with region). [3]

a. How many litres of water would a family of four use in a year on average?

b. One litre is 0.001 of a cubic metre. Using the depth of 537 mm, how many square metres would your roof have to be to satisfy the annual water needs from question a.? What does that tell you about water use and collection?

c. If you had a cistern that collected the rainwater, would a cylinder with a height of 2 metres and a radius of 1 metre be enough to hold the weekly water requirements from this family of four?

3. Create a pie chart showing typical water use in Canada based on the following statistics: toilet, 30%; bathing and showering, 35%; laundry, 20%; drinking and cooking, 10%; cleaning, 5%.[4] What strategies might you use to reduce your worst water guzzlers?

4. It is not uncommon for an Earthship to use 1,000 tires to create its walls, which means that they don't end up in a landfill. Tires are horrible for dumps because they take up so much space. One quarter of a billion tires a year are discarded.[5]

   a. How many million tires is a quarter of a billion?

   b. If each tire is 38 centimetres in radius and 15 centimetres in width, how many cubic metres of space are used by discarded tires each year?

   c. Compare your answer in b. to the volume in cubic metres of your school.

   d. 75% of the tire is empty air space! What is 75% of the volume in b.?

   e. Pounding earth into each tire takes about an hour. How many weeks would it take to fill in 1000 tires for the main walls. Because it's hard labour, assume you can work a 30-hour week and that you have three friends helping you.

5. Your windows must be on the correct angle to maximize the amount of sunlight that you receive. You take 90 degrees and subtract the latitude of your space, and that means that the sun will enter at 90 degrees on the winter solstice, which is what you want.[6]

   a. What latitude is your location currently?

   b. If you built an Earthship in your schoolyard, what angle would the windows have to be?

   c. Draw a sketch of your windows with the correct angle.

   d. Go back to the Earthship diagram in question 1. Based on the angle of the windows, figure out the latitude of this house.

6. Interior walls that are not load-bearing can be made by stacking colourful glass bottles on their sides and packing them with cement or clay. Take the dimensions of the wall below, and use a radius of a bottle of 5 cm, and design a wall using coloured bottles put on their sides (don't forget to colour them in). How many bottles can be positioned across the width? How many bottles will fit along the length of the wall?

Wall width: 1 metre

Wall height: 2.5 metres

7. Interior bottle walls are actually constructed by cutting the bottom 4 inches off of the bottle and then taking two of them and taping them together (so you are looking at the bottom of the bottle on both sides of the wall). How many bottles does the above wall need in total?

make it better

Attempt to build a small solar oven using the principles of the Earthship. You will need some scrap wood, a piece of glass, and a good design. Without any electricity, can you use the sun's energy to boil water?

Endnotes

1. https://sites.google.com/site/earthshipmanitoba/home/faqs#TOC-How-many-tires-did-you-use-
2. https://www.ec.gc.ca/doc/publications/eau-water/COM1454/survey2-eng.htm
3. http://www.tradingeconomics.com/canada/average-precipitation-in-depth-mm-per-year-wb-data.html
4. http://www.canadiangeographic.ca/magazine/mj00/water_use.asp
5. http://en.wikipedia.org/wiki/Tire_recycling
6. http://www.bluerockstation.com/earthship

Bay of the Beaver

"Our people and our Mother Earth can no longer afford to be economic hostages in the race to industrialize our homelands."

~ ERIEL DERANGER, ATHABASCA CHIPEWYAN FIRST NATIONS

 **setting the stage** Manitoulin Island in Ontario is considered sacred to the Anishinaabe people, including the Ojibwe, Odawa and Potawatomi tribes. The Island is particularly special because on the eastern side lies a peninsula that does not belong to the Canadian government.[1] It is called the Wikwemikong Unceded Indian Reserve.

In the 1930s, the British government, represented by Sir Francis Bond Head, tried to encourage First Nations peoples in Upper Canada to move to Manitoulin Island and created a treaty to designate the area as permanent Indian territory. On the surface, Sir Francis explained that this was to protect "these intelligent, simple-minded people" from white settlers and convert them to Christianity. In actual fact, he was trying to free up valuable farmland in Upper Canada for the European settlers.[2]

By 1860, the population on the Island had grown five-fold to 1,200, but this was far short of the 9,000 that the government had hoped for. White farmers ready to supply the growing markets of Toronto and Montreal started eyeing Manitoulin. Plans were drawn up to give each native family 100 acres of land, with cash bonuses as well. While most chiefs on the Island signed a new treaty in 1862, the people of

Wikwemikong refused. Perhaps not surprisingly, the new white settlers to the Island took the better farmland, and areas near rivers and shores, which were useful for mills. The government also took control of wharfs and harbours.

Just prior to the Treaty in 1862, fishing licenses were granted by the government to non-Indigenous groups in waters surrounding Wikwemikong. How do you think this might have contributed to the events in 1862?

1. Using the following map from Statistics Canada[3], estimate the land area of Wikwemikong.

2. The whole of Manitoulin Island has an area of 2,766 km². What percentage is Wikwemikong of the whole island?

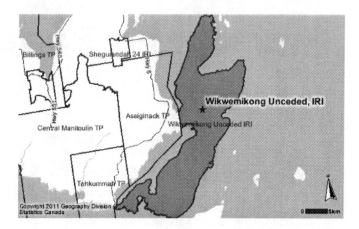

3. In the 1862 treaty, each family was offered 100 acres of land. How many hectares is 100 acres? Is there a comparable area in your community? Why might families see this amount of land as inadequate?

4. In the introduction, it says that the population increased five-fold from 1830 to 1860 and that the population in 1860 was 1,200. What was it in 1830?

5. Some First Nations leaders around Lake Huron and Lake Superior had, just earlier to the Manitoulin Treaties, sold 15 million hectares of land for $10,000 up front and $2,700 annually thereafter.

    a. Using an inflation rate of 3%, what would this offer be equivalent to today, if it was made in the year 1800?

    b. What is the algebraic equation that captures the offer, in current day terms?

6. Using the (fictitious map) on the next page, answer the following questions. Assume that each square is one kilometre by one kilometre.

    a. What is the land area of the mainland? What is the area of the island?

    b. How much mainland shoreline is shown on the map?

c. Why do you think area A would be taken by colonizers?

d. Why do you think area B might be taken by colonizers?

e. The area to the east of the river is the best farmland and is claimed by the government. Surveyors go in and divide the land into plots. Mark the angles within each plot of land.

f. Why is shoreline property valuable?

g. Without using a protractor, fill in the missing angle in the offshore island.

Dividing the Land

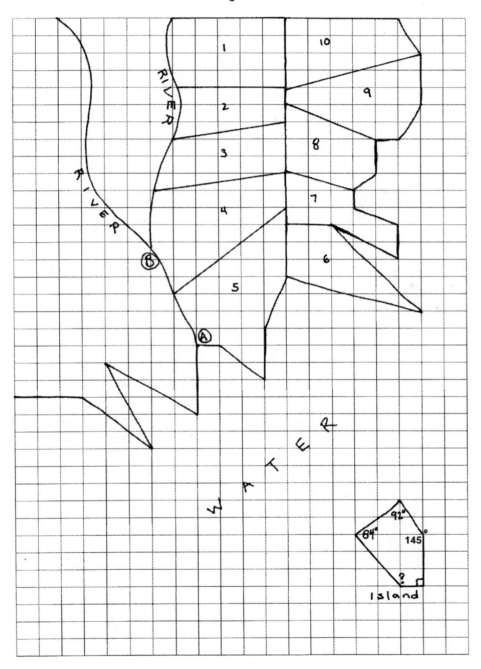

make it better ✌

Learn about the movement called Idle No More. There are many learning resources at their website www.idlenomore.ca as well as an action section for getting involved.

Recognize your own responsibility as a participant in the Treaty process.

Endnotes

1. http://en.wikipedia.org/wiki/Manitoulin_Island
2. Surtees, Robert. Treaty Research Report, Manitoulin Island Treaties. Indian and Northern Affairs Canada, 1986.
3. Ibid.
4. Statistics Canada. 2012. GeoSearch. 2011 Census. Statistics Canada Catalogue no. 92-142-XWE. Ottawa, Ontario. Data updated October 24, 2012.
http://geodepot.statcan.gc.ca/GeoSearch2011-GeoRecherche2011/GeoSearch2011-GeoRecherche2011.jsp?lang=E&otherLang=F
(accessed 2014-04-04)

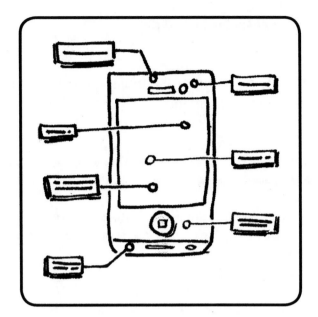

Tough Call

"People must be trained to desire, to want new things even before the old has been entirely consumed. We must shape a new mentality in America. Man's desires must overshadow his needs."

~ PAUL MAZUR

setting the stage

Five million, four hundred thousand people dead: that's the current count of the cost of civil war in the Democratic Republic of the Congo in Africa.[1] But how are the warring factions funded?

Deep within the earth, people living in desperate poverty, including children, dig for a mineral named cassiterite. Armed guards take a tax on the miners on their way in and out, and that money is used for weapons.[2] While the wealthy get wealthier, the people of the Congo sit at the bottom of the United Nation's Human Development Index, and have the lowest GDP per capita in the world.[3]

If companies were held accountable for the sourcing of their minerals, it's possible that the amount of conflict would drop considerably, but that means that tough laws have to be put in place to allow us to see the supply chain and penalize corporations and governments that place profits above human rights. The question is: why should I care about this problem on the other side of the planet? What does it have to do with me? The answer may be in your hand.

Cassiterite is the mineral used in all cell phones.

Discuss the meaning of the initial quote by Paul Mazur. On whose behalf is Mazur speaking?

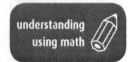

1. Seventy-five percent of Canadian households have at least one cellphone. Find the most current Canadian population and calculate the lowest number of cell phones in Canada.

2. China has 1,227,360,000 cell phones in use, Nigeria has 114,000,000 cell phones in use and Canada has 26,543,780 cell phones in use.[4] What further information would you need to know to figure out the relative impact of each country?

3. China has a population of 1,349,585,838, Nigeria is 165,200,000 and Canada is 35,160,000.[5] How many cell phones per person does each country have? What does this tell you about the relative impact of each country?

4. Children as young as 12 years old descend into the cassiterite mines to a depth of 100 metres. Find a comparable distance to understand what 100 metres means.

5. Armed groups fund 75% of their activities using the taxes they take from the mine sites. Create a graphic to show this information.[6]

6. Create a bar graph to show the comparative impact of this conflict.

Conflict	Casualties
World War I	68,000 Canadian military
World War II	47,000 Canadian military
War in Afghanistan	158 Canadian military
Civil war in the Democratic Republic of Congo	5.4 million

7. A new law in the United States, called the Dodd-Frank Wall Street Reform and Consumer Protection Act, now requires companies to show where the materials in their products come from. Of the 12,000 companies affected by this law, it is estimated that 1,200 are currently reporting on their products.[7] What percentage is that, and why do you think that all of the companies are not reporting?

8. There are 17 rare earth elements, some of which are mined for elements in cell phones. Although they are not actually scarce ("rare" means odd in this case) they are difficult to mine. China has most of these rare earth elements and increased production of them from 16,000 metric tons in the year 1990 to 73,000 metric tons in 2000.[8] What percentage increase in production is that?

9. Half of the weight of cell phones comes from the LDPE plastic. For every 1 kg of this plastic it takes 2 kg of oil to produce.

    a. What is the algebraic equation describing the relationship between the weight of plastic and the amount of oil to produce it?

    b. If each cell phone weighs 130 grams, and there are 26,543,780 cell phones in use in Canada, how much oil was used to make those phones?

10. Refining one ton of rare earth metals causes 75 cubic metres of acidic wastewater and one ton of radioactive residue.[9]

    a. What is the algebraic equation that describes the relationship between the amount of refined rare earth metal and the amount of acidic wastewater produced?

    b. What is the algebraic equation that describes the relationship between the amount of refined rare earth metal and the amount of radioactive residue that is created?

    c. World demand for rare earth metals is 136,000 tons per year.[10] Use your algebraic equations to find out the amount of acidic wastewater and radioactive residue that the world creates each year.

11. In the United States in 2009, 2.37 million tons of electronic waste was collected but only 25% was sent for recycling. How many actual tons were collected and how many recycled?[11]

12. Look at the following graphic by Barbara Reck.[12]

    a. What are the three variables in her model?

    b. What are the elements that are included in the model?

    c. Which element is rated as the highest environmental implication?

    d. Which element has a 50 for vulnerability to supply restriction, a 75 for supply risk and an 18 for environmental implication?

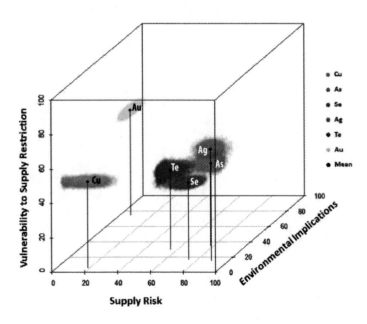

make it better

Make sure that your electronics are taken to accredited recycling facilities when you are done with them.

Pressure cell phone companies to disclose the source of the cassiterite that they use in their phones.

Call your local politician and ask how Canada's laws protect the human rights of people around the world who are mining minerals that end up in products that we use. Does Canada have the equivalent of the Dodds-Frank Act?

Endnotes

1. http://www.globalwitness.org/library/implementing-conflict-minerals-provision-cost-business-usual
2. http://www.theguardian.com/film/filmblog/2011/oct/10/blood-in-the-mobile-congo
3. http://www.globalwitness.org/all-regions/countries/democratic-republic-congo
4. http://en.wikipedia.org/wiki/List_of_countries_by_number_of_mobile_phones_in_use
5. Ibid.
6. http://www.sourceintelligence.com/what-are-conflict-minerals
7. http://www.sourceintelligence.com/what-are-conflict-minerals
8. http://www.pbs.org/wgbh/nova/next/physics/rare-earth-elements-in-cell-phones/
9. http://blogs.ei.columbia.edu/2012/09/19/rare-earth-metals-will-we-have-enough/
10. http://www.fas.org/sgp/crs/natsec/R41347.pdf
11. http://www.eastonline.eu/attachments/article/221/east%2047_Rare%20Earths%20and%20Microchips.pdf
12. http://www.yalescientific.org/2014/04/metal-fe

Scientific notation

WTF?
(What the Frack?)

"Natural gas is a dirty fossil fuel like the rest of them."

~ JOSH FOX

setting the stage

"If you take a shower, just remember to turn the fan on to clear the air from the bathroom. If there happens to be natural gas coming out of your faucet along with the water, we wouldn't want an...um...explosive situation."

Since the natural gas companies have come into the community and carved wells deep down into the shale to hunt for natural gas, strange things have been happening. "If you hear loud pops in the middle of the night you might want to get up and check out your front window to see if anything is on fire, or to make sure your shed isn't missing from an explosion," says the investigator who is inspecting your home.

"I'm sorry...say what?"

The investigator has taken out a cigarette lighter and turned on the tap in your laundry room. The small flame next to the jet of water looks a little amusing, until you hear a "floom" and your water catches on fire.

"Don't drink this water," she says.

You haven't been. It smells like turpentine. You've been filling up huge cisterns in town with fresh water each week, out of your own pocket and your own time.

"High volume slickwater hydraulic fracturing," the investigator says. "Short-form: fracking. Send a pipe deep in the earth, disrupt the shale with explosives, pump water and chemicals down, and up comes the natural gas."

"Any leaking into the groundwater where we pump our drinking water from?" you inquire.

"Most people's tap water doesn't catch on fire," she responds.

Watch the trailer to the documentary by Josh Fox, called *GasLand*. It can be found on YouTube at **http://www.youtube.com/watch?v=B9XJfCYDoMU.** What questions do you have?

Now watch the Canadian Association of Petroleum Producer's YouTube video at **https://www.youtube.com/watch?v=TGCOK9tPPTo&feature= player_embedded.**

Compare the two clips.

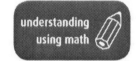

1. Create a drawing using the following information.[1] Be sure to take any measurements that are listed in imperial form and convert them to metric.

   a. Draw a line to represent the ground, with most of the space on your page under that line.

   b. Create a scale for your drawing that makes the distance from your ground line to the bottom of your page equivalent to 1.4 km.

   c. Find an object (like a tall building or tower that you know the height of- which is less than 1.4 kilometres high) and draw a sketch of it (to scale) downwards from your ground line. This is your comparison object.

Item	Dimensions- Imperial	Dimensions- Metric
Shale rock layer where natural gas is trapped	2 – 200 feet thick	
Distance of shale from surface	0 – 1 mile	
Airborne contaminants from drilling will go this distance from your drawing	Up to 200 miles	
Natural gas well	5000 – 9000 feet, turn 90 degrees and continue for up to a mile	
Water table- drinking water source	400 feet	

2. The planet was created about 4.6 billion years ago. Plankton and animals from 400 million years ago sank and under great pressure turned into methane (natural gas) locked within shale.

   a. Write out the numbers 4.6 billion and 400 million in standard form and scientific notation.

   b. Create a pie chart where the entire pie represents a clock, the entire clock representing 4.6 billion years. Indicate when this natural gas was created.

3. Each well requires the following raw materials to frack just once:

Resource Used	Imperial	Metric
Water (average)	5 million gallons	
Chemicals (average)	25,000 gallons	
Diesel truck trips	1,000	1,000

   Use the information above to fill in the chart below:

Location	Number of wells	Water	Chemicals	Diesel truck trips
New York State	Planned: 77,000 wells			
United States	450,000 wells			
Your community...				

4. The National Energy Board of Canada estimates that Canada has about 98 trillion cubic feet of marketable shale gas (British Columbia's share is more than 90%).[2]

   a. Write out 98 trillion in standard form and scientific notation.

   b. What is 90% of 98 trillion cubic feet?

5. Methane that is burned creates half of the greenhouse gases that burning coal creates. If, however, unburned methane escapes into the atmosphere, it is 20 times more powerful at trapping heat than carbon dioxide.[3]

   a. Although unburned methane traps heat more effectively, how mathematically could carbon dioxide be a greater contributor to global warming?

   b. Use hypothetical numbers to demonstrate your answer from part (a).

6. In his film *GasLand*, filmmaker Josh Fox describes the reason that some people lease their land to gas companies so that they can frack: money. Before any additional royalties, people are offered $4,750 per acre of land up front.

157

a. How much would a person receive if they had 25 acres of land to lease to the gas companies?

b. What algebraic equation describes the total amount of money that a landowner would receive, for any amount of acres?

c. Landowners are also due royalties based on the value of the natural gas that is pulled from under their property. In Pennsylvania, the law states that leases are not valid unless they have a minimum 12.5% royalty to the landowner.[3] Re-write the algebraic equation to include a 12.5% royalty along with the initial up front bonus.

d. If a landowner had 30 acres of land to lease, and negotiated a contract with 15% royalties, what would the algebraic equation be for their total remuneration? If the value of the natural gas turned out to be $120,000, what would the landowner receive?

e. Although the landowner may be receiving substantial sums of money, what costs might they incur that make the deal less valuable? Think broadly.

7. A group called the Endocrine Disrupter Exchange has written a report on the chemicals that they believe are used in the fracking process- up to 300 of them. Create an infographic that visually conveys their findings.[4]

Problem	Percentage	Actual number
Endocrine disrupters	40%	
Suspected carcinogens	33%	
Developmental toxicants	33%	
Chemicals that can harm the brain and nervous system	More than 60%	

8. When we use water, if what we mean when we say we "waste water" is that it is 'lost from the water cycle', that's inaccurate. Water will cycle around: it takes energy to make that happen, and water can certainly be contaminated along the cycle, but the water is not lost. In fracking, only half of the water pumped below the ground returns to the surface: the other half remains locked underground and removed from the water cycle permanently.

a. Use your answer in question 3 to calculate the amount of water that has been removed from the water cycle permanently.

b. Why do you think that the flow back water that comes to the surface during fracking is called "produced water" by the gas industry?

9. Containment ponds are sometimes used to store "produced water" when it comes to the surface.

a. If a pond is 150 metres by 100 metres, what is the surface area of the pond?

b. Sometimes the pond water is agitated and turned into mist so that the water can evaporate faster by the sun. If this mist sits 15 metres above the pond, what volume of airspace sits above the pond? Why might that be a problem?

c. Gas companies are quick to point out that the water table is unlikely to be contaminated by the drilling operation as it is so far below the water table and the wells are encased in cement. How do the containment ponds add into this equation?

Food for thought:

"Recent studies indicate the U.S. and world could rely 100% on green energy sources within 20 years if we dedicate ourselves to that outcome."[4]

make it better

Check out the Council of Canadians website at **candians.org/fracking**.

They have a Fractivist Toolkit, complete with case studies and education strategies. It's available at:

http://canadians.org/sites/default/files/publications/what-you-can-do.pdf.

Watch Josh Fox's film *GasLand* and become involved in local activism around this issue.

159

Endnotes

1. Steingraber, Sandra. Raising Elijah: Protecting Our Children In An Age of Environmental Crisis. Da Capo Press, 2011, pp. 269 – 284.
2. http://www.theglobeandmail.com/report-on-business/industry-news/energy-and-resources/canada-faces-hurdles-in-joining-shale-gas-revolution/article8900288/
3. Steingraber, Sandra. Raising Elijah: Protecting Our Children In An Age of Environmental Crisis. Da Capo Press, 2011, p. 272.
4. http://pubs.cas.psu.edu/FreePubs/pdfs/ua448.pdf
5. Steingraber, Sandra. Raising Elijah: Protecting Our Children In An Age of Environmental Crisis. Da Capo Press, 2011, p. 278.
6. Steingraber, Sandra. Raising Elijah: Protecting Our Children In An Age of Environmental Crisis. Da Capo Press, 2011, p. 282.

Scientific notation
volume
surface are

David and Goliath

"Facts do not cease to exist because they are ignored."

~ ALDOUS HUXLEY

160

setting the stage

The year was 1976. It was winter and a research team was out taking samples of the Ohio River. The results from the lab brought back a surprise: elevated levels of carbon tetrachloride in the water. A single carbon atom surrounded by four chlorine atoms, 'carbon tet,' has been used as a refrigerant, a dry cleaning solvent and a pesticide. It's also highly toxic to the human liver, which is why, in 1970, it was banned from all consumer products in the United States.[1]

Since the water samples were reading carbon tetrachloride as high as 340 parts per billion and the "safe" levels were listed at five parts, the race was on to find the source. The suspects: four companies upstream of the sampling site. Three opened their doors to the Environmental Protection Agency inspectors, leaving the guilty party exposed: the FMC plant on the Kanawha River.

This decades-old disaster spawned a monitoring system along the Ohio River that is one of the best in the United States. Today a new technology has been developed that uses microscopic particles to 'soak up' certain types of spills, including carbon tetrachloride. They are called nanoparticles. A nanometre is a billionth of a metre, so there's got to be something pretty special about these particles that gives them such fantastic clean up power.

It turns out that it's their surface area.

If you take the surface area of the tabletop you are sitting at and divided it into a billion pieces, do you think you could see one of the pieces? How could you find out?

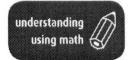

1. Nanoparticles are between 1 and 100 nanometres in diameter. Use scientific notation to express these values in metres.

2. Draw three rectangular prisms, all the same size on three separate sheets of paper. Make the dimensions 10 cm by 5 cm by 5 cm. Imagine that these are iron nanoparticles, and they are enlargements of a particle 10 nm by 5 nm by 5 nm.

3. What is the volume of the first 'nanoparticle'?

4. 'Cut' the second rectangular prism in half by drawing a line dividing the longest sides in two. Imagine that you have created two smaller nanoparticles out of the bigger one. Is the total volume still the same?

5. 'Cut' the third rectangular prism to create 1 nm³ blocks. Is the total volume the same or different than the other two particles?

6. Fill in the following chart:

	Particle #1	Particle #2	Particle #3
Total volume			
Total surface area			

   a. What happened to the surface area of the particles as you created smaller nanoparticles?

   b. How does this relate to absorption capacity for the clean up of spills?

7. Nanoparticles have been designed to soak up oil under the surface of the water when there is a spill. Nanoparticles can hold 10 times their own weight.

   a. If a barrel of oil weighs 300 pounds, how many pounds of nanoparticles are required to soak up a single barrel spill?

   b. How many kilograms is that?

   c. In the year 2010, the oil spill in the Gulf of Mexico was 4.9 million barrels.[2] How many kilograms of nanoparticles would be needed to clean up that amount of oil?

   d. Does that seem reasonable? What would likely need to take place before using the nanoparticles?

8. Federal funding for monitoring stations along a river has been approved. There is $1,680,000 to spend. Stations can be made of two types: those that require people in the station (for a cost of $35,000 each) and those that are completely automated (for a cost of $50,000 each). The funding requires you to build twice as many of the cheaper stations as the more expensive stations. How many of each station can you build? (See if you can show all of your work using algebraic equations.)

9. Over-spending and unanticipated costs mean that the cheaper stations end up costing $40,000 and the more expensive stations cost $55,000 each. You are still bound by the same funding amount and the same requirement to build twice as many as the cheaper stations. Re-work your algebraic equations to find out the new numbers, and based on what you find, make a recommendation.

10. Can you think of any possible reasons for concerns about releasing nanoparticles into a site that needs environmental rehabilitation?

make it better

Monitoring of engineered nanoparticles is an emerging field of study, one in which the location, concentration and consequences of environmental contamination are determined. Investigate which level of government is responsible for the protection of the water nearest where you live and contact them to find out if they have a plan in place to monitor nanoparticles.

Endnotes

1. http://en.wikipedia.org/wiki/Carbon_tetrachloride
2. http://www.insidescience.org/content/going-small-mop-big-oil-spills/1415

162

Trans[form]

"For every dark corner, there is a wall that the sun is shining on."

~ NICOLE MAINES, TRANS YOUTH.

163

For 19 months between 2007 and 2009, the Education Committee of Egale Canada connected with 3,607 high school students across the country. The subsequent report painted a picture of what school life was like for gender and sexual minority youth. And what they found was very disturbing: 70% of all students heard homophobic comments daily, and 79% of trans youth frequently heard inappropriate gendered remarks.[1] Even more shocking was that 22.5% of trans students reported hearing negative gender-related or transphobic comments *from teachers* daily or weekly.[2] And only one quarter reported staff intervening in transphobia most of the time.

Although it is difficult to know exactly how many people identify as transgender around the world, the most current estimates suggest about 15 million, amounting to 0.3% in the USA, or equivalent to one in 333 people.[3] But transphobia affects everyone: it's probably no surprise that 80% of LGBTQ youth report that the comments are upsetting,[4] but large numbers of non-LGBTQ youth are also harassed about their gender, and a full 58% of those youth report that they find homophobic comments distressing.[5]

The idea that we have multiple identities related to race, class, gender, ability, ethnicity, sexuality and many other factors, and that these identities overlap and influence our experience in school in complex ways is called **intersectionality**.[6] Transphobia in schools must be understood in terms of multiple systems of oppression that are connected.

In 2012, gender identity and gender expression became prohibited grounds for discrimination in the Ontario Human Rights Code.[7] It's time to transform our schools into safe places for everyone. No exceptions.

As a way to provide inclusive space within the school, City View Alternative School in Toronto created a multi-stall 'all-gender washroom' for students — any student is welcome to use it. Can you think of any advantages of multi-stall all — gender washrooms compared to offering students a single stall washroom (like perhaps one that the staff use)?

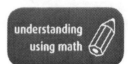

1. One part of the data collection for Egale's school climate survey was done over the internet. Can you suggest one reason why using the internet can be useful in collecting data?

2. If you are trying to reach students who are marginalized and as a result may not be "out", but you want to make sure that their experiences are captured by your survey, how could you make sure people know about it?

3. Many studies over the years have found that anywhere between 2.5 and 11% of students identify as LGBTQ. Egale's in-class component of the survey found that 14.1% of the students identified as LGBTQ.[8] What might account for the difference?

4. Participants in the Egale survey were asked to provide their sexual orientation, gender (male/female/ trans), ethnicity, and religion. Apply the idea of intersectionality to explain why this information is important.

5. Look at the following bar graph[9] and calculate the mean value of people in these groups experiencing verbal harassment, and then suggest why the mean alone is a less useful number than keeping the data separated into the three categories. How could the categories be further separated?

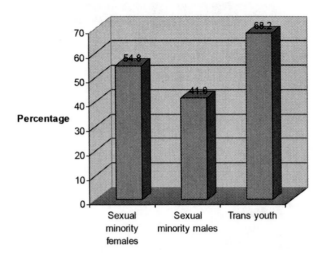

Verbal Harassment Due to Perceived Gender or Sexual Orientation

6. In looking at the consequences of victimization due to gender identity you decide to compare the number of students missing school in the past month. Looking at a number of schools, you find the following:

	School 1	School 2	School 3	School 4	School 5	School 6	School 7
Days missed by students who are victimized	101	268	68	89	160	245	301
Days missed by students who are not victimized	46	134	37	42	87	128	158

a. What general pattern do you see in the numbers, using words?

b. How did you figure out the pattern?

c. How would you quantify the pattern in numbers? Create an algebraic equation to capture the pattern.

d. If a school reported that non-LGBT students had collectively 70 days of missed school, how many days would you expect that the LGBT-identified students had missed?

e. What broader consequences might there be for missing school?

f. How might the school system address the safety of trans and gender non-conforming young people so that this pattern doesn't continue?

7. In looking at the consequences of victimization due to sexual orientation you compare the number of students missing school in the past month. Looking at a number of schools, you find the following:

	School 1	School 2	School 3	School 4	School 5	School 6	School 7
Days missed by students who are victimized	101	268	68	89	160	245	301
Days missed by students who are not victimized	33	84	25	34	57	78	98

a. What general pattern do you see in the numbers, using words?

b. How did you figure out the pattern?

c. How would you quantify the pattern in numbers- create an algebraic equation to capture the pattern.

d. If a school reported that non-LGBT students had collectively missed 100 days of school, how many days would you expect that the LGBT-identified students had missed?

8. Besides absenteeism rate, what other data could you collect so that you could quantify and therefore address the problem of homophobia and transphobia in schools?

9. The Gay, Lesbian & Straight Education Network in the United States did a National School Climate Survey in 2011. Two of the comparisons that they did between middle schools and high schools found the following:[10]

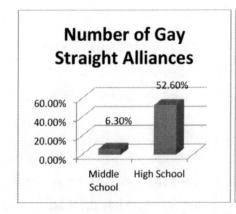

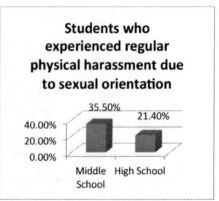

a. What do you think accounts for the differences between the middle schools and the high schools?

b. How would you use this data to address the problem?

Food for Thought:

In a report by GLSEN and Harris Interactive on school climate in the United States,[11] they found that only 34% of elementary school teachers engaged with the creation of safe and supportive classroom environments for gender non-conforming students.

make it better

Form a Queer Straight Alliance (QSA) at your school. There are many useful resources at the website www.mygsa.ca to help you, and posters can be found at **http://gsa13-14.tumblr.com/post/56909146499/our-posters-from-2012-2013**.

Once you have a QSA up and running, consider advocating for an all-gender washroom. You can read about City View Alternative School's all-gender washroom at **http://etfovoice.ca/article/its-the-small-things-that-matter-most/**.

Endnotes

1. Egale Canada Human Rights Trust. Every Class In Every School. 2011. P. 51.
2. Ibid, p. 50.
3. Erikson-Schroth, Laura. Trans Bodies, Trans Selves: A Resource for the Transgender Community. Oxford University Press, New York, 2014, p. 5.
4. Egale Canada Human Rights Trust. Every Class In Every School. 2011. P. 49.
5. Ibid, p. 26.
6. Erikson-Schroth, Laura. Trans Bodies, Trans Selves: A Resource for the Transgender Community. Oxford University Press, New York, 2014, p. 5.
7. Ontario Human Rights Commission. Policy on preventing discrimination because of gender identity and gender expression. www.ohrc.on.ca. 2014, p.6.
8. Egale Canada Human Rights Trust. Every Class In Every School. 2011. P. 39.
9. Egale Canada Human Rights Trust. Every Class In Every School. 2011. P. 60.
10. www.glsen.org The 2011 National School Climate Survey Executive Summary. 2012.

167

20/3

graph
equations
given a
formula
di
create
input /
output
table

Missing

"We're talking about so many layers of violence, so many generations of loss, and it's all covered up in layers of silence...in order for us to move ahead, we have to deal with all the things people don't want to talk about."

~ BEVERLEY JACOBS

setting the stage

Between 1980 and 2012 in Canada, 1,017 Indigenous women have been killed and at least 164 more are missing.[1] This has sparked 29 official inquiries that have collectively demanded more than 500 actions to resolve the problem. Now there are calls for a *national* public inquiry.[2] And the Prime Minister has recently promised to launch one.[3]

The historical record of the treatment of First Nations peoples in Canada is rife with human rights violations: Indigenous cultures and religion have been banned, voting rights were non-existent until 1960, emotional, physical and sexual abuse occurred within government mandated residential schools (1800s – 1996) , and laws have been made, like the Indian Act, that to this day limit and frame First Nations rights within this country.[4]

When widespread racism, poverty, sexism, misogyny, limited access to government services and radically different living conditions combine together, the risk of violence escalates. As Amnesty International writes: "This violence against Indigenous women and girls has deep roots in racism, marginalization and poverty."[5]

In 2010, after holding out for four years, Canada finally signed The UN Declaration on the Rights of Indigenous Peoples.[6] But federal government officials were quick to point out that the declaration was "aspirational in nature", rather than legally binding.

James Anaya, the United Nations Special Rapporteur on the rights of Indigenous people calls on the Canadian government to "undertake a comprehensive, nation-wide inquiry into the issue of missing and murdered Aboriginal women and girls, organized in consultation with Indigenous peoples." Now it is time to act.

Why are the historical record and the current reality of injustice *both* important to understanding the issue of missing and murdered aboriginal women and girls in Canada?

1. 4.3% of the roughly 32.9 million people in Canada are Indigenous. How many people is that?

2. In the Canadian Community Wellbeing Index, 96 of the bottom 100 communities in Canada are First Nations while only one First Nations Band is in the top 100 Canadian communities. (The Index measures education, labour force activity, housing and levels of income). Graph these two finding side by side and discuss. How does the act of juxtaposition help us to understand a topic?

3. The Native Women's Association of Canada has tracked missing and murdered Aboriginal women and girls. Since March 31st, 2010 there have been 582 cases, as follows:[7]

67% murder cases	4% suspicious deaths
20% missing women or girls	9% the nature of the case is unknown

   a. Find the actual number of each group of people based on the percentages.

   b. Graph the groups in a pie chart.

   c. Why do you think the category 'suspicious deaths' is included?

4. Aboriginal women are 4.3% of the female population in Canada. The total number of homicides across Canada between 1980 and 2012 was 20,313, of which 32% were female victims: 1,017 were Aboriginal women. What percentage is that of the total female victims and how does it compare to the percentage of Aboriginal women in Canada?

5. When involved in collecting information about a homicide, it can be difficult to establish Aboriginal origin or identity. Suggest one reason why you imagine this might be so.

6. From the RCMP report on Missing Aboriginal Women, the probable cause for missing Aboriginal women as of 2013 is as follows:

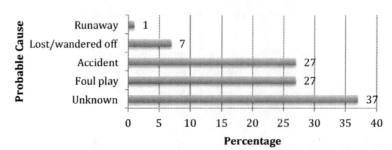

Probable Cause for Missing Aboriginal Women

a. These percentages refer to 164 missing Aboriginal women. Write in the actual numbers next to the percentages.

b. The total number of missing females in Canada is 1,455. What is 164 as a percentage of 1,455 and how does that compare to the percentage of Aboriginal females in Canada (4.3%).

c. The RCMP aggregate the data into suspicious/unknown circumstances and non-suspicious i.e. the last two categories and the first three categories respectively. What are the aggregated percentages and why do you think the RCMP does this?

7. Most of the violence occurs in urban areas rather than on-reserve (70% disappeared from urban areas versus 7% from on-reserve, the remainder from rural areas).[8] Why is knowing this distinction important in communicating the problem?

8. Women who have been pushed into sex trade work because of systemic racism and poverty may contribute to under-reporting of the problem of violence. Why?

9. A 2009 Canadian study of 10 provinces found that Aboriginal women are three times more likely to experience violent crime than non-Aboriginal women and the homicide rate for Aboriginal women is seven times more than non-Aboriginal women.[9] What are the two algebraic equations that represent this relationship, and how might knowing the relationship lead to action?

10. In Saskatchewan, the only province that has looked carefully at its Aboriginal missing persons cases, they find that while 60% involve Aboriginal women, only 6% of women in Saskatchewan are Aboriginal.[10] What might account for this huge discrepancy?

11. Heather King, who works with Northwest Alberta Child and Family Services, argues that spending money to prevent domestic violence is far more strategic than paying to intervene once the problem exists. She claims that for every dollar spent on prevention, seven dollars are saved on intervention.[11]

a. Where are some of the possible savings coming from?

b. Fill in the graph and the t-chart on the following page with the following information.

c. If you were willing to spend $20,000 on violence prevention initiatives, what would the potential savings be?

d. If you were willing to spend $60,000 on violence prevention initiatives, what would the potential savings be?

e. The Melissa Institute for Violence Prevention and Treatment estimates that the savings from acting proactively to stop domestic violence are much higher. For every dollar spent on prevention, they suggest that $28 is saved down the road.[12] Sketch in the $y = 28x$ line on the same graph. How does the slope compare?

Algebraic equation: _____   Slope:

y-intercept:

Variables:

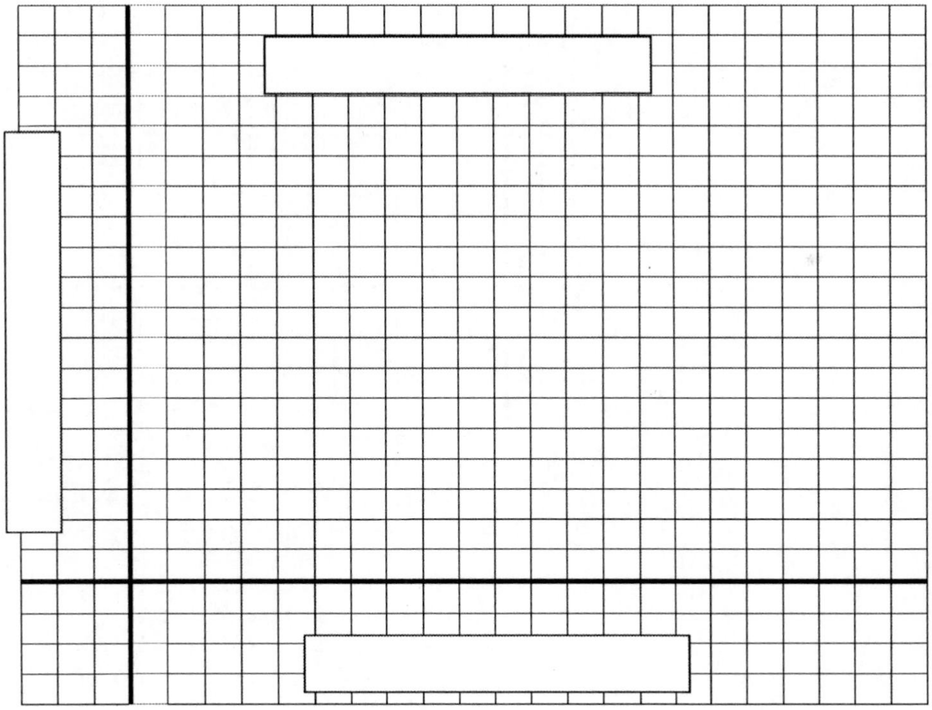

t chart:

When x is:	y is:

12. Creating women's shelters has been one way to address domestic violence. People assemble a Board of Directors, secure funding and a site, apply for insurance, and furnish the building's rooms. If the start up costs for a small shelter are $60,000 and the yearly costs (rent, food, upkeep, staff) are $40,000, fill in the following graph.

Algebraic equation
for total cost:

Slope:

y-intercept:

Variables:

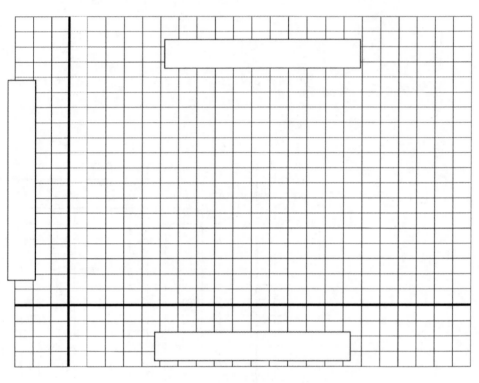

t chart:

When x is:	y is:

a. If you had $1,500,000 to run this shelter, how many years could you run it for?

b. If you had $3,500,000 to run this shelter, how many years could you run it for?

make it better

Download and distribute the Community Resource Guide from the Native Women's Association of Canada. It is available at the following site:
http://www.nwac.ca/sites/default/files/imce/2012-02-14_NWAC_ CommunityResourceGuide_full_e.pdf

Take a look at the REDress Project (**http://www.redressproject.org**), and consider an arts-based response to what you have been learning in mathematics. What are the benefits of mathematics and art working together to do social justice?

Endnotes

1. GLSEN & Harris Interactive. Playgrounds and Prejudice: Elementary School Climate in the United States; A Survey of Students and Teachers. New York; GLSEN. 2012
2. RCMP. Missing and Murdered Aboriginal Women: A National Operational Overview. 2014.
3. Anaya, James. Report of the Special Rapporteur on he rights of indigenous people. UN Human Rights Council. 27th Session.
4. http://www.cbc.ca/news/aboriginal/police-forces-need-culture-change-trudeau-1.3428530
5. Ibid.
6. http://www.amnesty.ca/sites/default/files/iwfa_submission_amnesty_international_february_2014_-_final.pdf
7. Anaya, James. Report of the Special Rapporteur on the rights of indigenous people. UN Human Rights Council. 27th Session.
8. Native Women's Association of Canada. Fact Sheet: Missing and Murdered Aboriginal Women and Girls.
9. Ibid.
10. http://www.amnesty.ca/sites/default/files/iwfa_submission_amnesty_international_february_2014_-_final.pdf
11. Ibid.
12. Callan, Patrick. Community comes together for 'Stop Family Violence' Campaign. Grande Prairie Daily Herald-Tribune, November 1, 2012.
13. The Melissa Institute for Violence Prevention and Treatment. The Dollars and Sense of Violence Prevention. 2009, p. 3.
14. http://www.getrichslowly.org/blog/2010/05/11/grow-your-savings-by-paying-in-full/

interest
writing
equations

Up Front

"Interests on debts grow without rain."

~ YIDDISH PROVERB

setting the stage ☞ The sign on the lawn says the house is for sale, and today you can step inside and take a look around. On the table in the kitchen is a piece of paper that describes the features of the house and the listed price: $300,000. You head to the bank. They say that if you can put a $30,000 down payment on the house, you'll pay $1,284 a month for 30 years. With a little calculator skill, you find that the $300,000 house is going to cost you $492,240!

Of course, the reason for this is that the bank will only loan you money if you pay interest on it. And that's the general idea: the longer you take to pay something, the more you'll end up paying. There are other reasons too — for small business, cash is usually easier to deal with, and the business may want to avoid their own payments to credit card companies or to work through cheques that bounce. As a result, you may be able to bargain for a better price.[1]

But at the end of the day, who has $300,000 to pay for a house up front? Probably not most of us. Even much smaller purchases like cars, or furniture, or laptops can be insurmountable financial barriers to people who live in poverty. And so the dilemma is that those with the least amount of money end up financing purchases that end up costing them more than people who have a lot of money and who can get those same things for less.

Might there be ways for social justice activists to leverage the idea of paying for things up front to reduce costs to those who need it most? Let's find out.

Ambrose Bierce is quoted as saying that debt is "an ingenious substitute for the chain and whip of the slave driver." What do you think he meant?

For each of the following scenarios:

1. Capture the ongoing costs in an algebraic equation.

2. Make the equation equivalent to paying up front and solve for the missing variable.

3. Explain how a social justice activist could use the idea of paying up front to address oppression, with specific reference to the scenario.

Scenario A:

A washer and dryer costs $800. A family without a washer and dryer goes to the local laundromat and pays $25 a week to wash and dry their clothes.

Scenario B:

A country finds that it is paying $25,000 a year in responding to climate disasters in its country. A study finds that if the country invested $230,000 immediately in disaster preparedness, it could reduce its likely response costs to $5,000 a year.

Scenario C:

A disaster response NGO has a choice of paying rent on an operations building that they will work out of, at a cost of $1500 a month over 20 years, or they can pay $200,000 up front to own the building. (Why is there a difference in the cost between the two options?)

Scenario D:

You can rent a laptop for $100 a month, or buy a reconditioned laptop for $800.

Scenario E:

As an individual you can buy food at $1.50 a kilogram. If you buy food in huge quantities you can pay 30% less. What would your savings be if you purchased 5000 kilograms of food all at once?

Scenario F:

A two-year magazine subscription up front costs $50. Buying the individual magazines each month in a bookstore costs $5.95.

Scenario G:

The one time costs to retrofit a house with more insulation costs $250. Monthly heating costs that were $20 a month then drop to $5 a month. Find out when you break even.

Scenario H:

You pay $350 a month to rent a car, for a period of four years, and then if you want to purchase it, it'll cost you $13,500. Or you can buy the car outright for $26,000.

Scenario I:

Write your own scenario, and share it with a partner. Remember to try and articulate how a social justice activist could use the idea of purchasing things up front to address oppression.

make it better ✌

Find out if your school might be able to use its capital to purchase something up front, that members in your school community could use to reduce their own spending that is locked into monthly payments.

176

Endnote

1. http://www.getrichslowly.org/blog/2010/05/11/grow-your-savings-by-paying-in-full/

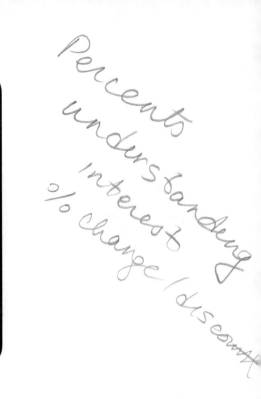

Mouseprint

"The large print giveth and the small print taketh away."

~ TOM WAITS

Every day, we are exposed to marketing messages. These ads plaster billboards, take center stage on our clothing, cover the products that we purchase, and fill newspapers, magazines and the internet. Depending on whom you believe, we see between 250 and 20,000 ads in a single day.

Understanding what these advertisements are saying can be very tricky. Take for example a study that was done on 100 people who had just purchased an HP inkjet printer. When asked how many had been informed about how much the replacement ink cartridges cost at the time of purchasing the printer, only 3% responded affirmatively. That's interesting, because 90% of the cost of owning an inkjet printer is paying for the ink.[1]

Think of all of the ways you've seen of obscuring the truth, and hiding additional costs. Having to sign long-term contracts. Penalties and fees. Connection costs. Super small footnotes. Terms and conditions that are hidden in pages of text, sometimes on different web pages. Objects in the ad that are not actually included in the purchase of the product.[2]

Truly, showing only part of the truth makes an excellent lie. In this lesson, you get to try your hand at it...

Have you ever purchased something and then realized that you didn't know the terms and conditions of your purchase? Share your story with the class.

1. One of the grand prizes on NBC's show *America's Got Talent* is a cool million dollars. But what isn't shared so openly is that the winner has to choose between a payment of $25,000 a year for 40 years, or a one-time lump sum right away of roughly $300,000.[3]

   a. What does $25,000 a year for 40 years amount to in total?

   b. Why is that total not really worth the full amount?

   c. Why is one of the options for winning one million dollars to take only $300,000?

2. An ad by American Express offered a deal that you would earn 5% on the purchases that you put on your credit card.[4]

   a. The mouseprint included the fact that the 5% only applied to purchases from supermarkets, drugstores and gas stations. Why is that an important limitation to understand?

   b. Another detail was that you only earn 5% on your purchases once you put $6,500 on your credit card. Why don't you want $6,500 on your credit card?

   c. You do earn 1% on your purchases up to $6,500. Does that make the deal significant enough to have $6,500 on your credit card? What kind of interest rates do many credit cards have?

3. A company offers a loan of $5,000. In the small print, the annual percentage rate (APR) is given as 116.73%, with 84 monthly payments.

   a. The monthly payments amount to $486.58. How much will you end up paying after the 84 payments?

   b. Find out if the province you live in has laws that restrict the APR.

4. Studies have been conducted to see if people read the terms and conditions of the purchase that they are making. Andy Greenberg writes in *Forbes.com* that 0.11% of users click on a link to get to the terms and conditions.[5]

   a. How many people in 1000 would be equal to 0.11%?

   b. If you need to click "I agree" to the terms, it turns out that even fewer follow the link: only 0.07%. How many people in 1,000 would be equal to 0.07%?

5. In a study done on visits to software retailers online, it was found that the mean number of seconds spent on the terms and conditions pages was 59.4 seconds, the median was 34 seconds, and 46% of users were lower than 30 seconds. 92% spent less than two minutes.[6]

   a. The average number of words used in retail products terms and conditions is 2,277 with a median of 2,187. The average reading rate is 250 to 300 words a minute. How many minutes would it take to read the terms and conditions?

b. Compare and discuss your answer in (a) with the amount of time people spend on the terms and conditions pages.

6. Design your own advertisement. In it, try to be as sneaky as possible. In addition to the ideas in the introduction, you might also think about:

a. What exclusions from the deal are there?

b. Whether the deal can be for a short period of time, and then revert to a much higher cost.

c. If you can use phrases like "as low as" or "up to ….% off".

d. Whether additional fees like transportation to and from the location can be conveniently missing (for example, airport taxes and taxi transfer to sunny all-inclusive resorts).

e. Whether rebates can be used to lure people in, but are difficult to follow through on.

f. Whether the deal applies only to a single person (so, for example, on many trip ads the price is posted per person, double occupancy required.)

You can pick any product: some common ones are credit cards, motor vehicles, travel, phones, internet providers, and television services.

7. Create a mouseprint gallery, and let everyone in the class see the different advertisements. Can you pick out the implications of the mouseprint?

---

make it better ✌

Visit **www.mouseprint.org** to see examples of advertising that is intended to deceive.

In Canada, false or misleading advertising is addressed under the Competition Act. At **www.consumerhandbook.ca** is a listing of contacts for the Better Business Bureau and other consumer groups where you can file complaints of misleading advertising.

Endnotes

1. Baker, Marotta-Wurgler and Trossen. Does Anyone Read the Fine Print? Consumer Attention and Standard Form Contracts. Journal of Legal Studies. Jan. 2014, p.9.
2. Bureau of Consumer Protection. Big Print. Little Print. What's the Deal?
3. www.mouseprint.org
4. Lin-Fisler, Betty. Truth of Ads Does Lie Beneath.
5. Greenberg, Andy. Who Reads The Fine Print Online? Less Than One Person in 1000. Forbes.com.
6. Baker, Marotta-Wurgler and Trossen. Does Anyone Read the Fine Print? Consumer Attention and Standard Form Contracts. Journal of Legal Studies. Vol. 43, No. 1, Jan. 2014, p. 22.

⁰/₀ change

Tipping Point

"Once we allow temperatures to climb past a certain point, where the mercury stops is not in our control."

~ NAOMI KLEIN

In 2009, at a climate summit in Copenhagen, big polluting countries finally agreed (in a non-binding way...) to keep global temperatures from rising more than two degrees Celsius. Scientists around the world have repeatedly pointed out that climate change is a threat to human civilization, and that if we intend to prevent catastrophic changes to the planet, we need to wean ourselves from burning fossil fuels.

One of the dangers is that humans could trigger a **negative feedback loop** that spirals out of control. Take the arctic ice as an example. Because it is white, it functions like a type of mirror, reflecting the sun's heat back into the atmosphere. As carbon dioxide in our atmosphere traps more heat, the artic ice melts, leaving less of a mirror. Which means more heat is absorbed by the earth. Which means the artic ice melts even more. And so on.

Although much focus has been placed on the problem of too much carbon dioxide in the atmosphere, methane is eighty six times more powerful at holding in heat.[1] Trapped in the Arctic permafrost is quite a bit of methane. So as you heat the earth, you melt the permafrost and release more methane. Which heats the earth, melting more permafrost, releasing more methane.

The oceans soak up atmospheric carbon, which might sound like a good thing at first, until you realize that it causes acidification of the water, a situation that has impacts on the ocean ecosystems.[2] If, for example, the ocean becomes too acidic for species at the bottom of the food chain, the loss of those species will ripple upwards through the entire ecosystem.

While countries have agreed to limit our planetary temperature rise to two degrees, The World Bank suggests we're currently on track to see an increase of four degrees and the International Energy Agency has projected a rise of six degrees.

We can't let that happen.

opening question **?**

Warming in the two to four degree range has a probability greater than 16% of causing at least one of five tipping points[3] (nine have been described). More than four degrees of warming has a probability greater than 56% of causing at least one of five tipping points. Discuss.

understanding using math

1. Watch the 33 second animation of the decrease in the Arctic icecap from 1979 to 2012 at the following link: https://www.youtube.com/watch?v=AztEry44A9A .

   a. The sea ice area in October of 2014 was 8.06 million square kilometres. The average between 1981 and 2010 was 8.91 million square kilometres. What is the difference as a percentage between the two numbers?

181

   b. The difference in square kilometres can be compared to the size of a country. Find the difference and make a comparison to a country of similar size. List some countries that are smaller in area than the difference.

   c. The National Snow and Ice Data Center have added a trend line showing the Arctic Ice extent between 1979 and 2014 (see chart). Is the trend line linear or exponential? Using values at 1979 and 2014, see if you can figure out the average loss of ice per year.

   d. At this rate, what year would you expect an ice-free Arctic?

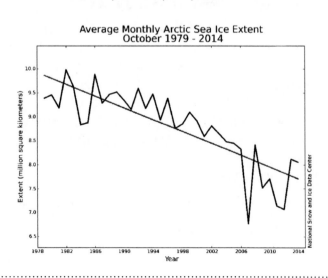

Average Monthly Arctic Sea Ice Extent
October 1979 - 2014

2. Increased absorption of solar radiation affects the top 66 feet of water.[4] How many metres is that? What is something else that is that same height?

3. If the Arctic ice melts, the resulting rise in global temperatures may have an effect on the release of methane from the permafrost. Frozen organic matter will melt, rot and release methane, or methyl clathrate frozen in ice crystals will be released.[6] The Earth's atmosphere has 850 gigatons of carbon in it.

   a. A gigaton is a billion tons. How many Titanics would it take to equal a billion tons?

   b. The carbon in the permafrost is estimated to be 1,400 gigatons. What is that as a comparison to the current atmospheric carbon?

   c. While it is unknown how much of the 1,400 gigatons would enter the atmosphere, a warmer Arctic would allow for plants to live for longer amounts of time each year. How would that decrease the carbon?

4. Look at the following graph and indicate whether the region is a carbon sink (it absorbs more carbon than it releases) or a carbon source (it releases more carbon than it stores).

	Region 1	Region 2	Region 3	Region 4
Carbon absorbed	346	2,378	19,237	3,590
Carbon released	356	2,456	18,125	3,789
Sink or source?				

5. Dr. Dwight Gledhill from the Cooperative Institute of Marine and Atmospheric Sciences, suggests that human impacts of increased carbon have come from the following:[5]

   4.1 pentagrams of carbon from deforestation and

   7.7 pentagrams of carbon from fossil fuel emissions

Not all of this carbon ends up in the atmosphere:

   1.1 pentagrams of carbon ends up in the atmosphere

   2.3 pentagrams of carbon ends up in the ocean

   2.4 pentagrams of carbon ends up in land plants and soils

Create some sort of graphic to show the various locations of carbon creation and carbon uptake. Include percentages.

6. Carbon dioxide from the air that ends up in the oceans creates a weak acid called carbonic acid. The pH scale goes from 0 (a strong acid) to 14 (a strong base).[6]

   a. What would a neutral pH be?

   b. The surface of the ocean has historically been 8.2. Is it acidic or alkaline?

   c. The pH scale is logarithmic: find out what that means.

d. The pH today is 8.1, which represents an increase in acidity of 30% over the past 350 years. Explain, using your answer in (c) how this change of 0.1 units can be 30%.

e. As the carbonate ions drop in quantity, what impact will that have on organisms that need calcium carbonate?

7. Eighty percent of the global fish catch come from about 10% of the world's oceans.[7] How would you create a bar graph to show this? Why does this matter?

8. Consider that multiple impacts on ocean systems may interact synergistically. Look at the following hypothetical table and explain synergy.

Impact Type	Impact Value
Ocean acidification	3
Overfishing	5
Ocean warming	2
Sea level rise	1
Pollution	1
Coral bleaching	2
Total:	25

make it better

The global environmental movement takes many forms, in many places. You might want to start at **www.350.org** to find your niche.

Endnotes

1. Klein, Naomi. This Changes Everything. Alfred A. Knoff Canada. 2014, p. 143.
2. Ibid. p. 259.
3. http://yosemite.epa.gov/ee/epa/eerm.nsf/vwAN/EE-0564-112.pdf/$file/EE-0564-112.pdf
4. http://nsidc.org/arcticseaicenews/
5. http://nsidc.org/arcticseaicenews/
6. https://nsidc.org/cryosphere/frozenground/methane.html
7. http://coralreef.noaa.gov/education/oa/presentation-videos.html.
8. UNEP. Emerging Issues: Environmental Consequences of Ocean Acidification: A Threat to Food Security. 2010, p. 2.
9. Ibid, p. 4.

*Reduce fraction/
ratio
slope
intercept*

Get Out the Lead

"For a prudent toxicological policy, a chemical should be considered guilty until proven innocent."

~ UMBERTO SAFFIOTTI

setting the stage

In the six years between 2008 and 2014, Torontonians tested their water 15,000 times. The reason? The pipes that deliver the city's water to households are oftentimes made of lead. And lead in the water can lead to health problems: attention deficit hyperactivity disorder, a drop in IQ, behavioural problems in children, and kidney failure and hypertension in adults.[1]

Lead is a naturally occurring metal that can also be found in old paint, cheap jewelry, and kids' toys. Sometimes it is more likely to be ingested: for example, when found on items that young people might put in their mouths, like crib toys or mouthpieces of musical instruments. In 2007, 45 million toys in the United States were recalled after the paint on them tested positive for lead.[2]

Safe levels for lead in humans depend on various factors, but always are in such minute quantities that it's impossible for us to see the danger. A renovation of an old home may disturb lead-based paint, and the resulting dust is simply inhaled. Lead paint on an old playground structure or fence finds its way into the soil as it decomposes, and can be absorbed by some of the vegetables that we eat.[3]

And while the World Health Organization pegs the safe level of lead at 10 parts per billion, some British researchers say it should be five,[4] and more than a few people always put the word "safe" in quotation marks. As in, no level of lead is safe for us.

How might a country with very high standards for eliminating lead from toys find itself with many toys that have been painted with lead based paints?

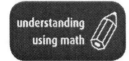

1. Safe levels of lead in drinking water are given as 10 parts per billion.

   a. Ten parts per billion is the equivalent to one part per what?

   b. Could you divide the table that you are working at into the same number of pieces as your answer in (a)? Don't show all of the pieces, but by marking the table in half and then half again and so on, can you come close to the size of one of the pieces?

   c. What does this mean about a concentration of 10 parts per billion?

2. You test your tap water and find it to be 32.4 parts per billion. The city is replacing its old lead pipes and finds that for each month of replacing lead pipes, the lead level in water drops by 1.2 parts per billion.

   a. Write an algebraic equation in the form $y = mx + b$ for the total parts per billion in your tap water over time.

   b. Why is the slope negative?

   c. If the safe level is 10 parts per billion, use your equation to solve for the number of months it will take to reach the safe amount.

   d. If you have kids, or someone pregnant in the house, 10 parts per billion is too high. Use your equation to see how long it would take to get down to 5 parts per billion. Why would infants who drink formula be at higher levels of risk?

   e. If you were a resident, would you think that this timeline was appropriate?

3. One solution that the city offers is that it will replace the water line along the street if you will replace the water line from the street to your house. The cost to you of replacing your part of the pipe is $3,000. The alternative is that you could buy a water filter (that removes lead) to put on your drinking water supply tap inside the house. It costs $60 a year.

   a. Write an algebraic equation in the form $y = mx + b$ to show the total cost to pay for water filters.

   b. How many years would it take to reach the cost to replace the pipe from the street to your house?

   c. Based on these numbers, which do you think is the better choice to make: buy the filters or replace the pipe?

4. Of the 50,000 tests conducted, 13% showed a failure rate.[5] How many homes does that represent?

185

5. The city would like to see 5,000 homes per year fixed, including the section between the street and the house.

    a. Write the equation for the number of homes in total to be fixed each year.

    b. If the number of homes to be fixed is 40,000, how many years would it take to reach all of the homes.

    c. The actual number of homes fixed is turning out to be about 3,500 per year. Write the new equation for total number of homes fixed.

    d. How long would it take to reach the 40,000 homes with lead pipes using the new equation?

6. Some municipalities offer loans to households if they fix the lead pipes. If the total loan is $3,000 and is interest-free, and you can pay it back monthly over the course of 10 years, how much are you paying each month? Write the algebraic equation for the total amount that you owe over time.

7. Some of the homes tested in Toronto showed lead levels 2,000 times greater than the 'safe level'.[6] How many parts per billion of lead did those homes have?

8. Sometimes while trying to implement good strategies you can cause more damage: it's called an iatrogenic effect. Can you think of why replacing some of the lead pipes led in some cases to higher levels of lead in the drinking water?

make it better

Call your Public Health Office to see if they offer a free water test for lead. Have your water tested and work make lead pipe removal a priority for your community. In the meantime, install a water filter with the capacity to remove lead. Run the cold water for several minutes before you use unfiltered water from old homes.

186

Endnotes

1. http://www.thestar.com/news/gta/2014/05/20/water_quality_tests_data_shows_elevated_lead_levels_in_toronto_homes.html
2. How much lead is too much? www.cbc.ca September 17, 2009.
3. Webmd.com 5 Surprising Sources of Lead Exposure.
4. How much lead is too much? www.cbc.ca September 17, 2009.
5. http://www.thestar.com/news/gta/2014/05/20/water_quality_tests_data_shows_elevated_lead_levels_in_toronto_homes.html
6. http://globalnews.ca/news/1341542/unsafe-levels-of-lead-in-toronto-tap-water-report/

Function
input/output
table

The Cat in the Coalmine

"Future warns us through current symptoms in nature."

~ TOBA BETA

Coal miners used to carry caged canaries into the mines, as an early warning system. If there were dangerous levels of methane or carbon dioxide present, the birds would be the first to perish, signaling to the miners that they should quickly escape.[1]

In Minamata, Japan in the 1950s, cats started to show bizarre behaviours: wobbling around in a type of 'dance', and falling over, sometimes dying. Within a few short years, the behaviour extended to the children, and then the adults. Researchers found their way back to the local Chisso factory, producing acetaldehyde for plastics. Mercury was being dumped into the bay, and was working its way up the food chain. Cats eating fish from the bay had been the canaries in the coalmine.[2]

In the end, methyl mercury in the fish took the lives of more than 100 people and many more suffered from brain damage.[3]

In 1975, researchers from Japan visited northwestern Ontario: Reed Paper Company had been forced to shut down by the government in 1970 after dumping 9,000 kg of mercury into the local waters. People in two First Nations communities, Grassy Narrows and Wabaseemoong were experiencing the same neurological symptoms as the people in Minamata. Compensation was less generous.[4]

On January 19, 2013, the United Nations introduced the Minamata Convention on Mercury to address the problems of mercury in everyday products, the soil, water and our atmosphere. There are currently 128 signatory countries.[5] Where are the others?

Find a definition for "environmental racism". Do you think that the case of poisoning in Grassy Narrows and Wabaseemoong qualifies? Why or why not?

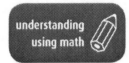

Minamata and Mercury Poisoning

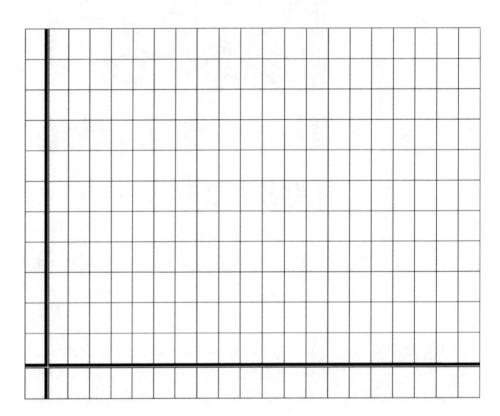

1. Fill in the t-charts layout for the level of mercury (Hg) in the water, in zooplankton, in small fish, large fish and humans. Then plot the points for each line on the above graph for the first 10 years of mercury being released into the water system

Levels of mercury in parts per billion (x represents number of years, y is mercury (Hg) levels in ppb)

Water levels		Zooplankton		Small fish		Large fish		Humans	
When x is...	$y = 3x$	When x is...	$y = 4x$	When x is...	$y = \frac{1}{2}x^2$	When x is...	$y = x^2$	When x is...	$y = 2x^2$
0		0		0		0		0	
1		1		1		1		1	
2		2		2		2		2	
3		3		3		3		3	
4		4		4		4		4	
5		5		5		5		5	
6		6		6		6		6	
7		7		7		7		7	
8		8		8		8		8	
9		9		9		9		9	
10		10		10		10		10	

2. Is the increase between trophic levels linear or exponential, and why?

3. If the 'safe' level of mercury in small fish 18 parts per billion, how many years would it take to reach this level? Make the two equations ($y = 18$ and $y = \frac{1}{2}x^2$ equal and solve for x).

4. If the 'safe' level of mercury in large fish is 49 parts per billion, how many years would it take to reach this level? Make the two equations and solve for x.

5. If the 'safe' level of mercury for humans is 162 parts per billion, how many years would it take to reach this level? Make the two equations and solve for x.

6. Can you think of some humans that might be more vulnerable to mercury than others? Which ones and why? If their 'safe' level of mercury is 50 parts per billion, how many years would it take to reach this level? Make the two equations and solve for x.

7. For compensation for being hurt, the people in Minamata received a payment in 1973 (let's say $5,000) and since then have been paid between $2000 and $8000 a month.[6]

   a. Write the algebraic equation for the compensation (use the average monthly payment as the coefficient and don't forget the payment from 1973).

   b. If the initial costs to deal with the disease are $15,000 and then ongoing costs are $4,000 a month, when does the compensation match the costs?

8. In 2010, researchers from Japan examined 160 people from Grassy Narrows and Wabaseemoong. They found that 57.8% of the people were still affected by mercury.[7] How many people is that?

9. The compensation for these First Nations is $250 to $800 a month, depending on the severity of the symptoms.[8]

   a. Compare that compensation to the compensation the victims in Japan are receiving.

   b. Why does the value of the monthly compensation drop as time passes, even though the amount stays the same? What implication does this have?

Food for thought:

It has been estimated that around the world, 10 million people are at risk of lead poisoning. The next most common toxic substance: mercury.[9]

make it better

Explore your community and find out which, if any, companies use mercury in the production of goods. See if you can find out what the local laws say about mercury release. Will a representative of the company visit your class to talk about how they deal with the mercury?

Endnotes

1. http://en.wiktionary.org/wiki/canary_in_a_coal_mine
2. www1.umn.edu/ships/ethics/minamata.htm
3. http://www.cbc.ca/news/canada/mercury-poisoning-effects-continue-at-grassy-narrows-1.1132578
4. Ibid.
5. www.mercuryconvention.org
6. http://www.cbc.ca/news/canada/mercury-poisoning-effects-continue-at-grassy-narrows-1.1132578
7. Ibid.
8 Ibid.
9. Guinness World Records 2015, p. 126

Pillaging the Public Purse (P3s)

"We have to choose between a global market driven only by calculations of short-term profit, and one which has a human face."

~ KOFI ANNAN

191

If you read the Canadian government's P3 (Public-Private-Partnership) website, you'll quickly notice that the solution to building and managing our public infrastructure (roads, hospitals, schools, waste water facilities) is to partner with private businesses. Risk is offloaded to the private sector, costs are clear before the project begins, and work gets completed on time and on budget.[1]

Except that not everyone agrees. In looking at some of the 180 P3 projects in Canada, journalist Barrie McKenna notes that while governments may love the idea of getting services up and running now and paying for them later, there is the sticky issue that P3s tend to cost an average of 16% more than regular contracts.[2] Part of the reason is that private business pays *more* to borrow money than public institutions. And then there's the fact that investors need to turn a profit.[3]

As a way to keep costs low, those private businesses can fire staff and hire them back without a union contract, meaning lower wages and fewer benefits. They can offer less service, use cheaper materials, and introduce user fees to the public.[4]

The Auditor General of Ontario released a report that said that the decision to use P3s depends on the value of the risks that are offloaded to the private corporations, but that "there is no empirical data supporting the key assumptions used by Infrastructure Ontario to assign costs to specific risks."[5]

What does it mean to say that there is no empirical data to support the key assumptions to assign costs to specific risks?

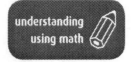

1. Both the Federal Liberals under Justin Trudeau and the Conservatives under Stephen Harper favour P3s as a solution to public infrastructure.[5]

   a. If the Auditor General in Ontario released a report saying that P3 projects caused the people of the province to pay $8 billion in extra costs,[6] why would the Liberal Party and the Conservative Party want them?

   b. If a P3 project can be recorded in accounting books as an operating lease instead of a capital expense, how does that change the impression of the provincial debt?

   c. How long would it take you to count to 8 billion?

2. In British Columbia, the privatization of some health services meant that the staff was hired at a rate of $9.50 per hour. The standard rate was $18.32 per hour.[7]

   a. If a workforce was made up of 500 people, each working 40 hour weeks, what savings does that mean for the corporation per week?

   b. What savings does that mean for the corporation over the course of a year? Use 50 weeks as your work year.

3. If payments to staff for benefits are cut by 22% from an annual amount of $732,000, what will the new amount spent on benefits be? Why is this important?

4. Ontario Infrastructure is a body designed to coordinate large infrastructure projects, using a P3 model.

   a. As of 2014, only 160 of the employees at Infrastructure Ontario agreed with P3 projects out of a total 493 full time staff.[8] What percentage is that?

   b. Seventy-five P3 projects have taken place in Ontario since the first in 2001. Forty-seven have been in health care, 10 in justice, six in transit, four in transportation, four in the Pan Am Games, three in education, and one in information technology.[9] Graph these projects using a bar graph and comment on anything that you notice.

   c. The Auditor General notes that the costs for 74 projects turned out to be 8 billion dollars more than if the public sector had delivered them, but that the risks associated with public sector delivery were $18.6 billion.[10] What conclusion did the government therefore draw? What do critics like the Auditor General say in response?

5. A report investigating the costs to build schools found that for every two you build using a P3 model, three could have been built financed by the public sector.[11]

   a. Write the algebraic equation that captures the relationship between funding the construction of schools under a public versus a P3 model. Use the form $y = mx + b$.

   b. What do you notice about the coefficient? And the constant?

   c. If the number of schools built using a P3 model was 10, how many could you have built in a public model?

   d. If the number of schools built using a P3 model was 20, how many could you have built in a public model?

   e. If the number of schools built using a P3 model was 45, how many could you have built in a public model?

6. If we imagine that for hospitals, for every five hospitals built using a P3 model you can build seven using a public model:

   a. Write the algebraic equation that captures the relationship between funding the construction of hospitals under a public versus a P3 model. Use the form $y = mx + b$.

   b. What do you notice about the coefficient? And the constant?

   c. What is the slope of the line? What is the y-intercept?

   d. If the number of hospitals built using a P3 model was 30, how many could you have built in a public model?

   e. If the number of hospitals built using a P3 model was 40, how many could you have built in a public model?

7. If the public municipal government can borrow money at an interest rate of 3.82% while private businesses can borrow at a rate of 6.2%, what would the difference in interest payments be per year on a loan of $75 million?

8. For a larger project, like a hospital, if the loan required was $400 million, calculate the difference in interest payments per year with the public institution compared to the private business.

9. Why can public institutions borrow money at much lower interest rates?

10. Have you had services that you use introduce a user fee? What were the services, how much was the user fee, and how might that fee prevent people from using the service? Which people are most affected?

193

make it better

Invite a local union representative to visit your class to talk about P3s and their impact on your community. What activism is being done by the unions to challenge P3s and how can you get involved?

Endnotes

1. www.p3canada.ca
2. McKenna, Barrie. The Hidden Price of Public-Private Partnerships. The Globe and Mail. Oct. 14, 2012.
3. www.reginawaterwatch.ca
4. www.policyalternatives.ca The Real Bottom Line: A Beginner's Guide to P3s.
5. www.auditor.on.ca 2014 Annual Report p. 198.
6. Butler, Michael. $8 billion down the drain in Ontario P3s. www.canadians.org. December 9, 2014.
7. Ibid.
8. Ibid.
9. www.auditor.on.ca Annual Report 2014 p. 194
10. Ibid. p.196
11. www.auditor.on.ca 2014 Annual Report p. 197-98.
12. www.cbc.ca Public-private school deals make 'no economic sense'; study

Damned

"The wise build bridges and the foolish build dams."

~ NIGERIAN PROVERB

setting the stage You are standing on a sandy beach. A rivulet of water is cutting a pathway across the sand, out to the sea. Carefully, you take small pebbles and put them on either side of the small stream, like little dwellings. A village grows up around your stream.

Closer to the lake, you begin to build a dam. Larger rocks slowly barricade the stream until it begins to back up, and form a reservoir. The higher you build the dam, the further back your reservoir reaches. All the way back to your village. Soon the dwellings are underwater.

In the same way, 13 cities, 140 towns, and 1,350 villages were swallowed by the rising waters behind China's Three Gorges Dam,[1] built between 2004 and 2012. Barricading the Yangtze River, it is the world's largest hydroelectric dam. And one massive trade-off: 1,200,000 people displaced, in return for 18,000 megawatts of power.

Along with people's homes, cultural sites were lost forever, and the factories, mines and dumps that were submerged have left a toxic legacy that swirls throughout the reservoir.

State violence initially squashed protests,[2] but now China's State Council has admitted to environmental, geological and social problems that the dam has caused.[3]

It's a damn shame it took so long to figure it out.

The hydroelectric power that is produced is meant to be the equivalent of burning 50 million tons of coal, or 25 million tons of crude oil.[4] Discuss.

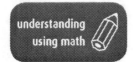

Use the topological map on the next page to answer the following questions.

1. Contour lines on this map connect points of equal elevation and have a contour interval of 10 feet. The lowest contour line on the map is listed as 10 feet below sea level. Use that line as a reference point and mark the elevation of all other contour lines on the map. Colour in the spaces between each contour line a different colour for each elevation.

2. What coordinates mark the highest point of elevation on the map?

3. What is the difference between the highest and the lowest points on the map?

4. Each of the following coordinates represents a village. Mark in a dot for each village:

(0, 6)	(-2, 9)	(-8, 7)	(-11, 8)	(-8, 3)	(-5, 1)	(-5, -5)	(-10, -9)	(-10, -15)
(-14, -12)	(-14, -19)	(-2, -14)	(7, 4)	(8, 6)	(8, 10)	(10, 14)	(13, 8)	(14, 3)
(13, -6)	(14, -12)							

5. A river flows from quadrant 2 down to quadrant 4. A dam is proposed in quadrant 4 between points (13, -16) and (7, -17). Mark the proposed dam and circle the villages above that would be put at risk if the dam was built in this place.

6. Would a dam between points (7, -9) and (2, -10) raise or lower the level of the reservoir compared to that last proposed location of the dam? Draw it in. If more communities are put at risk, put a square around them.

7. What is the difference between the height of the two dams?

8. Where would you be able to put a dam without putting communities at risk? What would be the reason that your dam might be rejected?

make it better

Research and report on the James Bay Cree hydroelectric plant in Quebec. What similarities are there to the three Gorges Dam? What differences? Did the government consult with the First Nations communities?

Endnotes

1. http://www.internationalrivers.org/campaigns/three-gorges-dam
2. http://news.bbc.co.uk/2/hi/asia-pacific/7042660.stm Oct. 12, 2007
3. http://www.bbc.com/news/world-asia-pacific-13451528
4. http://www.pbs.org/itvs/greatwall/controversy.html

Pad-dling Upstream

"Shame corrodes the very part of us that believes we are capable of change."

~ BRENÉ BROWN

199

setting the stage

Menstrual activists: people who refuse to feel shamed talking about normal bodily functions like having your period, who openly challenge the $3 billion a year feminine products industry,[1] and who understand clearly that 20 billion pads and tampons making their way into North American dumps each year just can't be good for the environment.[2]

But far from a bunch of armchair critics, menstrual activists go out and change the world: they purchase organic cotton tampons to avoid the pesticides put on conventional cotton, they make their own reusable pads, shift to reusable menstrual cups, and educate others about the choices they have made.

opening question ?

Why would being made to feel ashamed of your period work to the benefit of the $3 billion a year feminine products industry?

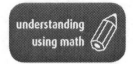
1. Let's say a period is five days long and you use four menstrual pads a day. The cost per pad is 25 cents and you have a 28-day menstrual cycle for 40 years of your life. What is the total lifetime cost of using disposable menstrual pads?

2. Do the same lifetime calculation with tampons, using 30 cents per tampon.

3. If you make your own reusable pads, using cloth from items you already have (pillowcases, towels, fleece), your costs can be non-existent. If you buy a set of re-usable pads you might pay $130. A menstrual cup can cost $50. By what factor are your answers in questions 1 and 2 greater than reusable pads or cups (which are marketed as five year and two year products, respectively — although some people write that cups can last 10 years). Filling in the following table may make it easier to figure out the factor of difference between categories.

Lifetime cost of disposable pads	Lifetime cost of tampons	Lifetime cost of reusable pads	Lifetime cost of menstrual cups

4. If a disposable pad is 20 centimetres by eight centimetres by 0.5 centimetres, what is the volume of one pad? What is the volume of 20 billion pads? Name something with comparable volume.

5. In a clean-up of ocean waters, a group called the Ocean Conservancy collected four million pieces of plastic garbage. 20,000 of those pieces were plastic tampon applicators.[3] What is that number as a percentage of the total?

6. If a clean up crew collected 3,000 kg of tampon applicators, how long would it take to biodegrade to less than 3 kg of plastic (use a half life of 2.5 years, and the following equation, where n is the number of half lives):

$$\text{End amount} = \frac{\text{Beginning amount}}{2^n}$$

7. Research the level of corporate profits for some of the big producers of tampons. Procter and Gamble makes Tampax, Johnson and Johnson makes o.b. and Kimberly-Clark makes Kotex. Are their chief executive officers (CEOs) men or women?

8. If a maker of reusable menstrual pads estimated that a single reusable pad replaces 120 disposable ones:

   a. What is the algebraic equation for how many disposable menstrual pads are saved by using reusable pads?

   b. How many disposable pads are saved by using 500 reusable pads?

   c. If you wanted to replace 1,500,000 disposable pads, how many reusable pads would you need?

9. For every woman who replaces a single package of 16 regular absorbency tampons with a package of organic cotton tampons, 17,000 pounds of pesticides are diverted from our waterways.

a. What is the algebraic equation for how many pounds of pesticides are diverted from waterways by using organic cotton tampons?

b. If you belong to an environmental group that wants to prevent five million pounds of pesticides from entering the water system from the process of growing cotton to make tampons, how many packages of regular cotton tampons would have to be replaced by packages of organic cotton tampons?

10. Of the top 10 pesticides used to grow cotton, three of them are considered acutely hazardous, and six of the remainder are considered moderately to highly hazardous.[4]

a. Express these numbers as probabilities.

b. What is the chance that cotton is grown with a pesticide that is not considered moderately, highly or acutely hazardous?

11. In October of 2013, Member of Parliament Irene Mathyssen introduced Bill C-282, an Act to Amend the Excise Tax Act. She argued that people who use menstrual products should not have to pay the GST tax (which is for luxury or non-essential items). The GST is 5%.

a. In 2014, people who used menstrual products between the ages of 12 and 49 spent $519,976,963. How much did they pay in taxes?

b. A Change.org petition was created to end the GST on menstrual products. Use the data in the table to graph the number of signatures to the petition over time. Is the trend linear or exponential?

Number of days	Number of signatures
0	0
1	200
2	3,000
3	5,000
7	7,000
8	15,000
9	30,000
10	40,000
23	50,000
30	54,000

make it better

Make your own pads! All you need is the design and a sewing machine. You can find some free designs here:

http://tipnut.com/free-pattern-for-washable-feminine-menstrual-pads/

Use 100% cotton non-chlorine bleached tampons that are fragrance free.

Endnotes

1. http://womensvoices.org/wp-content/uploads/2013/11/Chem-www.Fatale-Report.pdf
2. http://www.treehugger.com/health/reasons-why-you-should-switch-to-reusable-menstrual-products.html
3. http://www.thechicecologist.com/2010/04/the-environmental-impact-of-everyday-things/
4. bodyunburdened.com/is-your-tampon-toxic/

Group projects
%

Vice Grip

"The world has enough for everyone's need, but not enough for everyone's greed."

~ GANDHI

There are some people on the planet who have money to invest. And some of them choose socially responsible investing (SRI), putting their money into businesses that care about the environment, human rights, corporate transparency and social justice.[1]

On the other hand, there are those who invest in 'sin stocks', which are often tied to tobacco, alcohol, gaming, and the military. These investments can have a high rate of return, and an ongoing demand for these products even in times of economic recession. One group of investors even calls themselves The Vice Fund.

In Canada, we lose 100 people a day from smoking related illnesses.[2] Almost 20 people die a day due to alcohol related accidents.[3] The cost of war in Iraq, Afghanistan and Pakistan includes at least 174,000 civilians.[4] Problem gambling has been known to cause anxiety, depression, health problems and isolation.[5]

Has greed really caught investors in a vice grip? Is socially responsible investing the answer?

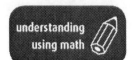

What do you think makes people invest in industries that are linked to human misery?

Divide the class into 10 groups. Each group is responsible for researching and preparing a one-page presentation on their topic. The use of mathematical data should be integrated in the presentation. Intersperse the presentations, linking the proponents and opponents for each industry. End with group nine and 10.

Group One: Opponents to Investing in the Tobacco Industry

To get you started:[6]

- Of the more than 230,000 Canadian deaths a year, 17% are from smoking.

- Smoke inhaled second-hand killed 831 Canadians in 2002.

- About 100 infant deaths a year are linked to smoking.

Group Two: Opponents to Investing in the Alcohol Industry

To get you started:[7]

- In Canada, 6,700 people die a year from accidents and incidents tied to alcohol.

- In instances of partner abuse, 35% of the time it is reported that the offender was under the influence of alcohol.

- Deaths due to alcohol are similar worldwide to those due to measles, tuberculosis and malaria, and higher than tobacco.[8]

203

Group 3: Opponents to Investment in the Military Industry

To get you started:

- In the war on Iraq, 70% of the deaths were civilian.[9]

- It has been estimated that 50% of most war deaths over the centuries have been civilian.[10]

Group 4: Opponents to Investment in the Gaming Industry

To get you started:

- Problem gambling ranges between 0.4% and 7.5% of the population, depending on the country, and increases in gambling availability lead to increases in problem gamblers following the introduction of casinos.[11]

- Twenty out of 22 studies found that gambling is a form of regressive tax, where the poor contribute more of their income (as a percentage) than the rich.[12]

Group 5: Financial Incentives to Investment in the Tobacco Industry

To get you started:

- Around the globe, smoking is very popular. Revenues are about $500 billion and the top six tobacco corporations took in $35.1 billion (equivalent to $1,100 a second).[13]

- Taxes that the government takes in from tobacco sales can be used for social services, like funding healthcare and education.

Group 6: Financial Incentives to Investment in the Alcohol Industry

To get you started:

- Considering only the top 10 brewers and top 10 distilled spirits corporations on the planet, sales are approximately $200 billion.[14]

- Beer sales alone worldwide are more than $500 billion.[15]

Group 7: Financial Incentives to Investment in the Military Industry

To get you started:

- War generates huge profit: Professor James Petras notes "No peaceful economic activity can match the immense profits enjoyed by the military-industrial complex in war." Returns on investment for three major arms manufacturers (Raytheon, Northrup Grumman and Lockheed Martin) have been 124%, 114%, and 149% respectively in the past three years.[16] (Compare with investment in stocks or real estate, where a rate of return might be 7%.)

Group 8: Financial Incentives to Investment in the Gaming Industry

To get you started:

- Globally, the revenues from casino gaming have risen from $99.88 billion in 2006, to $182.77 billion in 2015.[17]

- In general, the introduction of casinos leads to increased government revenue, which has been found to improve social services like health, education and social security.[18]

Group 9: Proponents of Socially Responsible Investing (SRI)

To get you started:

- It's now starting to be popular: one in every six dollars of professionally invested money in the United States falls under the SRI umbrella, to the tune of $6.57 *trillion*.[19]

- In 2014, shareholders in SRI investments went to annual shareholder meetings and made 400 resolutions related to environmental, social and governance concerns. This is called proxy voting.[20]

Group 10: Critics of Socially Responsible Investing (SRI)

To get you started:

- What counts as "socially responsible" is very vague. British Aerospace, for example, extolled the virtues of 'biodegradable plastic in missiles', and 'quieter warheads'.[21] Who decides what really counts?

- The corporation Apple, for example, often shows up on SRI lists but has been criticized for treatment of workers and the environment.[22]

Food for thought:

"Corporate Social Responsibility reports are public relations tools."
~ KEVIN SLATEN, CHINA LABOR WATCH

Research ethical funds at your credit union or bank.

If you ever do purchase investments in SRI funds, make your voice heard at annual shareholder meetings and demand better rights for workers, better treatment of the environment, and more transparent corporate governance.

Endnotes

1. http://en.wikipedia.org/wiki/Socially_responsible_investing
2. http://www.hc-sc.gc.ca/hc-ps/tobac-tabac/legislation/label-etiquette/mortal-eng.php
3. http://carleton.ca/studentaffairs/alcohol-awareness/its-your-body/alcohol-related-injuries-and-accidents/
4. http://costsofwar.org/article/civilians-killed-and-wounded
5. http://www.problemgambling.ca/EN/AboutGamblingandProblemGambling/Pages/TheEffectsOfGambling.aspx
6. http://www.hc-sc.gc.ca/hc-ps/tobac-tabac/legislation/label-etiquette/mortal-eng.php
7. http://carleton.ca/studentaffairs/alcohol-awareness/its-your-body/alcohol-related-injuries-and-accidents/
8. http://www.ias.org.uk/What-we-do/Publication-archive/Alcohol-Alert/Issue-1-1997/Global-alcohol-is-big-profitable-and-powerful.aspx
9 http://costsofwar.org/article/civilians-killed-and-wounded
10. http://en.wikipedia.org/wiki/Civilian_casualty_ratio
11. https://www.uleth.ca/dspace/bitstream/handle/10133/1286/SEIG_FINAL_REPORT_2011.pdf?sequence=1
12. https://www.uleth.ca/dspace/bitstream/handle/10133/1286/SEIG_FINAL_REPORT_2011.pdf?sequence=1
13. http://www.theguardian.com/business/2012/mar/22/tobacco-profits-deaths-6-million
14. http://www.ias.org.uk/What-we-do/Publication-archive/Alcohol-Alert/Issue-1-1997/Global-alcohol-is-big-profitable-and-powerful.aspx
15. http://www.valuewalk.com/2012/12/alcohol-sales-soar-worldwide-in-2012/
16. http://www.globalresearch.ca/the-soaring-profits-of-the-military-industrial-complex-the-soaring-costs-of-military-casualties/5388393
17. http://www.americangaming.org/industry-resources/research/fact-sheets/gaming-revenue-10-year-trends
18. https://www.uleth.ca/dspace/bitstream/handle/10133/1286/SEIG_FINAL_REPORT_2011.pdf?sequence=1
19. http://www.ussif.org/sribasics
20. http://www.ussif.org/sribasics
21. http://thenewpioneers.biz/2010/08/11/the-paradoxes-of-sustainable-business/
22. http://www.truth-out.org/news/item/26221-socially-responsible-capitalism-still-feeds-the-disease

circumference
%

The Drone of War

"Drones have replaced Guantánamo as the recruiting tool of choice for militants."

~ NEW YORK TIMES

setting the stage

They are called Seekers, Predators, Reapers and Sharp Swords. They drop bombs called Hell Fire missiles.[1] Unmanned aerial vehicles, or drones, fly tens of thousands of feet above the sky while below, civilians anxiously watch and wait for the next attack. In Pakistan alone between 2004 and 2012, independent journalists believe that between 474 and 881 innocent civilians, including 176 children, were killed by drones.[2]

But numbers depend on definitions. What constitutes a "militant" might surprise you, if you consider U.S. President Obama's definition: *military-age* males in a strike zone.[3]

Under international law, assassination and extrajudicial killing is illegal. Article 10 of the Universal Declaration of Human rights states that all people have the right to a fair trial, and that people are innocent until proven guilty before a public, independent and impartial court.[4] Even so, killing people is allowed under international law if the threat that they pose is "imminent", in "self defense", and requires lethal force to address. But how many drone deaths meet this standard?

206

The UN Special Rapporteur on Extrajudicial Killings, Christof Heyns, has been more blunt: drone strikes amount to war crimes.[5] Since Canada has both received drones and sold them, it's important we understand the issues, and the lives, at stake.

Watch the *Out of Sight, Out of Mind* graphic at http://drones. pitchinteractive.com and discuss as a group. How does the use of mathematics help to tell the story?

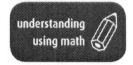

1. Drones drop bombs that kill people. Proponents of drone strikes say that they have "surgical precision".

   a. Why do you think that proponents want people to think of strikes as surgically precise? What do you think of when you hear those words?

   b. The Hellfire missile that is dropped from some drones has a blast radius of 20 metres. What is the diameter of the blast?

   c. What is the area destroyed by the blast?

   d. Go out into the schoolyard and, using pylons, create a circle with a radius of 20 metres.[6] Does this look like surgical precision?

   e. Shrapnel is small but dangerous pieces of metal from the bomb, that can explode to beyond the 20 metre radius. Create a second circle in the schoolyard with a radius of 30 metres. What is the area of this strike zone?

2. The Pew Research Center polled 44 countries to see what people thought of U.S. drone strikes against extremists in Pakistan, Yemen and Somalia.

   a. Thirty-nine of the countries had majorities or pluralities that opposed the strikes. What percentage is that?

   b. In Pakistan, 66% of those polled were opposed to the strikes. Only 3% approved.[7] Why would some people omit the percentage of Pakistanis that approved the drone strikes, and who might the other missing people be?

3. Of the 85 countries with armed and unarmed drones, only three have used armed drones: United States, United Kingdom and Israel.[8]

   a. What is three as a percentage of 85? Do you think this is likely to increase? Why or why not?

   b. The United States is going to start selling drones, pushing the market from $6.6 billion dollars annually to $11.4 billion annually.[9] How much of an increase is that?

   c. Israel is the largest exporter in the world of UAVs, having sold $4.6 billion dollars worth of systems between 2005 and 2012.[10] $4.6 billion is more than the annual GDP of how many of the world's 194 countries?

   d. If the sale in drones increases to $11.4 billion annually, how many countries' GDPs will be surpassed?

4. Look at the data on the number of people killed by drones and compare the figures. The first three sources are independent organizations.

Source	Years & Place	Civilian	Unknown	Militant
New America Foundation	Since 2004, in Pakistan	258 – 307	199 – 334	1,770 –2,971
Long War Journal	Since 2006	138	2,396	
The Bureau of Investigative Journalism	Since 2004	474 -881 including 176 children	Only list total deaths- including civilian, at 2,562 – 3,325	
United States Government		Classified		
Militant Groups like the Taliban				

    a. Why is there such a discrepancy between groups?

    b. What is the difference between independent groups and the United States and the Taliban?

    c. Why do you think that the United States refuses to release data on the drone strikes?

    d. What do you think militant groups like the Taliban, al-Qaeda, the Uzbek Islamic Movement and others would report for people killed?

    e. Why is the data on number of people injured important to add?

5. Based on unnamed U.S. officials, the number of low-level fighters killed by drones was 12 times the number of mid to high level "militants".

    a. Fill in the empty cell under 'low level fighters'.

    b. The New America Foundation states that since 2004, only 49 militant leaders have been killed, which amounts to 2% of all drone related deaths. What does that make the total?

Total "militants" killed since 2008	High level "militants"	Mid to high level "militants"	Low level fighters
500	14	25	

6. One civilian whose home was destroyed by a drone strike explains that the cost to build a new home is one million rupees.[11]

    a. How many Canadian dollars does one million rupees amount to?

    b. The civilian said that he only had 5,000 rupees. How many Canadian dollars is that?

    c. Does it seem likely that those who lose property in drone strikes will have the capacity to rebuild their homes?

7. In 2013 -2014, the per capita income in India (with wide variation depending on the region) was 74,920 rupees.[12]

    a. If the medical fees required to address injuries are thousands of dollars, how does this compare with India's per capita income? Use $3,000 as your reference for medical fees.

    b. Beyond physical injury, what other costs must be taken into account when you consider people's health?

make it better

All information about drone activity should be made public . Find out what the different political parties' positions are on drones.

Endnotes

1. http://securitydata.newamerica.net/world-drones
2. http://www.livingunderdrones.org
3. http://www.livingunderdrones.org
4. http://en.wikipedia.org/wiki/Right_to_a_fair_trial
5. http://www.theguardian.com/world/2012/jun/21/drone-strikes-international-law-un
6. http://www.livingunderdrones.org
7. http://blogs.reuters.com/data-dive/2015/01/30/drones-by-the-numbers/
8. http://securitydata.newamerica.net/world-drones
9. http://securitydata.newamerica.net/world-drones
10. http://securitydata.newamerica.net/world-drones
11. http://www.livingunderdrones.org

Visualizing %s

dividing %

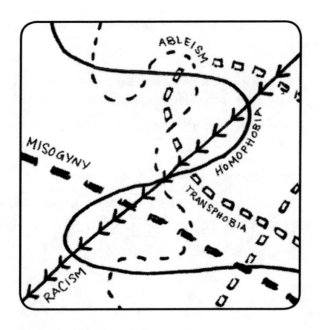

Layers

210

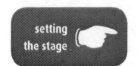
setting
the stage

"Every day of my life that I walk out of my house I am a combination of race, gender, class, sexual preference and religion...."

~ bell hooks

In the final half of the twentieth century, social movements sought to challenge oppression and fight for political freedom: the fight for civil rights, second-wave feminism, lesbian and gay rights, the American Indian movement, and the liberation of people with disabilities. The formation of these identity groups helped to give voice to and respond to social and cultural marginalization, violence, and domination.[1]

But identity politics are not without problems. Kimberle Crenshaw, best known for her work in race and gender issues, points out that "the problem with identity politics is not that it fails to transcend difference...but rather the opposite: that it frequently conflates or ignores intragroup differences."[2] The experience of oppression as a woman, for example, needs to take into account other simultaneous identities: race, sexuality, ability and so on. This concept is known as **intersectionality**.

Marxist critique of intersectionality suggests that even if we manage to deepen our understanding of oppression into multiple identities, it is not enough; that it is important to see the historical conditions that created these social conditions, and ultimately, the central role that capitalism has played in their creation.[3]

Have you ever had a time in your life where you experienced discrimination based on more than one of your identities?
The identity of "youth" is a possible starting point. Share your experiences with the class. Which identity was most salient when it happened?

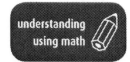

1. Draw either a rectangle or a circle to represent "all people".

2. Divide your shape into pieces that represent three ethnic groups. Label them A, B and C: A is 40% of the overall population, B is 35% of the overall population and C makes up the remaining 25%.

3. In group A, 5% of the population lives in poverty. What is 5% of 40%? Shade in those living in poverty.

4. In group B, 30% of the population lives in poverty. What is 30% of 35%? Shade in those living in poverty.

5. In group C, 40% of the population lives in poverty. What is 40% of 25%? Shade in those living in poverty.

6. A researcher says that although 40% of population C lives in poverty, there are more people living in poverty in population B, even though the poverty rate is 30%. Explain.

7. In group A, 50% of those living in poverty experience depression. Shade in this group.

8. In group B, two thirds of those in poverty experience depression. Shade in this group.

9. In group C, 40% of those in poverty experience depression. Shade in this group.

10. One in eight of those in group A identify as LGBTQ. Of that group, 20% live in poverty, and half of that group suffers from depression. Shade in all subgroups of the LGBTQ community within group A.

11. One in seven of those in group B identify as LGBTQ. Of that group, 40% live in poverty, and half of that group suffers from depression. Shade in all subgroups of the LGBTQ community within group B.

12. One in eight of those in group C identify as LGBTQ. Of that group, 50% live in poverty, and half of that group suffers from depression. Shade in all subgroups of the LGBTQ community within group C.

13. Highlight the people most at risk within each community. How could this understanding help policy makers develop strategies to address the problem?

14. What other factors having to do with one's identity could be further considered in your multi-layered drawing?

211

15. How might these layers of identities that are often marginalized and oppressed have an impact that is more than the sum of their total?

---

make it better ✌

In Toronto, 20% of homeless youth self identify as LGBTQ, and it could be as high as 40%. In response, the city allocated $600,000 to open two homeless shelters with 54 beds specifically for queer youth.[4] How is the intersectionality between homelessness, youth, and LGBTQ-identified people in your community being addressed?

Endnotes

1. http://en.wikipedia.org/wiki/Income_in_India
2. http://plato.stanford.edu/entries/identity-politics/
3. http://funnel.sfsu.edu/students/luyilin/Courses/M420/Lu_Yilin/other/wgs/Crenshaw1991_intersectionality.pdf
4. http://www.thestar.com/news/gta/2015/01/27/advocates-praise-funding-for-lgbtq-homeless-shelters.html

wages / minimum wage % change

The Threat of a Good Example

"They are not afraid of me. They are afraid that what I say may help the poor to see."

~ JEAN BERTRAND ARISTIDE

(213)

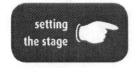
setting the stage

Over two hundred years ago, in 1804, the tiny Caribbean country of Haiti declared its independence from France. It was the first ever successful slave revolt and it wasn't without a fight: slaves that had been brought from Africa to work in French-owned plantations managed to fend off Great Britain, France and Spain. In the end, France demanded 150 million francs to pay back the losses of the slave owners.[1]

Fast forward to 2002, and the formation of the Group of 184, an organization presenting itself as the voice of Haitians. Except that it really represented the business interests of the big corporations and was led by millionaires Reginald Boulos and Andy Apaid Jr.[2] They were not happy with Haiti's democratically-elected president, Jean Bertrand Aristide.

Artistide had dismantled the military,[3] pushed against privatization in his country, was doubling minimum wage, and had begun a campaign to get $22 billion back from France. Some of Apaid's factories made t-shirts for Montreal-based Gilden Activewear, employer to nearly 5,000 workers in Haiti's capital, Port-au-Prince.[4]

In early 2003, Canada hosted the Ottawa Initiative, a collaboration between France, the United States and Latin American officials to decide Haiti's fate. Ominously, Haitian government officials were not invited.[5] On February 29, 2004, U.S. troops removed Aristide from power and deposited him in the Central African Republic.

Human rights violations in Haiti quickly followed.

What does "the threat of a good example" mean?

1. One franc is worth $1.30 Canadian. How much is 150 million francs worth in Canadian dollars?

2. At an annual inflation rate of 2.5% and 190 years, what is 150 million francs in 1804 worth in Canadian dollars now?

3. If you increase something by 100% it sounds like you are increasing it a lot! (Consider that typical wage increases might be 3%.) Imagine you make 75 cents an hour. What is a 100% wage increase? How can increasing something by a big percentage still be a tiny number?

4. If Gilden Activewear employed 5,000 Haitians at $1 an hour, for 10 hour days, five days a week, how much more money would they have to pay in a week if the minimum wage increased to $2 an hour? In a year?

5. How can very low wages in one country serve to control workers in other countries?

6. Before the overthrow, fewer than 100 bodies were entering the state morgue each month, but following the overthrow it jumped to 1,000. By October of 2004, the morgue was declared off-limits.[6]

   a. What is the factor of difference of deaths before and after the coup?

   b. Why do you think that the morgue was declared off limits? Why is what we measure a political act?

7. The prison in Port-au-Prince was used to hold people following Aristide's overthrow.

   a. There were about 1,100 prisoners. Less than 20% were charged with a crime.[7] How many prisoners were being held without charge?

   b. When a riot broke out in the prison, the official number of prisoner deaths was reported as 10.[8] Later independent reports suggested three to four times as many deaths. Why was the official report low?

   c. One estimate was 110 deaths. How many times greater is that than the official estimate?

   d. Why are independent reports important?

8. Both Canada and the United States claimed that there were voting irregularities in Aristide's 2000 election. But in the uncontested lower house, Aristide took 72 of the 83 seats.[9] What percentage is that?

9. In the years between 2000 and 2002, money from the Canadian International Development Agency (CIDA) to Haiti was cut from $39 million to $19 million.[10] How much of a cut is that as a percentage? How would cutting aid money destabilize a country?

10. Two Canadian mining companies, KWG Resources and St. Genevieve Resources, were ready to exploit Haiti's mineral resources following the coup. One mineral deposit had an estimated five billion pounds of copper.[11]

    a. If copper is worth $2.80 a pound, what is the deposit worth?

    b. Why do countries nationalize their resources?

make it better

Check out the resources and suggestions for action at Canada Haiti Action Network (**http://canadahaitiaction.ca**). The Institute for Justice and Democracy in Haiti also has suggestions for action (**http://www.ijdh.org**).

Endnotes

1. Engler, Yves and Anthony Fenton. Canada in Haiti. Fernwood Publishing Company, Vancouver, B.C. 2005, p. 6.
2. http://coat.ncf.ca/our_magazine/links/62/62_50-53.pdf
3. http://www.huffingtonpost.ca/larry-rousseau/haitian-coup_b_4860630.html
4. Engler, Yves and Anthony Fenton. Canada in Haiti. Fernwood Publishing Company, Vancouver, B.C. 2005, pp. 97-104.
5. http://en.wikipedia.org/wiki/2004_Haitian_coup_d'état#Ottawa_Initiative_hosted_by_Canada
6. Engler, Yves and Anthony Fenton. Canada in Haiti. Fernwood Publishing Company, Vancouver, B.C. 2005, pp. 73, 78.
7. Ibid, p. 80.
8. Engler, Yves and Anthony Fenton. Canada in Haiti. Fernwood Publishing Company, Vancouver, B.C. 2005, p. 79.
9. http://www.huffingtonpost.ca/larry-rousseau/haitian-coup_b_4860630.html
10. http://www.huffingtonpost.ca/larry-rousseau/haitian-coup_b_4860630.html
11. Engler, Yves and Anthony Fenton. Canada in Haiti. Fernwood Publishing Company, Vancouver, B.C. 2005, p. 98.

Ratios
percents
conversion
(metric)
& standard

Sweet and Dangerous

"In order to change, we must be sick and tired of being sick and tired."

~ AUTHOR UNKNOWN

setting the stage

Have we been tricked? A long time ago, a decision was made to focus on the dangers of fats in the diet. Fatty foods led to fatty arteries, which led to heart disease and stroke. And obesity. Or so the argument went. But powerful sugar industry lobbyists had been working behind the scenes to direct the spotlight away from another possible culprit: sugar.

In the opening scene of the film *Sugar Coated* it says that in the past 30 years obesity rates have doubled to 600 million people and diabetes rates have tripled to 347 million people worldwide. This, in spite of the fact that the rate of dietary fat intake had been steadily decreasing in that same time. But our rate of sugar intake has steadily increased.

Glucose and fructose (called monosaccharides) and sucrose (which you know as table sugar, or disaccharide) are everywhere. Many processed foods have sugar added to them: canned fruit, granola bars, pasta sauce, yogurt, cereal, and even ketchup.

In 2015, the World Health Organization published a new health guideline called "Sugars intake for adults and children". Of the 56 million deaths in 2012, 38 million were from non-communicable diseases. And poor diet is listed as one of the causes of those diseases.[1] It's time to look at sugar.

What is the difference between correlation and causation? Watch the first two minutes of the film *Sugar Coated* at http://tvo.org/video/documentaries/sugar- coated and discuss what Gary Taubes is saying.

1. List 10 foods that you enjoy eating and then do research to find out how many grams of sugar are included in a serving of each food.

2. The new WHO guidelines say that reducing free sugars in the diet to less than 5% of total energy intake is desirable. 5% amounts to 25 grams, or 6.25 teaspoons.[2] How does your list of foods compare to the suggested guideline?

3. One can of soda may contain up to 40 grams of sugar.

   a. How many teaspoons is that?

   b. What percentage of the daily guideline is a can of soda?

   c. If a can of soda is 355 mL, how many teaspoons of sugar would be in a 2 litre bottle of soda?

   d. What percentage of the daily guideline is a 2 litre bottle of soda?

4. What is the algebraic formula for the total teaspoons of sugar intake from drinking soda if the soda has 40 grams of sugar in it? How many cans of soda would you need to consume to reach 500% of the daily guideline from the WHO?

5. If you go out and purchase a snack, and first have a chocolate bar that has 36 grams of sugar, and then start drinking cans of soda, what does the algebraic equation for total teaspoons of sugar look like? After how many cans of soda would you reach 100 teaspoons of sugar?

6. A glass of juice (12 fluid ounces) has 36 grams of sugar.

   a. How many teaspoons is that?

   b. What percentage of the daily guideline is a glass of juice?

   c. What is the difference between drinking a glass of apple juice and eating an apple?

217

7. Here are the grams of sugar in some common chocolate bars and candy.[3] Fill in the percentage of the WHO sugar guideline in the final column.

Chocolate Bar	Grams of sugar	Percentage of daily WHO guideline
Hershey's Milk Chocolate	31	
Kit Kat	22	
Reese's Peanut Butter Cups	25	
Snickers	30	
3 Musketeers	40	
Milky Way	35	
Skittles Original Fruit	47	
M & M's Milk Chocolate	31	

8. Three quarters of the 38 million deaths attributed to non-communicable diseases are in low and middle-income countries.[4] Why might this be the case? What is three quarters of 38 million?

9. Eighty-two percent of premature deaths attributed to non-communicable diseases are in low and middle-income countries.[5] What is 82% of 38 million?

10. Sugar causes diseases of the teeth, which you know as cavities. Cavities are the most common non-communicable disease in the world. What possible problems can you imagine stemming from dental diseases? Why might these be more pronounced in low-income countries?

make it better

Watch the entirety of the film *Sugar Coated*. Consider the amount of sugar that you put into your body and its possible impacts.

Endnotes

1. Engler, Yves and Anthony Fenton. Canada in Haiti. Fernwood Publishing Company, Vancouver, B.C. 2005, p. 98.
2. http://apps.who.int/iris/bitstream/10665/149782/1/9789241549028_eng.pdf?ua=1
3. http://www.who.int/mediacentre/news/releases/2015/sugar-guideline/en/
4. http://www.acaloriecounter.com/candy-chocolate.php
5. http://apps.who.int/iris/bitstream/10665/149782/1/9789241549028_eng.pdf?ua=1

Unplug

"Because of the feed, we're raising a nation of idiots. Ignorant, self-centered idiots."

~VIOLET, IN M.T. ANDERSON'S BOOK *FEED*

setting the stage

Sedentary. Stationary. Desk-bound. Inactive. Idle. That's what we are. At least most of us. In Canada, only 19% of 10-16 year olds meet the criteria for non-sedentary status, specifically, limiting recreational screen time to less than two hours a day and minimizing extended sitting, indoor time and motorized transportation. For 12-17 year olds, the quantity of screen-based time is a stunning 3.5 hours a day on average.[1]

In the homes of eight to 18 year olds you'll now find an average of 3.8 televisions, 2.8 DVD players, a digital video recorder, two computers, and 2.3 video game devices. But the big change has been the increase in multimedia cell phones, with the average number of texts per day sitting at 118, or about an hour and a half of time.[2]

Screen time is linked to all sorts of consequences: from increased food intake and childhood obesity, to sleep disturbance, hyperactivity, emotional and conduct problems and difficulty with academics.[3] While some effects are likely causative (for example, the exposure to thousands of advertisements for unhealthy food and the rise in purchase of those foods), it may also be that the loss of what screen time is replacing is equally a problem (for example, the reduction in physical activity and socializing with family and friends).

Perhaps we should consider taking time to unplug.

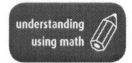

Shambare, Rugimbana & Zhowa (2012) are researchers who have suggested that cell phones are a kind of paradox: something that is "both freeing and enslaving".[4] Discuss.

1. In a research study by the Kaiser Institute, it was found that eight to 18 year olds in the United States consumed seven hours and 38 minutes of media per day. However, the actual exposure time is listed as 10 hours and 45 minutes.[5] How can this be so?

2. In 2009, the median number of texts sent by teens in a Pew Research study in the United States was 50. By 2011 it was 60. But a subset of the participants, age 14 to 17, were averaging 100 texts a day. How is this possible?

3. Why do you think that the research above reported the results using the median instead the mean?

4. In research studies, you have to be cautious about correlation and causation. It's very difficult to prove causation (for example, more media exposure causes more depression) because the two things may simply be occurring together, with other confounding variables as the real cause. One way around this is to stratify your data collection (separating the different variables). If data is collected that separates the participants into four different age categories, the gender categories boy, girl, and transgender, and five socioeconomic ranges, how many substrata will there be?

5. Why will the higher number of substrata be more and more difficult?

6. What is the algebraic equation for total media exposure, using the seven hours and 38 minutes a day figure? How many hours of media exposure does that make in one week? In one year? In the years between age eight and 18?

7. Video games saw a rise from 26 minutes in 1999, to 49 minutes in 2004, to one hour and 13 minutes per day in 2009.[6] What is the percentage increase between 1999 and 2009?

8. The probability of eight to 18 year olds having a cell phone has gone from four chances in 10 to two chances in three in the five years between 2005 and 2010. What do you think it is now?

9. The Kaiser Family study found differences between media exposure with respect to race and ethnicity, with White youth reporting 8.5 hours of media exposure per day, and Hispanic and Black youth reporting 13 hours per day. Why might there be this disparity in the findings?

10. In providing opportunities for increased physical activity, policy makers need to consider the needs of different groups, including adolescent girls, First Nations youth, young people with disabilities, and low-income families. What is it called when you take into account the multiple layers of a person's experience?

Food For Thought:

46% of Canadian young people get three hours of active play per week or less.[7]

make it better

Think about choices that you can make around the time that you are exposed to screen, the content on those screens and the places where you view those screens (for example, screens in bedrooms are linked to poorer sleeping patterns).

Get outside and get active. The Canadian recommended guidelines are 60 minutes a day of moderate exercise. Research your own community to find out if there are groups that get together to play pick-up sports at a local field.

Endnotes

1. Report Card on Physical Activity for Children and Youth. Active Healthy Kids Canada. 2013.
2. https://kaiserfamilyfoundation.files.wordpress.com/2013/01/8010.pdf
3. www.commercialfreechildhood.org
4. https://en.wikipedia.org/wiki/Nomophobia
5. https://kaiserfamilyfoundation.files.wordpress.com/2013/01/8010.pdf
6. http;//www.away.gr/wp-content/uploads/2012/03/PIP_Teens_Smartphones_and_Texting.pdf
7. https://kaiserfamilyfoundation.files.wordpress.com/2013/01/8010.pdf
8. Highlights from the 2012 Active Healthy Kids Canada Report Card on Physical Activity for Children and Youth.

Paying for It

"We should make every man in this country take a 20% pay cut. Overnight, we'd go from the status quo to pitchforks in the street, all-out political fury."

~ DAVE MCGINN

setting the stage 👉

It's interview day. You've applied for a new 60-hour a week job and the description of the duties you'll be performing looks a little daunting. The interviewer, Sylvia, goes over the list. "Event planning, managing financials, cooking, landscaping, carpentry, nursing, child care, teaching, cleaning, laundry, chauffeuring. And other duties as assigned." 'Other duties as assigned' is always the kicker.

Things are going smoothly until the end of the interview when she asks you if you have any questions.

"I notice that you didn't list the salary for this position in the posting," you say, eyebrow raised. Blank stare from Sylvia.

"You know," you continue undaunted, "how much I'll be paid?"

"Oh, were you unaware?" she says with shock. "This isn't a *paid* position. We don't pay people who stay at home and manage all of the duties of the household. If you end up as the lucky successful applicant, you'd be working for free."

Globally, men do less housework and child care. Everywhere, they do more of the paid work, and are paid better for it.[1] And so you know who's paying for it...

Helen Clark, from the United Nations Development Programme, suggests that an aging global population will have more impact on women.[2] Explain.

1.a. Enter the following information from OECD[3] into a spreadsheet program and use the program to calculate the missing numbers in columns four and six. (India is not a member of the OECD, but put in for comparison)

Country		Minutes per day of unpaid work	Women's minutes as a percentage of men's minutes	Minutes per day of paid work	Women's minutes as a percentage of men's minutes
Canada	Men	159.6		341.4	
	Women	253.6		267	
Japan	Men	61.9		471.5	
	Women	299.3		206.4	
Turkey	Men	11.64		360.3	
	Women	376.7		123.7	
Sweden	Men	154		321.9	
	Women	206.5		268.7	
Finland	Men	159		249	
	Women	232		210	
OECD Avg	Men	137.6		328.5	
	Women	271.7		215.3	
India	Men	51.8		390.6	
	Women	351.9		184.7	

1.b. In which country do women do more of the unpaid work compared to men? What are the women's minutes as a percentage of the men's minutes? What do you think accounts for the huge discrepancy in the minutes of unpaid work?

1.c. In which country do the women and men's unpaid work minutes most closely match? What do you think accounts for the greater match?

223

1.d. In which country do women's minutes of paid work least match men's minutes of paid work? In which country do women's and men's minutes of paid work most closely match?

1.e. In addition to knowing the average values of men's and women's paid work per day, what other information would be important to know about that work?

2. The wage gap for full time employees across the 35 OECD countries varies from a high of 36.6% (Korea) to a low of 5.62% (New Zealand). Canada is 18.97% and the OECD average is 15.46%. New Zealand attributes differences in men's and women's pay to gender discrimination, women performing more unpaid work than men, as well as occupational segregation and vertical segregation.[4] Find definitions for the last two terms.

3. In Canada, averages hide the reality of the wage gap for different groups of women. While women earn 73.5 cents for every dollar that men earn, racialized women working full time make 68 cents for every dollar made by non-racialized men. Calculate how many additional hours of work that women have to do each year to match men's pay.

4. Maternity leave is the amount of time that a mother can take immediately before and after having a child, and have the job protected. The following is the data for the number of weeks of maternity leave in different countries, as well as an average rating of satisfaction with life (out of 10).[5]
   (The United Kingdom is not a part of the OECD countries)

	1990	2000	2010	2015	Life Satisfaction
Canada	17	17	17	17	7.4
Japan	14	14	14	14	5.9
Turkey	12	12	16	16	5.5
Sweden	0	11.3	15.6	15.6	7.3
Finland	17.5	17.5	17.5	17.5	7.4
OECD Average	14.5	15.8	18.5	19.1	6.5
United Kingdom	40	40	52	52	

a. What do you notice about the data?

b. Does Turkey's low "life satisfaction" rating seem to be explained by the maternity leave data? Why or why not?

5. In the same five countries, the paid leave for fathers in number of weeks is listed in the following chart:

	1990	2000	2010	2015
Canada	0	0	0	0
Japan	0	0	52	52
Turkey	0	0	0	0
Sweden	1.4	5.8	10	10
Finland	0	3	7	9
OECD Average	0.2	3.4	8.7	9.1

a. What do you notice about the data?

b. Do you think that adjusting the paid leave for fathers could have an impact on women's participation in the workforce? If so, how?

6. The United Nations published a report in 2015 that found that three out of every four hours of unpaid work are done by women, and men do two out of every three hours of work that is paid.[6]

a. Transform these findings into algebraic equations.

b. If women did, on average, 15,600 minutes of unpaid work a year, how many hours would the average man do?

c. What are some of the benefits of working for pay?

7. For a full day, log how many minutes of time your parent(s) at home do work that is unpaid. Fill in the following chart:

Category of work	Minutes per day
Housework and cleaning	
Meal planning, grocery shopping, cooking	
Yard work	
Laundry	
Planning activities for the family	
Budgeting, finances	
Playing with children	
Helping children with schoolwork	
Taking care of kids' health and hygiene	
Shuttling kids to different events	

Public Radio international is a non-profit organization trying to make change in the world, and they have developed a calculator to figure out how much money the above-unpaid work is worth.
Go to their calculator and input the minutes your parent(s) do and find out what it is worth (http://www.pri.org/stories/2016-05-07/domestic-work-deserves-salary-and-how-much-we-should-pay-moms). Are you surprised?

8. Work-life balance is the idea that the time spent 'at work' is balanced with time 'away from work' or 'leisure time'. In the table below, column two lists the percentage of people who work more than 50 hours in a workweek, and column three is a rating, out of 10, of the satisfaction level that the average person in that country feels.

Country	% of employees working over 50 hours/week	Life Satisfaction Rating
Australia	13.39	7.3
Austria	7.32	7.1
Belgium	4.73	6.9
Canada	3.83	7.4
Chile	13.84	6.5
Czech Republic	5.99	6.6
Denmark	2.21	7.5
Estonia	3.29	5.6
Finland	3.6	7.4
France	7.77	6.4
Germany	4.96	7
Greece	6.37	5.6
Hungary	3.76	5.3
Iceland	13.79	7.5
Ireland	4.11	6.8
Israel	14.74	7.1
Italy	3.83	5.8
Japan	21.89	5.9
Korea	23.12	5.8
Latvia	2.45	5.9
Luxembourg	3.27	6.7
Mexico	28.28	6.2
Netherlands	0.044	7.3
New Zealand	13.78	7.4
Norway	3.05	7.6
Poland	7.25	6
Portugal	9.77	5.1
Slovak Republic	6.23	6.2
Slovenia	5.5	5.7
Spain	5.61	6.4
Sweden	1.1	7.3
Switzerland	6.34	7.6
Turkey	39.26	5.5
United Kingdom	12.83	6.5
United States	11.69	6.9

a. Which country has the lowest life satisfaction rating, and what percentage of the workforce works more than 50 hours a week? (Investigate what things are happening in that country that might account for the low life satisfaction score.)

b. Which country has the highest life satisfaction rating, and what percentage of the workforce works more than 50 hours a week?

c. Enter the data into a spreadsheet and use Excel to calculate the correlation coefficient for the two columns of data. What is the correlation coefficient? What does the number mean?

Food for thought:

In Sweden, parental leave is a full 480 paid days: 390 of which are at 80% of the parent's salary.[6]

make it better

More than 60 million girls in the world do not go to school, leading to early child-bearing, marrying young and becoming trapped in poverty.[7]

Watch the video *Keeping Girls in School*, by Plan International Canada and learn more about the "Because I Am A Girl" campaign. List five upstream solutions to keeping girls in school and make a plan to put one solution into effect.

Endnotes

1. Highlights from the 2012 Active Healthy Kids Canada Report Card on Physical Activity for Children and Youth.
2. http://www.pri.org/stories/2016-05-07/domestic-work-deserves-salary-and-how-much-we-should-pay-moms
3. http://www.pri.org/stories/2015-12-23/should-you-make-doing-less-housework-your-new-years-resolution-calculator-might
4. http://stats.oecd.org/index.aspx?queryid=54757
5. http://women.govt.nz/work-skills/income/gender-pay-gap
6. http://www.huffingtonpost.ca/2016/03/08/canada-gender-pay-gap_n_9393924.html
7. http://stats.oecd.org/index.aspx?queryid=54757
8. http://hdr.undp.org/en/content/speech-launch-2015-human-development-report
9. http://hdr.undp.org/en/content/speech-launch-2015-human-development-report
10. http://plancanada.ca/6-things-keeping-girls-out-of-school

Maththatmatters 2
Answers

Canada: Peacekeeper or Profiteer? – Answers

Opening question:

Chomsky is suggesting that the definition of 'crime' and who commits crime is determined by those who have power, and who will ensure that they themselves will not be implicated.

Understanding using math:

1.

Who is hurt by landmines?				
People killed and injured annually by landmines	Number of Civilians	Number of Combatants	Number of Civilians (Children)	Number of Civilians (Adults)
20,000	16,000	4,000	6,667	9,333

2. The formula is asking the computer to find 80% of the number that exists in cell A3, or specifically, to find 80% of 20,000.

3. There are two options: "=A3-B3" or "=A3*0.2".

4. It's not possible to have a fraction of a human, so decimals don't make sense.

5. 9,333, using the formula "=B3-D3".

6.

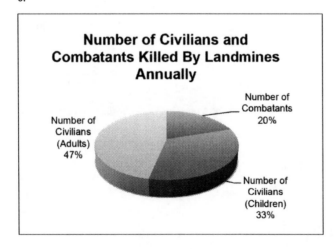

7.a.

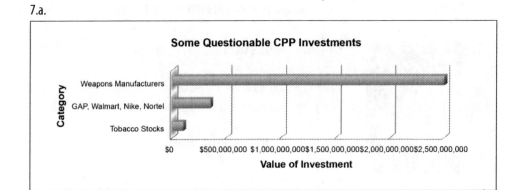

7.b.   Pacifists are one group that could oppose investment in weapons manufacturers. Union organizers are people who could oppose investment in GAP, Walmart, Nike and Nortel. Cancer survivors, or doctors might oppose investment in tobacco stocks.

8.a-d.

Canadian Pension Plan Investments In Corporations Producing Landmines	
Corporation	Investment
General Electric Company	$137,326,000
Texas Instruments (subsidiary Unitrode)	$17,059,000
Raytheon	$2,940,000
Rockwell (subsidiary Allen-Bradley)	$1,176,000
Total:	$158,501,000
Mean:	$39,625,250
Median:	$9,999,500

8.e.

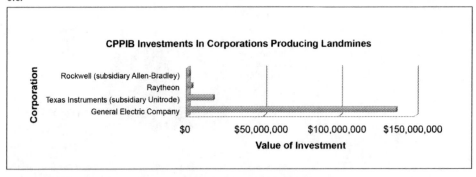

8.f.   You could argue that divesting from General Electric would have the most impact, due to the large amount invested in them, but it is unclear how much of the investment dollars actually end up supporting landmine development and the number of lawyers that they have might make it very difficult. On the other hand some of the smaller investments might be exclusively directed towards landmine development, and it might be easier to pressure the CPPIB to divest from them. More information is required.

9.a. No law is set in stone. Laws that are unethical can and have been fought and changed.

9.b. Although technically this statement is true, it is also likely that a vast majority of the 16 million people would vote for divestment because of specific reasons. For example, children dying due to the investment is one persuasive argument for divestment.

10.a. Someone who tells others not to smoke and then themself smokes.

b. Answers will vary but consider that the role that the Canadian government played in the Ottawa Treaty seems incongruent with the CPPIB's decision to invest in corporations that produce landmines.

11.a. One percent of a large number can be more than 40% of a small number. So for example 1% of 5,000 is 50, while 40% of 80 is 32.

11.b. If Raytheon had a very high percentage of landmines as its products, while General Electric had a very low percentage, Raytheon could produce more landmines than General Electric.

11.c. Rockwell is a smaller company than General Electric and so has fewer lawyers to protect its interests.

Tarnished – Answers

Opening question:

"Tar sands" sounds a lot dirtier than "oil sands". If members of the public picture dirty tar, they may be more likely to resist its extraction.

Understanding using math:

1. 170,000,000,000 barrels $\times$ 0.158987295 m³ / barrel = 27,027,840,150 m³.

2. 27,027,840,150 ÷ 1,600,000 = 16,892 Skydomes.

3. 170,000,000,000 ÷ 175,000,000,000 $\times$ 100 = 97.14%.

4. Answers will vary. An adult giraffe is about 2,000 kg.

5. 525,000 barrels $\times$ 2,000 kg/barrel = 1,050,000,000 kg extracted per day. A blue whale, the largest animal to have ever lived on the earth, is about 150,000 kg. So the amount is equivalent to 7,000 blue whales. This is roughly the number of blue whales alive today in the oceans.[1]

6 Oil spills threaten coastal communities, both in terms of the ecosystem and peoples' livelihoods. The remaining 20% figure is not defined, so it could include both people who approve of the oil tankers, or those who are indifferent. For those that approve, they may hope that the pipeline will bring jobs to their communities.

7.   525,000 barrels $\times$ 0.158987295 m^3 / barrel $\times$ 4 m^3 tailings/m^3 bitumen= 333,873 m^3 of tailings.

8.   Without knowing the five results, it's impossible to know if 11 million litres is the mean, or possibly the median value of the reports on seepage.

9.   11,000,000 litres/day $\times$ 365 days / year = 4,015,000,000 litres of seepage per year. An Olympic-sized swimming pool is 2,500,000 litres of water, so the seepage amounts to 1606 Olympic pools.

10.a.   The ratio is very close to 1:5. ($0.0147 \div 0.0029 = 5.06$).

10.b. $0.0147 \div 0.005 = 2.94$ times over the safe level of arsenic.

11.

Substance	Nanograms per sample of river sediment		Effect Ratio	Difference
	Upstream	Downstream	Down-Up	Down-Up
C1-Dibenzothiophenes	27.4	197.9	1:7	170.5
C3-Dibenzothiophenes	58.3	874.6	1:15	816.3
C3-Flourenes	83.2	1007.2	1:12	924

12. $26 \div 28 \times 100 = 92.9\%$ showed increases downstream.

13.a. $0.041 \div 0.32 \times 100 = 128$, so a 28% increase from the levels in 1976.

13.b. $0.41 \div 0.20 = 2.05$ times Health Canada's guideline for safe levels of mercury.

13.c.   People eat the fish, and so can ingest the dangerous substance, becoming sick.

14.   185,000,000 m^3 $\times$ 2 = 370,000,000 m^3.

15.   Ecosystems along the shorelines would be affected, and other water systems that are fed by the Athabaska River could be cut off as the water level drops.

16.   If y = total barrels of water and x = the number of barrels of pit-mined oil, then $y = 12x$ and if $x = 525,000$ then $y = 12 \times 525,000$. The amount of water to process the daily oil is 6,300,000 barrels of water per day.

17. $175 \div 15 = 11.7$ times more expensive at the low end. $230 \div 15 = 15.3$ times more expensive at the high end. In both cases, it's more profitable to pay the carbon tax, which means that the carbon will continue to enter the atmosphere.

18.   525,000 barrels of oil per day $\times$ 35 kg of CO2 per barrel = 18,375,000 kg of CO_2 per day.

19. $55 \div 35 \times 100 = 157$, which means 57% more, due to the increased energy demands of extracting tar sands from deeper in the earth.

20. The graph on the right shrinks the distance between the different values, making it look less dramatic.

21.a. $766,000,000,000 taxes / 25 years ÷ 25 = $30,640,000,000 per year.

21.b. That amount is less than the cost of the BP spill in the Gulf of Mexico.

22. What kinds of jobs? Are they part time? Permanent? Well paid? Unionized?

23. $5,500,000 ÷ 3,571,000,000 \times 100 = 0.15\%$.

1. https://en.wikipedia.org/wiki/Blue_whale#Population_and_distribution_today

Lesson 3

Pointed Questions – Answers

Opening question:

This is a good example of intersectionality. Access to health clinics, access to information material in a language other than English or French, and ability to use health services legally are all important obstacles to consider.

Understanding using math:

1. People in the "developed" world may have better access to health services and having regular Pap tests, which would catch the infection before its possible progression to cervical cancer.

235

2.a-c.

Cancer	Number of deaths (in 2015)
Lung	7,000
Breast	5,000
Colorectal	3,800
Pancreas	1,650
Ovary	1,600
Non Hodgkin Lymphoma	1,200
Leukemia	880
Stomach	770
Body of uterus	690
Brain	650
Multiple myeloma	600
Kidney	550
Bladder	430
Oesophagus	390
Cervix	360
Oral	330
Melanoma	290
Total:	26,190
Mean:	1540.588235
Median:	690
Percentage of cervical cancer deaths compared to total:	1.374570447

2.d.

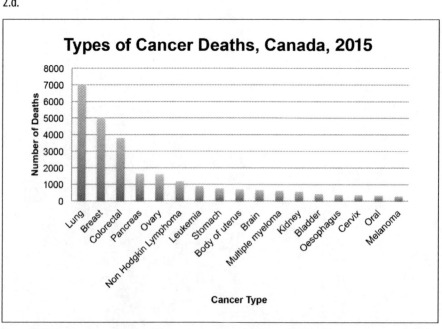

2.e. $0.4 \times 360 = 144$

2.f. $144 \div 26{,}190 \times 100 = 0.55\,\%$

3.

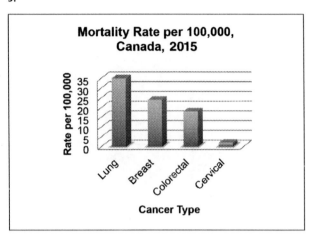

4. $1 \div 153 \times 100 = 0.65\%$

5. $1 \div 445 \times 100 = 0.22\%$

6.a.   "=0.95*(A2)"

6.b.   Either "=A2 – B2" or "=A2*0.05"

6.c.   "=C2*0.2"

6.d.   "=C2*0.8"

6.e.   "=D2/A2*100"

Total HPV infections in Canada (2002)	Number of HPV infections that the body naturally clears in 2 years	Number of HPV infections that aren't cleared by the body	Number of people who progress to invasive cervical cancer in 5 years	Number of people who don't progress to cervical cancer in 5 years	Percentage of those who get invasive cervical cancer as compared to total infections
1,350	1282.5	68	13.5	54	1

6.f.

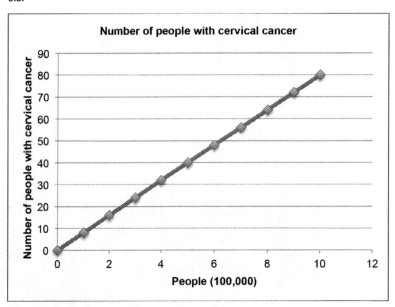

People with and without cervical cancer

Number of people who progress to invasive cervical cancer in 5 years
1%

Number of people who don't progress to cervical cancer in 5 years
4%

Number of HPV infections that the body naturally clears in 2 years
95%

7. Cervical cancer is most often slow to progress, and if people are getting regular Pap testing it should be caught over this time frame.

8.a.

Number of people with cervical cancer

People (100,000) — horizontal axis

Number of people with cervical cancer — vertical axis

8.b. The slope of the line would be steeper.

8.c. There are 100 hundred thousands in 10 million. The difference in rate of six people per hundred thousand multiplied by 100 makes an increase of 600 people in a population of 10 million.

9. 934,000 vaccinations × $400 = $373,600,000. Treating HPV over that time is $54,000,000. The vaccinations are 6.92 times more expensive.

238

Little Do We Know – Answers

Opening question:

When Procter and Gamble use their own data, but stand to gain financially from a particular conclusion, it is a conflict of interest. An independent third party who does not stand to gain or lose anything from whatever conclusion is found avoids conflict of interest.

Understanding using math:

1. All lines are graphed below. If d represents the amount of resource used per disposable diaper and r represents the amount of resource used per reusable diaper, then d = 60r for the amount of waste created.

2. Using the same variables, the three other algebraic equations are:

   d = 20r for raw materials used
   d = 3r for energy used and
   d = 2r for the amount of water used

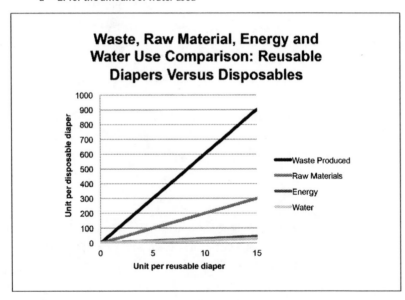

3. The coefficients are 60, 20, 3 and 2. Another name for the coefficient is the slope.

4. The y-intercept for all four lines is zero. Another name for the y- intercept is the constant.

5. m = -0.03n – 500

6. m = -0.40n

7. 8 diapers/day × 365 days/year × 2 years = 5,840 diaper changes in two years.

8.

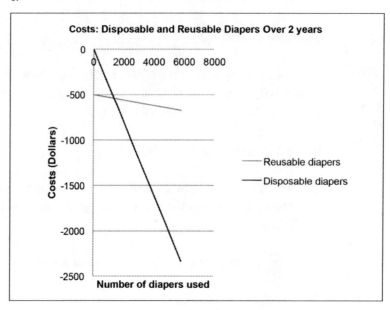

Costs: Disposable and Reusable Diapers Over 2 years

9.

$$m = -0.03n - 500 \text{ and } m = -0.40n$$
$$-0.03n - 500 = -0.40n$$
$$-500 = -0.37n$$
$$1351 = n$$

After 1,351 diaper changes, the two lines are equal.

10. For disposable diapers m $= -0.40 \times 5840 = $ -\$2,336$ and
for reusable diapers m $= -0.03 \times 5840 - 500 = $ -\$675.20$ so disposable diapers cost more over that period of time, by \$1,660.80.

Bonus:

For reusable diapers, m $= -0.03n - 500$, where n $= 5,840 \times 3$ so m $= $ -\$1,025.60$.
For disposable diapers m $= -0.40n$, where n $= 5,840 \times 3$ so m $= $ -\$7,008$.
The difference is \$5,982.20.

Lesson 5

Fear – Answers

Opening question:

Items that are shocking will be most prominent in the news media. Shocking news is sometimes shocking because it is rare, but seeing rare events lead the news can convince people that they are more commonplace than they actually are. When the events are murder or assault, for example, people may become overly fearful.

Understanding using math:

1. Answers will vary.

2.

Cause	Absolute Number	Percentage
Heart diseases and stroke	60,910	25.2
Lightning	10	0.004
Murder	575	0.243
Cancer	72,476	29.9
HIV	407	0.172
Unintentional Accidents Including Motor Vehicle Accidents	10,716	4.4
Suicide	3,728	1.5

Comparing the student perceptions in the first questions with the actual numbers from question two is a way to highlight and explore how perception and reality can be vastly different.

3. Police could use public perception to argue for more tax dollars. Security companies may try to sell home security systems to the public. In some countries, gun sales could go up.

4. Companies that profit from selling health products could benefit. The pharmaceutical companies who produce vaccinations make money.

5. Eight people die per hour in Canada from cancer. 0.07 people are murdered per hour in Canada (or roughly one death every 15 hours).

6. Any industry that may be linked to products that cause cancer and heart disease. The fast food industry, the tobacco industry, companies that produce environmental toxins and many more.

7.

Cause	Number of males	Percentage of males	Number of females	Percentage of females
Motor vehicle accidents	1,863	71	765	29
Murder	452	79	123	21
Accidental Drowning	225	82	50	28
Suicide	2,777	75	928	25

8. It's possible to speculate, but causal relationships are hard to substantiate. One reason may be that masculinity is associated with risk taking behaviour and aggression, while femininity is less so. In terms of suicide, femininity is associated with asking for help, while masculinity is less so.

9. The absolute population sizes are different in each of the regions, which means that comparisons are hard to make. If the incidents are listed as a rate per 100,000 people, you can compare them. In this case, at first glace it may appear that Ontario has the biggest problem of the listed regions, with 1,025 suicides. But due to the fact that the Northwest Territories and Nunavut have smaller population sizes, the rates end up being much higher than Ontario.

10. First Nations peoples live in the north of Canada and have experienced colonization, racism, abuse within government residential schools, lack of support from the government, and the resulting poverty and lack of access to services. All of these and more could influence the suicide rates.

11. All of these groups are hidden within the data, which means that if those groups were listed separately (the data was "disaggregated"), you would likely see higher numbers for typically marginalized groups. Without disaggregating the data, it can be difficult or impossible to design policy and direct resources to the groups that need them the most.

Lesson 6

All That Glitters – Answers

Opening question:

Other issues could include land disputes, particularly with First Nations groups, the environmental impact of mining, the working conditions for the miners, the age of the miners, the possibility of precious resources fuelling conflict within the region.

Understanding using math:

Environmental assessment:

In the roll of the two dice, the probability that a sum of 2, 3 or 4 will appear is 6 in 36, which is 16.7%. The chance that the sum of 2, 3 or 4 will not appear is the complementary probability, which is 30 in 36, or 83.3%.

The probability that a sum of 9 will appear is 4 chances in 36, which is 11.1%. The chance that the sum of 9 will not appear is the complementary probability, which is 32 in 36, or 88.9%.

Environmental laws would make it tougher or easier to do damage to the environment. Whether or not the existing laws are enforced is also an important question.

Clean-up costs:

Rolling a sum of 4, 5, or 6 on a single die has a 50% chance of happening. In some countries, lower or non- existent levels of enforcement mean that companies can avoid responsibility for clean up.

Exhaust-ed – Answers

Opening question:

Kennedy is suggesting that both public health and public transportation should be priorities, and that public transportation should not come at the cost of poor health.

Understanding using math:

1.

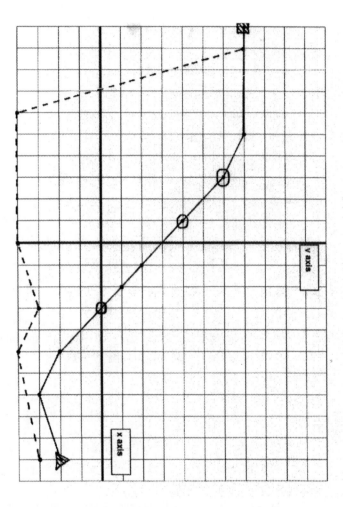

2. Various answers are possible, including the fact that Canada has 0% of its rails electrified, while other countries like Italy, Austria and Sweden have close to 60% of their rails electrified.

3. Since the rail corridor already exists, complete with tracks, the costs to build an entirely new line would be prohibitive.

4. $5,000,000/\,km \times 30\,km = \$150,000,000$

5. $875,000,000 \times 0.17 = \$148,750,000$

6. $150,000,000 \div 10 = $15,000,000 per year savings.

7. 4,000 trucks/day $\times$ 365 days/ year $= 1,460,000$ trucks per year.

8. $40 \times 0.375 = 15$ that are likely carcinogenic.

9.

Particle type	Diameter	Diameter in metres
Chain agglomerate of soot particles	40 nanometres up to 500 nanometres	0.000 000 04
		0.000 000 5
Metallic ash particles from lube oil	10 nanometres up to 20 nanometres	0.000 000 01
		0.000 000 02
Hydrocarbon particles	10 nanometres up to 30 nanometres	0.000 000 01
		0.000 000 03
Chain agglomerate of soot particles with adsorbed/ condensed layers of hydrocarbon and sulphate and metallic ash	40 nanometres up to 500 nanometres	0.000 000 04
		0.000 000 5
Comparison: diameter of human hair	40,000 nanometres	0.000 04

10. All particles in the above chart are fully or partially within the 100 nanometres or less range, making them "ultrafine".

11. Some of the chain agglomerate of soot particles, all of the metallic ash particles, all of the hydrocarbon particles and some of the soot particles with layers of hydrocarbon and sulphate and metallic ash would be considered nanoparticles.

12. $0.000\ 04 \div 0.000\ 000\ 02 = 2,000$ times bigger than the largest metallic ash particles and 4,000 times bigger than the smallest metallic ash particles.

13. Children and elderly people have lungs that are most sensitive to these particles. That's the reason for the concern about the diesel trains running alongside schools and homes for the elderly.

14. $t = 75h$ where h is the number of hours that the trains run, and t is the total amount of diesel used in gallons.

15. $75 \times 58.3 = 4,372.5$ gallons of diesel per day.

16. 4,372.5 gallons $\times$ 22.38 pounds of carbon dioxide per gallon $= 97,856.55$ pounds of carbon.

Spilled - Answers

Opening question:

Our driving requires oil and gas, and so we are responsible for the tankers that spill and destroy coastal ecosystems.

Understanding using math:

1.

When the radius is.....	The area is....
R	A
10 m	314 m²
20 m	1256 m²
30 m	2826 m²
40 m	5024 m²
50 m	7850 m²
60 m	11,304 m²
70 m	15,386 m²
80 m	20,096 m²
90 m	25,434 m²
100 m	31,400 m²
110 m	37,994 m²
120 m	45,216 m²
130 m	53,066 m²
140 m	61,544 m²
150 m	70,650 m²

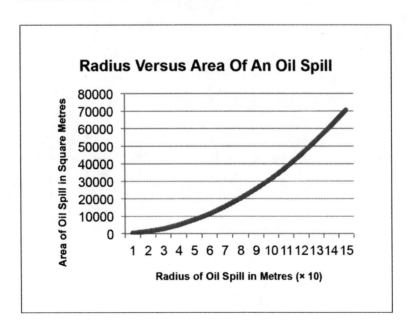

2. The growth of the area around the oil tanker is exponential.

3. $\sqrt{(18{,}000 \div 3.14)} = 75.7$ metres is the radius.

4. $C = \pi d$ so $C = 3.14 \times 75.7 \times 2$ and $C = 475.4$ metres.

5. $\sqrt{(23{,}000 \div 3.14)} = 85.6$ metres is the radius.

6. $C = \pi d$ so $C = 3.14 \times 85.6 \times 2$ and $C = 537.6$ metres.

7. 85.6 metres $\div$ 0.5 metres / minute $= 171.2$ minutes, or 2.85 hours. Spill clean up crews and materials would have to be close and ready to respond in that short amount of time.

8. The amount of wave action would impact the dispersal of the oil, which wouldn't likely progress at a constant rate.

9. $200{,}000{,}000 \times 0.14 = 28{,}000{,}000$ litres of oil was cleaned up (172,000,000 litres remained).

10. 200,000,000 litres $\div$ 159 litres/barrel $= 1{,}257{,}861$ barrels of oil.

11. 1,257,861 barrel $\times$ \$4,300 / barrel $= \$5{,}408{,}802{,}300$.

12. $t = 4{,}300b + 100{,}000$ where t is the total fine and b is the number of barrels spilled.

Lesson 9

Thin – Answers

Opening question:

Groups that are further marginalized, such as women escaping from domestic violence or people with added health care costs could depend on the Special Diet Allowance even more.

Understanding using math:

1. $442{,}599 \times 1.0144 = 448{,}980$

2. Answers will vary. In a class of 30, and assuming all had lost their jobs, nine would receive employment insurance and 21 (or 70%) would end up on welfare.

3.a.

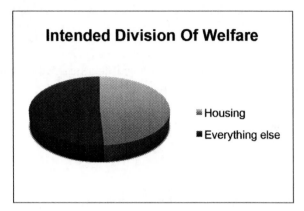

Intended Division Of Welfare

■ Housing
■ Everything else

3.b.

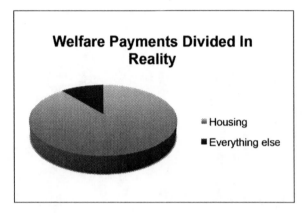

Welfare Payments Divided In Reality

■ Housing
■ Everything else

The amount left for food and everything else turns out to be $132 a month. It's clear that the cost of housing is an enormous piece of the welfare payment.

4.a. $10 \times 12 = $120

b. $42 \times 12 = $504

c. $250 \times 12 = $3,000

d. We know, for example, that people living with diabetes have "medical costs that are two to three times higher than those without diabetes."[1] The lifetime healthcare costs for someone living with HIV are estimated to be $250,000.[2] These yearly supplements are likely far below the actual costs individuals must take on.

5.a. $800 \times 0.6 = $480

b. Inflation is where the costs of living rise over time, which means the food and accommodation costs that you have in 1995 will be higher in 2010. If you are receiving a payment that doesn't increase, then you're purchasing power is reduced. Activists suggest indexing (or tying) welfare payment increases to inflation.

6.a. 246,880

b. 446,537

c. Cases can include more than one person. If the person has dependants, for example, it will be reflected in the higher beneficiaries total.

d. 54,000

e. $446,537 \div 54,000 = 8.3$

f. Over the year, the number of beneficiaries dropped by 1%, or 4,638 people.

g. Answers will vary.

h. 448,515

i. An increase of 1,186 people, or 0.3%.

1. https://www.diabetes.ca/getmedia/4873c9cc-1105-4c11-9e90-230ea52a9c60/ontario-financial-assistance-programs.pdf.aspx
2. http://www.cdnaids.ca/cost-of-hiv

Lesson 10

Unsettling – Answers

Opening question:

Idle No More is a group of people committed to establishing nation to nation relationships between First Nations groups and the Canadian government. They care about peaceful revolution to encourage sovereignty, and to protect the land and water.[1] Treaties are agreements between nations and are meant to capture the idea that while the land is shared, First Nations people maintain rights related to land and resources.[2]

Understanding using math:

1.a. Answers will vary.

1.b. Answers will vary.

1. http://www.idlenomore.ca/vision
2. http://www.idlenomore.ca/manifesto

Beyond Left & Right – Answers

Opening question:

Once people reach voting age, understanding the political platforms of the different parties will enhance peoples' ability to align their values with their political representatives.

Understanding using math:

1. Answers will vary.

2.

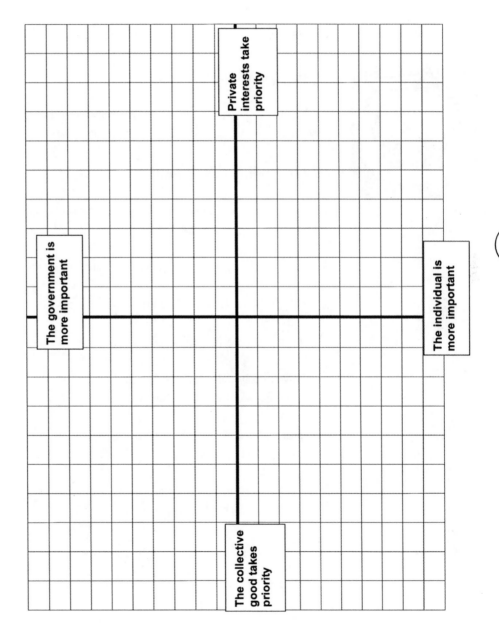

3.

Media source	Which Canadian political party do they often endorse?
The National Post	Conservatives (2004, 2006, 2011)
The Toronto Star	NDP (2011) & Liberal (2011)
The Globe and Mail	Conservatives (2011)
Rabble.ca	NDP

3. Quadrant III
4. Quadrant II

Well Spoke-n – Answers

Opening question:

Possible advantages might include deeper community ties and feelings of support, while disadvantages might be a lack of exposure to different and possibly beneficial ideas.

Understanding using math:

1. A recreation centre, a library, a school, a government or community council office, a park, an emergency response centre, a clinic.

2. d= 2r   so d = 2 × 400 = 800 metres. 1.5 minutes/ 100 m × 800 m = 12 minutes.

3. $A = \pi r^2$ $A = \pi (400)^2$ A = 502,640 m^2

4. $C = \pi d$ so C = 3.14 × 800 = 2,513 m

5. 8 roads × 6 m/road = 48 metres for roads
    (2,513 m – 48 m) ÷ 15 = 164 houses

6. Area of total circle – area of hub = area of housing
    $\pi (450)^2 – \pi (400)^2 = 133,514$ m^2 for the housing

7. $C = \pi d$ so C = π 900 = 2,827 m
    2,827 – 48 m for roads = 2,779 m
    2,779 ÷ 164 homes = 16.94 metres

8. Farmland area + housing area and hub = total area
   $1,500,000 \text{ m}^2 + \pi (450)^2 = 2,136,154 \text{ m}^2$
   $\sqrt{(2,136,154 \div 3.14)} = 825 \text{ m radius}$
   Total radius − radius of housing area and hub = depth of farmland
   $825 \text{ m} - 450 \text{ m} = 375 \text{ metres}$

9. 825 metres

Lesson 13

Jux-tice – Answers

Opening question:

Answers will vary.

Understanding using math:

1.a. Possibly that the cost to end illiteracy is far less than the spending on fast food in the United States.

b. Both the word 'would' and 'fries' are spelled incorrectly, drawing attention to the idea of illiteracy.

c. Answers will vary.

2.a. Comparisons must share the same timeframe. Therefore you could compare the number of bikes produced in a year with the number of cars produced in a year, or compare the daily production of bikes and cars.

b. It is important to know who produces statistics so that you can assess the bias.

Lesson 14

Bridge Over Troubled Waters – Answers

Opening question:

The islands that fill the Douglas Channel are missing from the Enbridge depiction of the waterway. This is important because the huge tankers carrying the oil will have to navigate the islands.

Understanding using math:

1. See map on next page.

2. See map on next page.

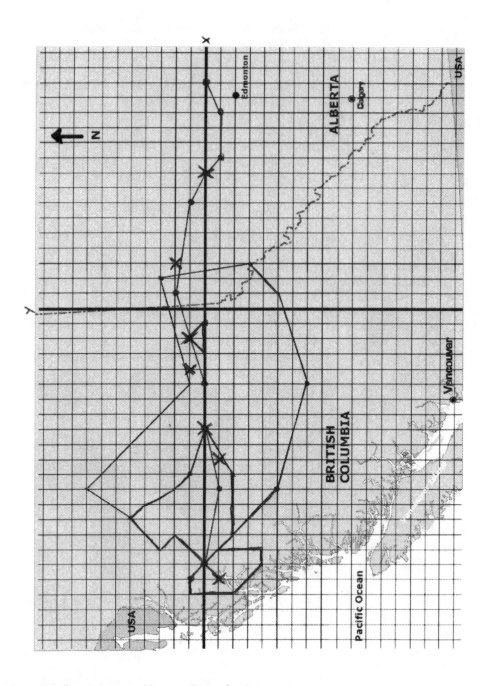

3. 80 spills per year or roughly one spill every five days.

4. Some of Canada's national parks are close to 1,000 km². For example, Cape Breton Highlands in Nova Scotia is 949 km², Grasslands in Saskatchewan is 907 km² and Yoho in British Columbia is 1,313 km².

5. The First Nations Reserves are not marked, nor the lakes and rivers that cover the province. The impact of oil spills on any of these sites explains the resistance to the pipeline, and may suggest a reason to omit them from the Enbridge map.

6. Successful opposition to the Keystone pipeline could inspire and motivate those opposed to the Northern Gateway Pipeline. On the other hand, if the Keystone pipeline is not available for transport of the oil, it may motivate proponents of the Northern Gateway Pipeline to ensure that it is built.

Exit Strategy – Answers

Opening question:

Hot water spraying can damage plants and animals along the shoreline, and can make tiny oil particles airborne, which is hazardous to clean-up crews.

Understanding using math:

1. $A = \pi r^2$ $A = \pi (100)^2$ $A = 31,415 \, m^2$

2. It would be a cylinder.

3. $V = \pi r^2 h$ $V = 31,415 \times 60 = 1,884,900 \, m^3$

4.a. $585 \, km^2 / cm^2 \times 40 \, cm^2 = 23,400 \, km^2$

b. $23,400 \, km^2 \times .08 \, km = 1,872 \, km^3$

c. $500,000 \times 0.05 = 25,000$ barrels

    $500,000 \times 0.1 = 50,000$ barrels

5.a. $V = \pi r^2 h$ $V = \pi (5)^2 (20) = 1571 \, cm^3$

b. A lower LC50.

c. $8 \div 1571 = 0.005$ and $4,000 \div 1,000,000 = 0.004$ so the sample is toxic to the fish.

6. $V = 4/3 \, \pi r^3$ $V = 4/3 \, \pi (5)^3 = 524$ cubic microns

7.

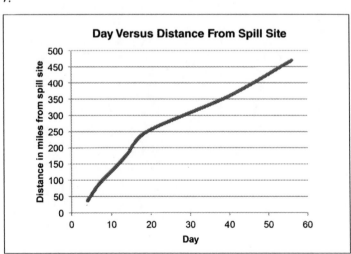

Day Versus Distance From Spill Site

(Graph: x-axis "Day" from 0 to 60, y-axis "Distance in miles from spill site" from 0 to 500)

253

8.a. $128 \div 0.32 = 400$ times the exposure rate

8.b. $3 \div 26 \times 100 = 11.5\%$

9.a. Smaller oil particles mean larger surface area. More surface area means more exposure to bacteria that biodegrade oil.

9.b. In the absence of Correxit, the Marenobacter increase in number and that allows the oil to be broken down more quickly. With dispersant, the Colwellia increase (which eat the dispersant), while simultaneously preventing the bloom of Marenobacter. This is an argument against Correxit.

Lesson 16

Cross Roads – Answers

Opening question:

The gas masks worn by the actors and the shot of the factories emitting pollutants indicate that the issue has to do with poor air quality.

Understanding using math:

1. Since there are 40 factories on the map, the circle should surround 32 of them (80%).

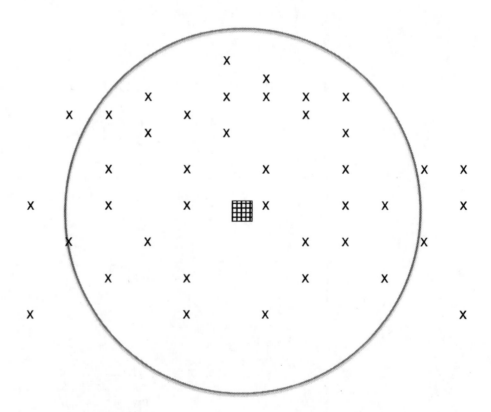

2. The radius is 4.2 cm and the scale is 4.3 cm: 5 km. Therefore the radius is 4.3 ÷ 5 × 4.2 = 3.6 km.

3. $A = \pi r^2$ $A = \pi (7.7)^2$ $A = 186.3$ km²

4. $V = \pi r^2 h$ $V = \pi (7.7)^2 (2)$ $V = 372.5$ km³

5.

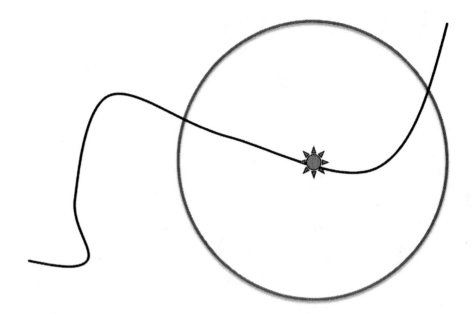

a. If 1.84 km is 4.3 cm, then 1.5 km is 3.5 cm and the diameter would be 7 cm.

b. $A = \pi r^2$ $A = \pi (1.5)2$ $A = 7.1$ km²

c. $V = \pi r^2 h$ $V = \pi (1.5)^2 (0.8) = 5.7$ km³

6. a. $V = \pi r^2 h$ $V = \pi (3.5)^2 \, 15 \times 3$ tankers $= 1,731.8$ m³

b. $4.3 \div 4 \times 5 = 5.4$ cm radius

c. $A = \pi r^2$ $A = \pi (5)^2$ $A = 78.5$ km²

d. $V = \pi r^2 h$ $V = \pi (5)^2 (2)$ $V = 157$ km³

Take a Peak – Answers

Opening question:

Other forms of energy production will begin to be more economically competitive to pursue, like solar and wind power. Alternatives to products made with oil could be far more environmentally friendly.

Understanding using math:

1.

x	y
0	0
1	7
2	12
3	15
4	16
5	15
6	12
7	7
8	0

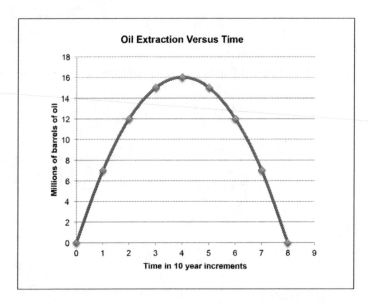

2. 40 years.

3.

x	y
0	0
1	2
2	4
3	6
4	8
5	10
6	12
7	14
8	16

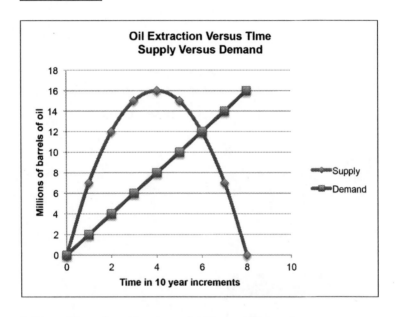

In this model, supply matches demand at 60 years, when $x = 6$.

$y = 2x$ $y = -x^2 + 8x$

$\qquad\qquad 2x = -x^2 + 8x$

$\qquad\qquad x^2 - 6x = 0$

$\qquad\qquad x(x-6) = 0$ so $x = 0$ or 6

4.

x	y
0	0
1	1
2	4
3	9
4	16
5	25
6	36
7	49

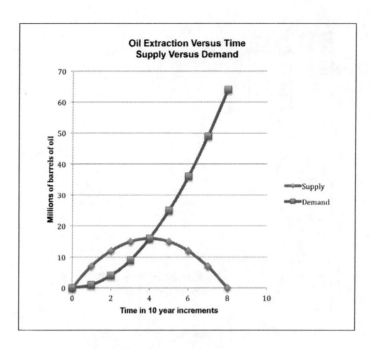

Oil Extraction Versus Time
Supply Versus Demand

Demand matches production after 40 years, when x = 4.

$y = x^2$ $y = -x^2 + 8x$

$x^2 = -x^2 + 8x$

$2x^2 - 8x = 0$

$2x(x-4) = 0$ so $x = 0$ or 4

5.a.

x	y
0	100
1	50
2	25
3	12.5
4	6.25
5	3.125
6	1.5625
7	0.78125
8	0.390625

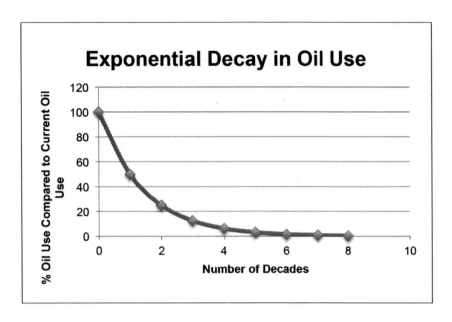

Exponential Decay in Oil Use

5.b.   The amount of oil use is dropping exponentially rather than linearly.

5.c.   Oil use drops below 20% of current use in the 23rd year.

5.d.   The base of 0.5 would have to be lower. For example, a base of 0.25 would see oil use drop below 20% of current use in the 11th year.

6.a.   It would take 10 decades, or 100 years.

6.b.

x	y
0	100
1	92
2	84
3	76
4	68
5	60
6	52
7	44
8	36
9	28
10	20

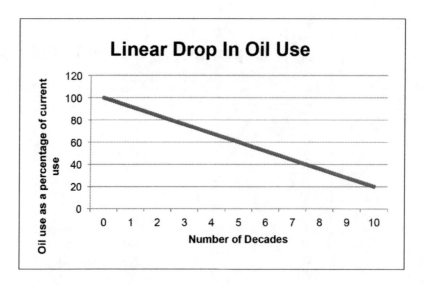

Linear Drop In Oil Use

(y-axis: Oil use as a percentage of current use; x-axis: Number of Decades)

6.c.   Answers will vary.

7.   Saudi Arabia, Canada, Russia, Iraq, Iran and Venezuala.

8.   A country or corporation might understate oil reserves to drive the price of oil up (less oil means a higher cost for oil). A country might overstate its oil reserves to seem powerful. Countries that have a lot of oil have historically faced the possibility of invasion or control by other countries looking to control that oil.

260 Lesson 18

Shark Infested Waters – Answers

Opening question:

Payday loan centres will point to the fact that people taking these short-term loans are more at risk, on average, of defaulting on those loans. In order to cover the costs of money that can't be recouped, the logic goes, higher interest rates must be charged.

Understanding using math:

1.   1.31

2. $280 \times 1.31 = \$366.80$ is the total payback so $\$366.80 - \$280 = \$86.80$ for the loan fee.

3. $((86.80 \div 280) \times 365 \text{ days/year}) \div 14 \times 100 = 808.2\%$ APR

4.

Type of credit	Loan (or $)	Loan fee	# of days of the loan	APR
Bank Loan	$200,000	$6,000	365	3
ATM Machine	$100	$1.00	1	365
Credit card	$350	$9.00	30	31.3
Payday loan (Ontario)	$100	$21	14	547.5
Payday loan (Nova Scotia)	$100	$31	14	808.2
Payday loan (Online)	$100	$33	14	860.4

5.

Week	Original Loan	Set up fee	Finance Fee	Payday loan default charge	Bank overdraft fee (NSF)	Second Loan	Finance Fee	Processing Fee
1	-$500	-$10	-$100					
2								
3			-$100					
4				-$20	- $45			
5			-$100			-$200	- $50	
6								- $8

6. $(-500) + (-200) = -700$

7. $(-500) + (-10) + (-100) + (-100) + (-20) + (-45) + (-100) + (-200) + (-50) + (-8) = -1,133$

8 $(-1,133) - (-700) = -433$

9. $(-433) \div (-700) \times 100 = 61.9\%$

10.a. It means that both are occurring together (that you see higher numbers of payday loan centres in higher levels of lower household income levels, and lower numbers of payday loan centres with lower levels of lower household income levels. This is an example of positive correlation.

10.b. Living in poverty can be associated with all sorts of systemic barriers: ableism, racism, transphobia, sexism and other forms of discrimination that may, for example, limit certain people from certain jobs.

10.c. Roughly $40,000.

10.d. Payday loan centres want people who can still pay back their loans. They may feel that the lowest income levels will lead to higher levels of default on their loans.

Mapping Access – Answers

Opening question:

Convenience stores and fast food outlets tend to have food that is high in fat, sugar and salt. These are all things that are problematic for people's health.

Understanding using math:

2. 3.

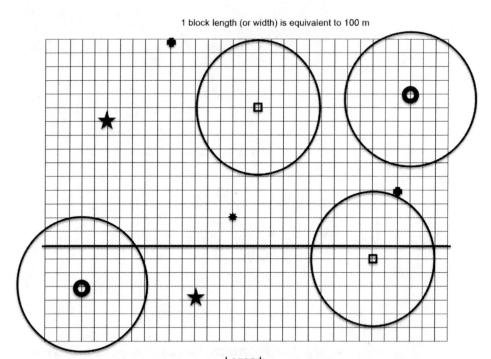

1 block length (or width) is equivalent to 100 m

Legend:

Feature	Symbol	Reasonable Distance	Distances		Average Distance
Your residence	✹				
High end grocery stores	▫		824.6 m	1,140.2 m	982.4 m
Affordable grocery stores	◉		1300 m	1,664.3 m	1,482.2 m
Libraries	✛		1,315.3 m	1,392.8 m	1,354.1 m
Community centers	★		670.1 m	1,220.1 m	945.1 m
Public transit line	▬				

3.b.　$A = \pi r^2$　　$A = \pi (500)^2$　　$A = 785{,}375 \text{ m}^2 \times 4 \text{ circles} = 3{,}141{,}500 \text{ m}^2$

4.　Answers will vary, but there can be a maximum number of line segments used, found by
$\$1{,}250{,}000{,}000 \div \$120{,}000{,}000 \times 10 = 104$

5.　Answers will vary, but there can be a maximum number of line segments used, found by
$\$1{,}250{,}000{,}000 \div \$300{,}000{,}000 \times 10 = 41.7$

a.　Light rail allows further reach because it costs less per kilometer to install.

b.　Subways avoid surface traffic and inclement weather and so the conveniences are used to justify the additional costs.

Unity – Answers

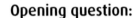

Opening question:

Answers will vary.

Understanding using math:

1.a.　4,716 borrowers funded this week $\times$ 52 weeks/ year = 245,232 borrowers funded / year.
3,808 new lenders this week $\times$ 52 weeks/ year = 198,016 new lenders / year.
13,820 lenders made a loan this week $\times$ 52 weeks/ year = 718,640 new loans/ year.
$1,747,150 loaned this week $\times$ 52 weeks/ year = $90,851,800 loaned this year.

1.b.　These are all signs that many people use Kiva, and so these statistics provide hope that this is a way to make meaningful change easily.

2.　If the system is set up with no accountability for repayment, lenders will be reluctant to lend. Also, the repayment time on loans is made long enough to create success.

3.　Local institutions may want to ensure Kiva funding in the future and so may cover defaulted loans to keep their success rate high.

4.　$763,077,250 $\div$ 1,342,681 = $568.32

5.　$1,000,000 $\div$ $25 = 40,000

These loans make it even easier to get involved because the lender doesn't need to loan any of their own money, and perhaps will experience how easy it is to do, resulting in further loaning behaviour.

6.　$1{,}342{,}681 \times 0.8046 = 1{,}080{,}321$

7.a. Both scores are out of 70. Kiva's score for accountability and transparency is 70 out of 70 and Kiva's financial score is 68 out of 70. Both of these are extremely high scores.

7.b. It would be good to know who Charity Navigator is, what connections if any they have with Kiva, and how they have created their rating scale.

8. Weighting means making a decision about how important a particular piece of data is, which in inevitably a human endeavour and one which is always susceptible to bias. The class may have different ideas about the relative value of each category, or may indeed have other categories that they would want included in a rating scale.

9.

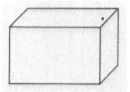

10.

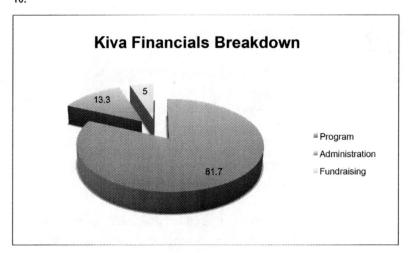

Lesson 21
....

The Bottom Line – Answers

Opening question:

Offshore boundaries will have an impact on the resources that a country can use (for example, fish or underwater oil resources).

Understanding using math:

1.a. Georgetown: Latitude 6.8000° N Longitude 58.1667° W.

1.b. Paramaribo: Latitude 5.8236° N Longitude 55.1697° W.

1.c.   The North Atlantic Ocean.

2.a.   The sum of internal angles of a triangle is 180 degrees, so the missing angle must be 60 degrees.

2.b.   A = ½ bh
       A= ½ × 162 km × 177 km
       A= 14,337 km²

2.c.   This land is internal to the country, and so some sort of natural resource is one plausible option, as well as control over the river for transportation or commerce.

3.– 6.

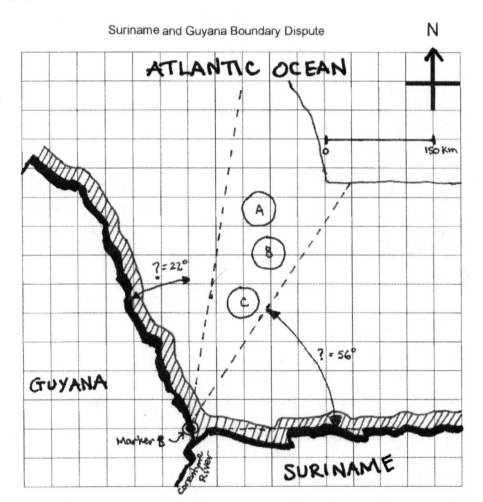

Suriname and Guyana Boundary Dispute

7. $A = \frac{1}{2}\, bh$
     $A = \frac{1}{2} \times 500\ km \times 150\ km$
     $A = 37{,}500\ km^2$

8.   See above map.

9.   56 degrees

10. The equidistant line would put the ocean oil reserves into Guyana's territory.

11. Area A: Formula: $(L1 + L2) \div 2 \times h$ Area: 52 km²
     Area B: Formula: ½ bh   Area: 17.5 km²
     Area C: Formula: $(L1 + L2) \div 2 \times h$ Area: 24.5 km²

12. $33{,}152 \div (33{,}152 + 17{,}871) \times 100 = 65\%$ went to Guyana
     $17{,}871 \div (33{,}152 + 17{,}871) \times 100 = 35\%$ went to Suriname

Lesson 22

Fare Prices - Answers

Opening question:

Moving people around a city or community can reduce isolation, increase participation in the workforce, and allow community members to get services that they need. Financing free transportation may be difficult.

Understanding using math:

1.   See chart next page.

2.   A parabola.

3.   Revenue increases because the public is paying more fare.

4.   At a certain point, the fare becomes too expensive for people and so ridership decreases, decreasing overall revenue.

5.

When x is...	...y is equal to...
0	0
1	8
2	14
3	18
4	20
5	20
6	18
7	14
8	8
9	0

6.   See graph below.

7.   At points (2, 14) and (7, 14).

8. $y = 14$ $y = -x^2 + 9x$
      $14 = -x^2 + 9x$ so $x^2 - 9x + 14 = 0$ so $(x - 2)(x - 7) = 0$ and $x = 2, 7$ while $y = 14, 14$
      (Same answer as in question 7).

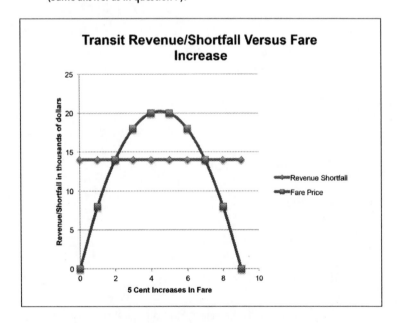

9.   Two fare increases, meaning 10 cents more per fare.

10.   Revenue peaks at 4.5 increases. $y = -x^2 + 9x$ so $y = -(4.5)2 + 9(4.5) = 20.25$ or $20,250.

Bitter – Answers

Opening question:

Governments likely have financial arrangements with the chocolate industry and benefit from those companies working within their borders.

Understanding using math:

1.a. Answers will vary.

1.b. 0.75

2.a. Answers will vary.

2.b. 0.43

3.a. Answers will vary.

3.b. 0.3333333

4.a. 3,000,000

4.b. 1,500,000

4.c. 0.5

4.d. $1,500,000 \times 0.5$

5. $6,000,000 \div 12,000,000,000 \times 100 = 0.05\%$

6. 1:30

7. $230 \times 1.5 = \$345$ Canadian

8. $90 \div 40 \times 100 = 225\%$

9.a. Direct trade partners engage in communication directly with each other and figure out what price is fair for the product. It is a response to fair trade practices that may exclude particular farmers or that may not provide sufficient remuneration for the product.

9.b. Approximately 4,540 km by road.

9.c. The boat and train route is a longer route than by road.

9.d Boat and train transport has lower carbon dioxide emissions (which cause global warming) than truck transport.

10.a. If the workweek is 40 hours, five batches of chocolate could be made.

10.b. $5 \times 52 = 260$ batches per year.

10.c. It's possible that they do it in order to reduce carbon dioxide emissions from multiple deliveries.

Lesson 24

Washed Up – Answers

Opening question:

Aid money that is funnelled through governments and institutions may not end up getting to the people who need it.

Understanding using math:

1. – 6. See map

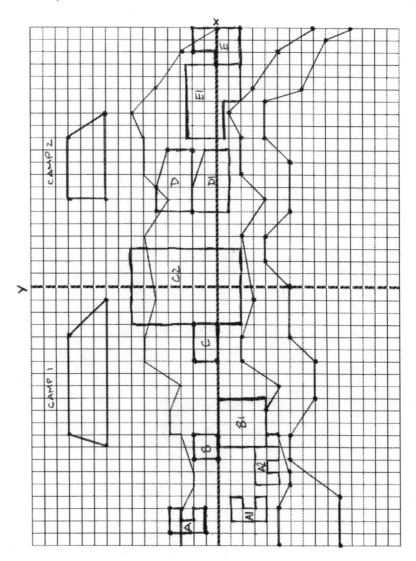

7. Refugee camp one: $(200 + 300) \div 2 \times 75 = 26{,}250 \, m^2$
Refugee camp two: $(125 + 175) \div 2 \times 75 = 11{,}250 \, m^2$

Camp one: $2{,}250 \div 26{,}250 = 0.09$ people per m^2
Camp two: $1{,}850 \div 11{,}250 = 0.16$ people per m^2 (more crowded)

8. $26{,}250 \, m^2 \div 30 \, m^2 /$ person $= 875$ people allowed (too crowded in camp one)
$11{,}250 \, m^2 \div 30 \, m^2 /$ person $= 375$ people allowed (too crowded in camp two)

9. $13{,}000{,}000{,}000$ seconds $\div 60$ seconds/ minute $\div 60$ minutes/ hour $\div 24$ hours / day $\div 365$ days / year $= 237{,}443$ years

Lesson 25

Under Threat – Answers

Opening question:

If you were trying not to fail, you might feel anxious or worried. If you were seeking success you might feel confident and motivated.

Understanding using math:

1.a. False.

1.b. True.

2.a. 60

2.b. 90

2.c. $(90 - 60) \div 11.54 = 2.6$

2.d. Large.

3. $96 \div 124 \times 100 = 77.4\%$

3.a. Yes.

3.b. Yes.

3.c. Yes.

4. The studies that would be reported by the media would be the ones where a sex difference was found.

5.a.

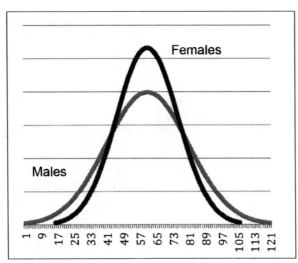

b. The mean values for each group are the same.

c. Yes.

d. Yes.

e. It would call into question the Male Variability Hypothesis, because you don't see it universally. It suggests that some systemic difference is leading to more variability in the Netherlands, Germany and Lithuania.

f. The difference in space between the bell curve for the boys at the upper end and the girls at the upper end would be 4.6 times less.

6. As we find fewer and fewer women at the higher levels of mathematics, there are fewer role models for people of the same sex.

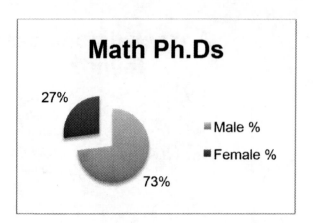

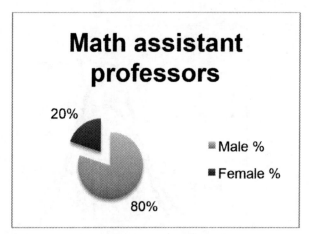

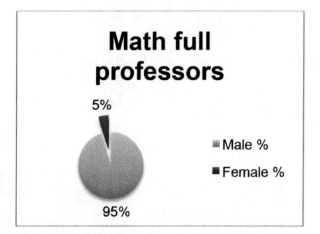

7.a. When the test takers are told that boys do better on this test, a clear difference in the results happened: the men did roughly five times better than the women. But when the test takers were *not* told that boys do better on the test, the achievement levels are almost the same.

7.b. Teachers and others administering tests should never make gender-based comparative statements. Even having to tick off a box indicating your sex can reinforce stereotype threat.

8.a.

Country	Females/Total[1]	%	Gender Gap Index[2]
Canada	13/120	10.8	18
USSR	15/120	12.5	45
United Kingdom	13/120	10.8	11
Romania	7/120	5.8	47
China	4/114	3.5	73
Japan	2/114	1.8	91
Iran	3/120	2.5	118
India	4/119	3.4	114
Israel	3/118	2.5	36
Korea	9/120	7.5	97
France	4/120	3.3	51
USA	5/120	4.2	31
Germany	8/120	6.7	7

8.b.   Very clearly, the greater the female participants, the lower the gender gap index is for the country that they come from.

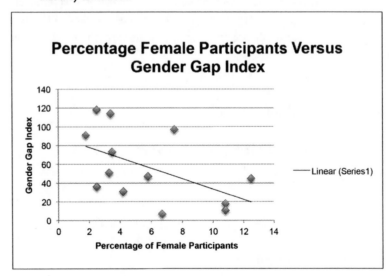

8.c.   See best fit line above.

8.d.

Saudi Arabia		0- 2%	124
Pakistan		0-2%	126
Sweden		15+%	1
Norway		15+%	2
Finland		15+%	3

9.a.   Negligible.

9.b.   Those are grades where girls outperformed boys on average (and in a negligible way).

1. Hyde, Janet and Jandet Mertz. Gender, Culture, and Mathematics Performance. www.pnas.org/cgi/doi/10.1073/pnas.0901265106
2. http://www3.weforum.org/docs/WEF_GenderGap_Report_2007.pdf

Lesson 26

Collapse – Answers

Opening question:

Discussion will vary.

Understanding using math:

3.   For example: $350,000 \times 0.0075 = \$2,625$

4.   For example: $350,000 \times 0.035 = \$12,250$

Homebuyers are willing to pay interest to a lending institution as the cost to borrow money, as most people cannot purchase a home outright. Lending institutions sometimes do not give loans to people if they feel the people will be unable to pay back the loan and if what they are purchasing could lose value, the lending institution might be left with nothing.

Round 2:

1.a. $1,000 or 10% profit.

1.b.   You have $1,000,000 (interest will be 1% or $10,000)

1.c.   100.

1.d.   You'll make $1,100,00, a profit of $100,000 or 10% (same as in part a).

1.e. $100,000.

1.f.   If you can use your money to borrow large amounts of money at low interest rates, you can use your money to create larger amounts of profit.

2.a.   So that they no longer have to worry about the risk of the mortgages defaulting.

2.b.   The investment banks.

3.   The greatest rate of return comes from risky mortgages because they are most likely to default, while the lower rate of return comes from the safe mortgages because they are least likely to default.

Round 3:

1. Investors will shift to CDOs rather than regular investments, in order to maximize profit.

2. They will reduce the standards for people applying for mortgages to encourage more people to get a mortgage.

3. The risk of the mortgage defaulting doesn't matter to the lender because they sell them to the banks.

4. Sub-prime loans are loans made to people who may not be able to repay the loan on schedule due to their financial situation.

Round 4:

2. The investment banker will take the house and try to sell it to recoup the investment.

3. As more houses go on the market, it drives the price of houses down. The houses are worth less, which means it is more difficult to sell them.

4. Investment banks will not be able to remain solvent — the banks begin to collapse.

Lesson 27

Where Can They Bee? – Answers

Opening question:

The precautionary principle is the idea that if a product has suspected or unknown risks, people should not be able to introduce it to the market.

Understanding using math:

1. $(20,000 + 60,000) \div 2 = 40,000$

2. $5,000,000 \times 40,000 = 200,000,000,000$ bees.

3. $100 \times 0.43 = 43$ pounds less.

4. The third row is demonstrating synergy because the total impact is more than the sum of the impact of the individual parts. If you are considering the interactive effects of hundreds of different chemicals, it would be very tricky to understand the inter-relationships between the chemicals because there would be so many.

5. $31 \div 22 \times 100 = 141\%$ which is a 41% increase.

6. From the winter of 2006 to the winter of 2012, the trend line is overall downwards, which means less colony loss, which is a good sign.

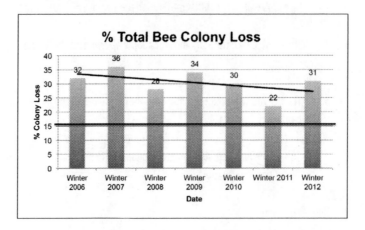

7. If you chart only the last two years, a different trend line appears. This isn't a significant amount of time to establish a trend, but it looks more ominous.

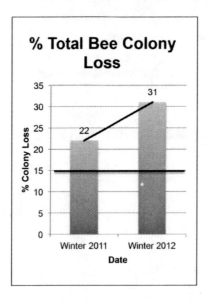

8. See the charts above for the 15% line.

9. Hive 2, and hive 5 is close.

10. With the possibility of the seven pesticides having a synergistic effect on the hive, you might have concerns about hive 3, 5, and 2.

11. $14,000,000,000 \div 60$ seconds/minute $\div 60$ minutes/hour $\div 24$ hours/day $\div 365$ days/year $= 444$ years.

Buffet – Answers

Opening question:

Answers will vary.

Understanding using math:

1.a. $370 \div 33 = 11.2$ times better, although transportation by boat takes longer.

1.b.   Distant food sources: $(9.42 \times 3,562 \times 160) \div 1,000,000 + (1.15 \times 6,016 \times 370) \div 1,000,000 = 7.93$

   Local food sources: $(9.42 \times 117 \times 160) \div 1,000,000 + (1.15 \times 142 \times 160) \div 1,000,000 = 0.2$

1.c. $7.93 \div 6 = 1.32$ per family member versus $0.2 \div 6 = 0.03$ per family member.

1.d. $7.93 \div 0.18 = 44.1$ green garbage bag equivalents for the distant food and $0.2 \div 0.18 = 1.1$ green garbage bag equivalents for the local food.

1.e.   All of the production of the food, which includes the burning of fuel for farm machinery, the emissions from the production of fertilizer and pesticides, and the fuel required to grow the feed that is fed to the animals.

1.f.   If local conditions are not as optimal as growing conditions in places further away, it may take more energy inputs to produce the same amount of food. Also, if you heat greenhouses during the off season it will create further carbon emissions.

1.g.   Canada is such a large country that there are many sources of food from the United States that are closer than moving food from one area of Canada to another.

2.a.

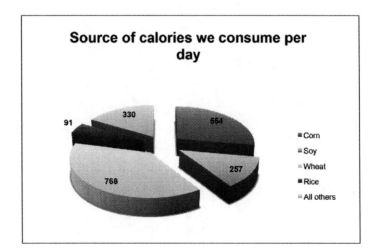

2.b.   Wheat $768 \div 2000 \times 100 = 38.4\%$

2.c.   A diversity of foods provides a diversity of nutrients.

3.   Answers will vary.

4.   Answers will depend on the length of the unit of measure.

5.   1000 grams $\div$ 150 grams $= 6.666$ $6.666 \times 2,300$ litres of water $= 15,333$ litres per kilogram
     The water used in the production of beef is not only the water that the cows drink, but also the water
     that goes into the production of the food that is being fed to the cows. That's not true with rice.

6.a.   Each level up on the food chain eats many of the organisms below it, and if the toxin collects in the
       fatty tissues, it builds over time.

6.b.

	Primary Producers	Primary Consumers	Secondary Consumers	Tertiary Consumers
Primary Producers	1	5.75	51.75	345
Primary Consumers		1	9.43	60
Secondary Consumers			1	6.66
Tertiary Consumers				1

6.c. This is an exponential pattern of growth

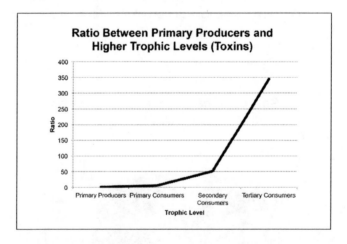

6.d.   The lower that you eat on the trophic levels, the less toxin that there is in the food.

7.a.   The general trend is an increase in spending on lobbying.

7.b.   Spending peaked in 2013 at roughly $150 million dollars.

7.c. $121,360,788 ÷ 1,151 lobbyists = $105,439 per lobbyist

7.d.

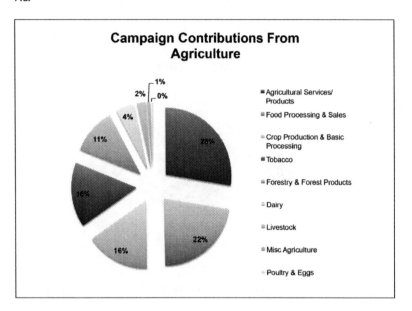

Lesson 29

Earthship – Answers

Opening question:

Answers will vary.

Understanding using math:

1.a. They must be facing the sun. In the northern hemisphere that would mean south.

1.b. It looks like the water is used for sinks, and then funnelled to plants, and then used for the toilet.

2.a. $274 \times 4 \times 365 = 400,040$ litres of water per year.

2.b. 400,040 litres $\times$ 0.001 cubic metres per litre = 400 cubic metres.
400 m³ ÷ 0.0537 m = 7,450 m² which means we use vast amount of water.

2.c. 274 L/day/person $\times$ 4 people $\times$ 7 days = 7,672 Litres / week.

$V = \pi r^2 h \quad V = \pi (1)^2(2) \quad V = 6.3 \, m^3 \quad 1 \, m^3 = 1000 \, L \, so \, 6.3 \times 1000 = 6,300 \, L$

The cistern wouldn't be able to hold the weekly water requirements for the family.

3. If you want to address the worst water use, you could flush the toilet less often or switch to a high efficiency toilet that only uses 6 L of water per flush (older toilets used 18 L!). Put a low flow showerhead on your shower and a 10 minute shower will use half the amount of water that a bath does.

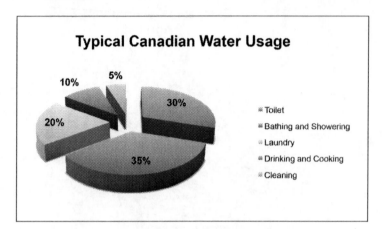

4.a. A quarter of a billion is the same as 250,000,000.

4.b. $V = \pi r^2 h$ $V = \pi (0.38)^2 (0.15) = 0.068$ m^3 per tire $\times$ 250,000,000 tires $= 17,011,223$ m^3

4.c Answers will vary.

4.d. 17,011,223 m3 $\times$ 0.75 $= 12,758417$ m^3

4.e. 1,000 hours total $\div$ 4 people $= 250$ hours
250 hours $\div$ 30 $= 8.3$ weeks

5.a. Answers will vary.

5.b. Answers will vary.

5.d. 90 degrees – latitude = window angle 90 – latitude = 58 so latitude = 32 degrees

6. d = 2r = 10 cm so 10 bottles will fit across the 1 metre width
d = 10 cm so 25 bottles will fit across the 2.5 metre height of the wall

7. $10 \times 25 \times 2 = 500$ bottles.

Bay of the Beaver – Answers

Opening question:

Seeing that the government was privileging non-Indigenous fishers may have contributed to the resistance to the treaty.

Understanding using math:

1. About 400 km² (It is the fifth largest reserve in Canada).

2. $400 \div 2{,}766 \times 100 = 14.5\%$

3. 100 acres = 40.5 hectares (1 acre= 0.4047 hectares)

4. $1{,}200 \div 5 = 240$ people

5.a. $\$10{,}000(1.03)^{215} = \$5{,}754{,}443$
    $\$2{,}700(1.03)^{215} = \$1{,}553{,}700$

5.b. $y = 1{,}553{,}700x + 5{,}754{,}443$ where $x =$ the number of years and $y =$ total compensation

6.a. Area of mainland: 328.5 km²
    Area of island: 9 km²

6.b. Shoreline: 65.1 km

6.c. The mouth of the river could provide increased opportunities for water mills, or docking or transport.

6.d. The convergence of the two rivers might be ideal for a water mill.

6.e. See map on the next page.

281

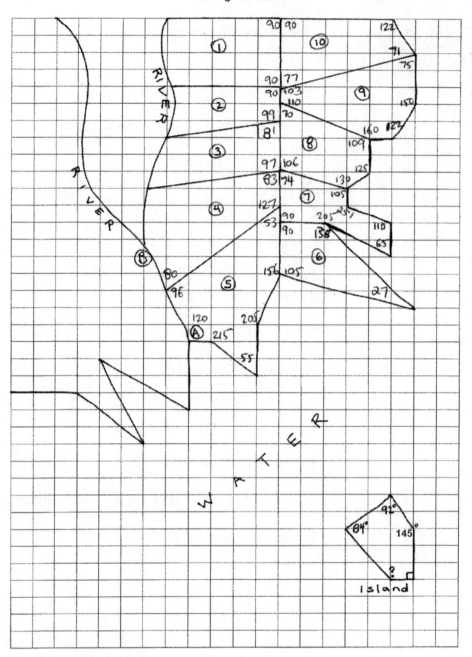

6.f. Shoreline allows easier access to the water for transportation and fishing

6.g. A pentagon has 540 total internal degrees. 540 − 90 − 145 − 92 − 84 = 129 degrees

Tough Call – Answers

Opening question:

Paul Mazur is a Wall Street banker, speaking on behalf of the wealthy. He is suggesting that the drive to consume ever more must be encouraged in people (in order to increase corporate profitability).

Understanding using math:

1. $35,160,000 \times 0.75 = 26,370,000$ phones

2. If you had the population for each country, you could determine the cell phones per capita, which would allow you to make comparisons between countries.

3. China: $1,227,360,000 \div 1,349,585,838 = 0.91$ phones/person
   Nigeria: $114,000,000 \div 165,200,000 = 0.69$ phones/person
   Canada: $26,543,780 \div 35,160,000 = 0.75$ phones/person

   Comparing the three countries, China has the most phones per person, followed by Canada and then Nigeria.

4. Answers will vary.

5. Answers will vary.

6.

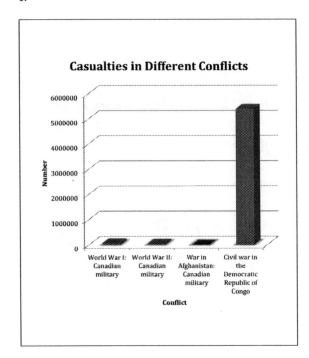

7. $1,200 \div 12,000 \times 100 = 10\%$

Some companies might not be reporting because of the potential negative publicity that it would create on their products, and the potential that customers might subsequently boycott products.

8. $73,000 \div 16,000 \times 100 = 456\%$

9.a. $y = 2x$ where $x =$ the weight of the plastic and $y =$ the weight of the oil to produce the plastic.

9.b.   26,543,780 phones $\times$ 0.065 kg $\times$ 2 kg oil/kg plastic $= 3,450,691$ kg oil.

10.a. $y = 75x$ where x is the number of tons of rare earth metals that are refined and y is the total cubic metres of wastewater produced.

10.b. $y = x$ where x is the number of tons of rare earth metals that are refined and y is the total tons of radioactive residue produced.

10.c. $y = 75(136,000) = 10,200,000$ cubic metres of wastewater
       $y = 136,000$ tons of radioactive residue

11. $2,370,000 \times 0.25 = 592,500$ tons were recycled out of the total.

12.a. Vulnerability to Supply Restriction, Supply Risk, Environmental Implications.

12.b. Copper, arsenic, selenium, silver, tellurium, and gold.

12.c. Gold.

12.d. Selenium.

Lesson 32
....

WTF? (What the Frack?) – Answers

Opening question:

Note the differences and discuss.

Understanding using math:

1.   Drawings will need metric:

Item	Dimensions – Imperial	Dimensions – Metric
Shale rock layer where natural gas is trapped	2 – 200 feet thick	0.6 m – 60.96 m
Distance of shale from surface	0 – 1 mile	1,609 m
Airborne contaminants from drilling will go this distance from your drawing	Up to 200 miles	
Natural gas well	5000 – 9000 feet, turn 90 degrees and continue for up to a mile	1,524 m – 2,743 m
Water table- drinking water source	400 feet	121.92 m

2.a. 4,600,000,000 or 4.6×10^9
      400,000,000 or 4.0×10^6

2.b.

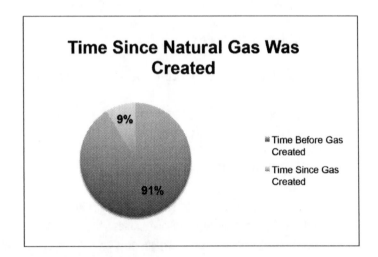

3.

Resource Used	Imperial	Metric
Water (average)	5 million gallons	18,927,059 litres
Chemicals (average)	25,000 gallons	94,635 litres
Diesel truck trips	1,000	1,000

Location	Number of wells	Water Required	Chemicals Required	Diesel truck trips
New York State	Planned: 77,000 wells	1,457,383,500,000 litres	7,286,895,000 litres	77,000,000
United States	450,000 wells	8,517,176,600,000 litres	42,585,750,000 litres	450,000,000
Your community...				

4.a. 98,000,000,000,000 or 9.8×10^{13}

4.b. $98,000,000,000,000 \times 0.9 = 88,200,000,000,000$

5.a. If more carbon dioxide was entering the atmosphere than methane it could be (and is) a greater contributor to global warming.

5.b. 5000 units of methane $\times$ 20 effect factor = 100,000
350,000 units of carbon dioxide $\times$ 1 effect factor = 350,000

6.a. \$4,750 per acre $\times$ 25 acres = \$118,750

6.b. $y = 4,750x$ where x is the amount of acres and y is the total compensation.

6.c. $y = 4,750x + 0.125v$ where x is the amount of acres, v is the total value of the gas from under the property and y is the total compensation.

6.d. $y = 4,750(30) + 0.15(120,000) = \$160,500$

6.e. If they become responsible for bringing in a fresh water supply it would cost money. If the value of the land dropped due to the fracking, future profit from the land might be less. If it was farmland and animals were affected by any damage to the water supply, it could be costly.

7.

Problem	Percentage	Actual number
Endocrine disrupters	40%	120
Suspected carcinogens	33%	100
Developmental toxicants	33%	100
Chemicals that can harm the brain and nervous system	More than 60%	More than 180

8.a. 18,927,059 litres $\times$ 0.5 = 9,463,530 litres

8.b. It sounds less dangerous than 'contaminated water'. Or 'toxic soup' for that matter.

9.a.   150 m × 100 m = 15,000 m²

9.b.   V = lwh   = 150 m × 100 m × 15 m = 225,000 m³

The chemical contaminants in the 'produced water' are made airborne, which then becomes a possible danger to humans breathing the air.

9.c.   Containment ponds have been known to rupture, which then releases 'produced water' into the local watershed.

Lesson 33

David and Goliath – Answers

Opening question:

It would be imperceptible. Try dividing the table with tape strips and it will become quickly apparent.

Understanding using math:

1. 1.0×10^{-9} to 1.0×10^{-7}

2.   Each rectangular prism should look something like:

3.   10 nm × 5 nm × 5 nm = 250 nm³

4.   The total volume remains the same.

5.   The total volume remains the same.

6.

	Particle #1	Particle #2	Particle #3
Total volume	250 nm³	250 nm³	250 nm³
Total surface area	250 nm³	300 nm³	1500 nm³

a.   The smaller the nanoparticle, the more surface area appears compared to the overall volume.

b.   Imagine having more sponge surface – it allows greater absorption of spills.

7.a.   300 ÷ 10 = 30 pounds

7.b.   13.6 kg

7.c.   4,900,000 ÷ 10 = 490,000 pounds which is 222,260 kilograms

7.d.   A full environmental assessment of the impact of that quantity of nanoparticles being introduced into the ecosystem should be required.

8.   y = the number of cheaper stations and x = the number of more expensive stations and y must be 2x to satisfy the funding.
1,680,000 = 35,000y + 50,000x
1,680,000 = 70,000x + 50,000x
1,680,000 = 120,000x so x = 14 and y = 28

9.   y = the number of cheaper stations and x = the number of more expensive stations and y must be 2x to satisfy the funding.
1,680,000 = 40,000y + 55,000x
1,680,000 = 80,000x + 55,000x
1,680,000 = 135,000x so x = 12.4 and y = 24.8

Recommendation: make 12 of the more expensive stations and 24 of the cheaper ones.

10.   There is some discussion about the unintended, unknown possible impacts of introducing nanoparticles into the environment. People must be cautious not to create more problems than they began with.

Trans[form] – Answers

Opening question:

One of the problems with a single stall all-gender washrooms is that it can 'spotlight' the person using it, which may be unsafe. If only certain students are allowed to use it, it prevents the entire community from having to consider the issue, or take responsibility for creating safer spaces.

Understanding using math:

1.   The internet has the advantage of reaching people in geographically distant places. It also allows a level of anonymity, which is important for safety.

2.   You could make the survey available in as many online places as possible, as well as promoting it in community hub sites where many people would see it.

3.   It's possible that people are becoming less fearful of identifying as LGBTQ. It's also possible that the survey participants understood that Egale Canada was a queer-positive organization that could be trusted with personal information.

4.   For example, a person of colour who is also trans identified will face different barriers than someone who is not a person of colour but who is trans identified. It will help to locate specific systemic oppressions so that they can be addressed.

5. $(54.8 + 41.6 + 68.2) \div 3 = 54.9$
    The mean hides the fact that more trans youth are experiencing verbal harassment. The data could be further disaggregated by including youth of colour, for example.

6.a.   The general pattern is that the number of days of school missed by students who are victimized is about double the number of days of school missed by those students who are not.

6.b.   Answers will vary.

6.c. $y = 2x$ where x is the number of days missed by students who are not victimized and y is the number of days missed by students who are victimized.

6.d.   Roughly 140.

6.e.   One possible consequence is a higher drop-out rate

6.f.   Answers will vary, but having a strong trans inclusion policy at the system level is important.

7.a.   The general pattern is that the number of days of school missed by students who are victimized is about three times the number of days of school missed by those students who are not.

7.b.   Answers will vary.

7.c. $y = 3x$ where x is the number of days missed by students who are not victimized and y is the number of days missed by students who are victimized.

7.d.   Roughly 300.

8.   Carefully collecting information about where homophobia and transphobia are occurring in the building would be valuable.

9.a.   Perhaps middle schools are reluctant to start GSAs for fear of the parental response.

9.b.   It's clear that there is a negative correlation between number of GSAs and the amount of physical harassment, so increasing GSAs would be a good start.

Lesson 35
....

Missing – Answers

Opening question:

The history of colonialism has deep and lasting intergenerational effects and cannot be separated from the racism and violence that First Nations communities face today.

Understanding using math:

1. $32,900,000 \times 0.043 = 1,414,700$

2.   Juxtaposition can highlight inequity, as in the chart below.

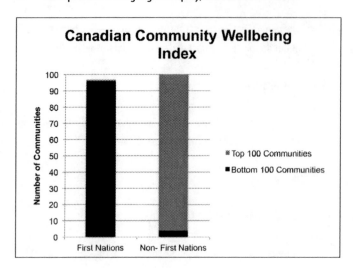

3.a.   Murder: $582 \times 0.67 = 390$
       Missing: $582 \times 0.2 = 116$
       Suspicious: $582 \times 0.04 = 23$
       Unknown: $582 \times 0.09 = 52$

3.b.

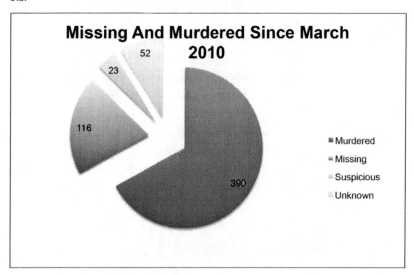

3.c.   Although perhaps it cannot be proven conclusively, the circumstances suggest that these people may have been murdered.

4. $1,017 \div (20,313 \times 0.32) \times 100 = 15.6\%$

       Aboriginal women make up 4.3 % of the female population but account for 15.6% of the murder victims.

5. Some Aboriginal people may be reluctant to share that information with the police, if they don't trust the police.

6.a.
Runaway:	$1 \div 164 \times 100 = 0.61\%$
Lost/wandered off:	$7 \div 164 \times 100 = 4.27\%$
Accident:	$27 \div 164 \times 100 = 16.46\%$
Foul play:	$27 \div 164 \times 100 = 16.46\%$
Unknown:	$37 \div 164 \times 100 = 22.56\%$

6.b. $164 \div 1{,}455 \times 100 = 11.27\%$ which is again higher than the percentage of Aboriginal women.

6.c. $35 \div 3 = 11.67$ non-suspicious and $64 \div 2 = 32$ suspicious/unknown

7. There may be good reason to focus on solutions within urban areas if the violence is 10 times more common in those areas.

8. Sex workers may be reluctant to report violence because they may not trust police.

9. $y = 3x$ where x is the amount of violent crime experienced by non-Aboriginal women and y is the amount of violent crime experienced by Aboriginal women.

$y = 7x$ where x is the homicide rate for non-Aboriginal women and y is the homicide rate for Aboriginal women.

Seeing these patterns should offend, disgust and enrage people, who may take action as a result.

10. There may be significant amounts of racism in Saskatchewan toward First Nations people.

11.a. Policing costs, court costs, health care costs, and social assistance.

11.b. $y = 7x$ where x is the amount of money spent on prevention, y is the savings, 7 is the slope and the y-intercept is 0. The variables are x and y.

When x is:	y is:
0	0
1	7
2	14
3	21
4	28
5	35

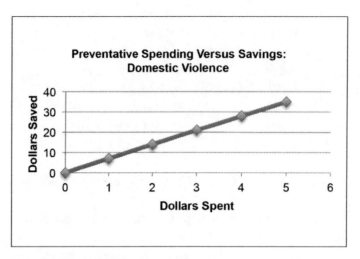

11.c. $y = 7x = 7 \times 20,000 = \$140,000$

11.d. $y = 7x = 7 \times 60,000 = \$420,000$

11.e. The slope is 4 times as steep

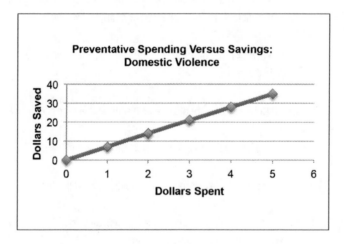

12. $y = 40,000x + 60,000$ where x is the number of years, y is the total cost, 40,000 is the slope and the y-intercept is 60,000. The variables are x and y.

When x is:	y is:
0	60,000
1	100,000
2	140,000
3	180,000
4	220,000
5	260,000

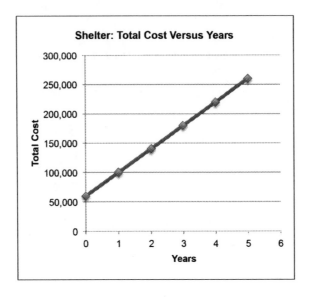

Shelter: Total Cost Versus Years

12.a. $1,500,000 = 40,000x + 60,000$
       $1,440,000 = 40,000x$
       $x = 36$ years

12.b. $3,500,000 = 40,000x + 60,000$
       $3,440,000 = 40,000x$
       $x = 86$ years

Up Front – Answers

Opening question:

Debt enslaves people financially: people need not be subjected to physical torture to be exploited financially.

Understanding using math:

Scenario A:

> $y = 25x$ where x is the number of weeks and y is the total cost of doing laundry.
> $800 = 25x$ so $x = 32$ weeks to break even.
> A community centre might purchase a washer and dryer for local residents to use for free.

Scenario B:

> $y = 25,000x$ where x is the number of years and y is the total cost of responding to climate disasters.
> Up front payments would reduce the yearly costs by $20,000.
> $230,000 = 20,000x$ so the upfront costs would be paid off in 11.5 years
> A country could reduce its ongoing costs by doing disaster preparedness.

Scenario C:

$y = 1,500x$ where x is the number of months and y is the total cost of rent.
Over 20 years, $x = 240$ months so $y = \$360,000$.
Purchasing the office up front will save \$160,000 over 20 years, so the NGO should purchase the office up front if they have the capital.

Scenario D:

$y = 100x$ where x is the number of months and y is the total cost.
$800 = 100x$ so the buying the laptop up front will mean that you will break even in 8 months.
If you have the capital, purchasing the laptop up front makes more financial sense. Activists could purchase and provide laptops.

Scenario E:

$y = 1.5x$ where x is the number of kilograms of food and y is the total cost of the food.
In bulk the equation is $y = 1.05x$ for a savings of 45 cents per kilogram.
$y = 0.45x$ so if $x = 5000$ kilograms $y = \$2,250$ dollars of saving.
Buying things in bulk is usually better, as long as the food can be used.

Scenario F:

$y = 5.95x$ where x is the number of months and y is the total cost.
If $x = 24$ months, $y = \$142.80$.
The two-year subscription saves you \$92.80. Activists could stock lending libraries and pay the two-year subscription to save the money.

Scenario G:

$y = 15x$ where x is the number of months and y is the total savings.
$250 = 15x$ so $x = 16.7$ months to break even on a one time retrofit.
Activist organizations could retrofit their buildings to reduce overall costs, creating more money for their mission.

Scenario H:

$y = 350x + 13,500$ where x is the number of months and y is the total price of the car
$26,000 = 350x + 13,500$.
$12,500 = 350x$ so after 35.7 months it makes more sense to buy the car outright.

Mouseprint – Answers

Opening question:

Answers will vary, but discuss cell phone contracts that turned out to be surprising.

Understanding using math:

1.a. $25,000 \times 40 = \$1,000,000$

1.b.   The value of money decreases over time due to inflation. Another way of saying this is that $1,000,000 today will not have the same purchasing power as $1,000,000 40 years from now.

1.c. $300,000 up front is better than $25,000. It probably isn't worth the million dollars spread out over 40 years — depending on how you calculate it, it's probably closer to $375,000.[1] Taking the money up front also ensures that you will be alive in order to claim your prize.

2.a.   Large purchases that you might make would mean that the 5% was significant: imagine buying $10,000 worth of furniture, or a vehicle. Five percent of supermarket or drugstore purchases amounts to much less money.

2.b.   You pay interest on your credit card balance. The more you have on the balance, the more you pay. The benefits from the 5% are far reduced by your interest payments.

2.c.   Let's say the credit card has an interest rate of 18%. $0.18 \div 12 = 0.015$ per month.
$0.015 \times \$6,500 = \$97.50$ interest per month.
$\$6,500 \times 0.01 = \$65$ so your interest payment on $6,500 is $32.50 more than your 1% bonus.

3.a. $\$468.58 \times 84 = \$39,360.72$

3.b.   Answers will vary.

4.a. $1000 \times 0.0011 = 1.1$

4.b. $1000 \times 0.0007 = 0.7$ (Not even one in a thousand people.)

5.a. $2,277 \div 300$ words/minute $= 7.59$ minutes

1. http://www.realityblurred.com/realitytv/2007/08/americas-got-talent-2-prize/

295

Tipping Point – Answers

Opening question:

Sixteen percent is still relatively unlikely- you might liken it to rolling a two on a six-sided die. Fifty-six percent is far more likely: it's like rolling a one, two or three on a six-sided die.

Understanding using math:

1.a. $8.06 \div 8.91 \times 100 = 90.5\%$

1.b.   850,000 km^2
Afghanistan (653,000 km^2), Austria (82,409 km^2) Chile (743,532 km^2), Finland (303,890 km^2), France (547,561 km^2), Greenland (410,450 km^2), Mozambique (786,380 km^2), Venezuela (882,050 km^2) are all examples.

1.c.   Linear. (9,900,000 km^2) – (7,700,000 km^2) $\div$ 35 years = 62,857 km^2 per year.

1.d.   If the trend continues to be linear, an ice-free Arctic would appear roughly in the year 2140.

2.   20.1 metres.

3.a.   The Titanic was 52,310 tons. 1,000,000,000 $\div$ 52,310 = 19,117 Titanics.

3.b. $1,400 \div 850 \times 100 = 165\%$ or 65% more than the atmospheric carbon.

3.c.   Plants use carbon dioxide in order to grow, which means that they pull carbon from the air.

4.

	Region 1	Region 2	Region 3	Region 4
Carbon absorbed	346	2,378	19,237	3,590
Carbon released	356	2,456	18,125	3,789
Sink or source?	Source	Source	Sink	Source

5.

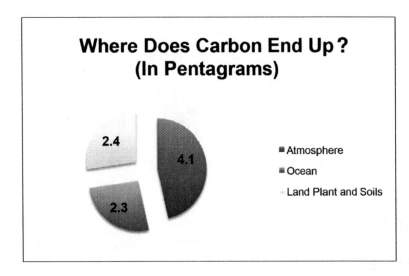

6.a. 7

6.b. Alkaline.

6.c. The scale on a graph that is plotted logarithmically is such that each tick mark is multiplied by a number to get the next tick mark.

6.d. pH works such that every value is 10 times greater (or less than) the next higher (or lower) value. In other words, a pH of 5 is ten times more acidic than a pH of 6 and 100 times more acidic than a pH of 7.

6.e. Urchins, coral, algae and some plankton use the calcium to make their external skeletal structure. If they were unable to do so, they put the ecosystem at risk because without them, the organisms that feed on them lose that food source.[1]

7.

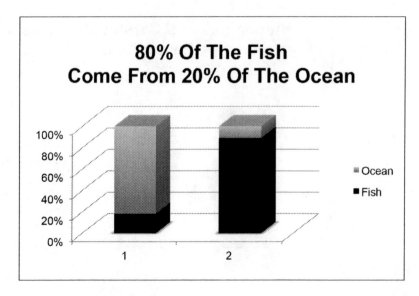

8. If you add up all of the individual impacts you have a sum of 13, and yet the total impact is listed as 25. This means that the interaction between impacts produces a total impact that is greater than the sum of its parts.

1. https://www.whoi.edu/main/news-releases/2005?tid=3622&cid1.a.=7388

Lesson 39

Get Out The Lead – Answers

Opening question:

Toys are imported from other countries that have lower standards (or no standards) for lead, and so may be painted with lead-based paints.

Understanding using math:

1.a. 1 part per 10 billion.

1.b. You'd be unable to see 1 piece in 10 billion.

1.c. It's extremely small.

2.a. $y = -1.2x + 32.4$ where x is the number of months and y is the total amount of lead in parts per billion.

2.b. The amount of lead is going down, so the slope is negative.

2.c. $10 = -1.2x + 32.4$
$1.2x = 22.4$
$x = 18.7$ months

2.d. $5 = -1.2x + 32.4$
$1.2x = 27.4$
$x = 22.8$ months
Infants who drink formula are possibly using tap water with the formula.

2.e. Answers will vary.

3.a. $y = 60x$ where x is the number of years and y is the total cost of the filters, in dollars.

3.b. $3000 = 60x$ so $x = 50$ years

3.c. As long as the filters are doing their job effectively, they make more economic sense.

4. $50,000 \times 0.13 = 6,500$

5.a. $y = 5000x$ where x is the number of years and y is the total number of homes fixed.

5.b. $40,000 = 5000x$ so x is nine years.

5.c. $y = 3500x$

5.d. $40,000 = 3500x$ so x is 11.4 years

6. 10 years $\times$ 12 months/year $= 120$ months
$\$3,000 \div 120 = \$25$
$y = -25x + 3000$ where x is the number of months and y is the remaining amount that you owe.

7. 10 ppb $\times$ 2000 $= 20,000$ parts per billion

8. Replacing the street lead pipes disrupted the connection between the street pipes and the pipes leading up to the house — creating more lead in the water.

The Cat in the Coalmine – Answers

Lesson 40

Opening question:

Environmental racism has to do with finding patterns between where minority groups (or groups with less power) live and where environmental toxins are put. At least two significant factors are involved: the inability of low income groups to move away from the danger, and the lack of political power to keep the toxins out or remove them once there.[1]

Understanding using math:

1. Levels of mercury in parts per billion (x represents number of years, y is mercury (Hg) levels in ppb)

Water levels		Zooplankton		Small fish		Large fish		Humans	
When x is...	y = 3x	When x is...	y = 4x	When x is...	y = 1/2x²	When x is...	y = x²	When x is...	y = 2x²
0	0	0	0	0	0	0	0	0	0
1	3	1	4	1	0.5	1	1	1	2
2	6	2	8	2	2	2	4	2	8
3	9	3	12	3	4.5	3	9	3	18
4	12	4	16	4	8	4	16	4	32
5	15	5	20	5	12.5	5	25	5	50
6	18	6	24	6	18	6	36	6	72
7	21	7	28	7	24.5	7	49	7	98
8	24	8	32	8	32	8	64	8	128
9	27	9	36	9	40.5	9	81	9	162
10	30	10	40	10	50	10	100	10	200

Chart, see below

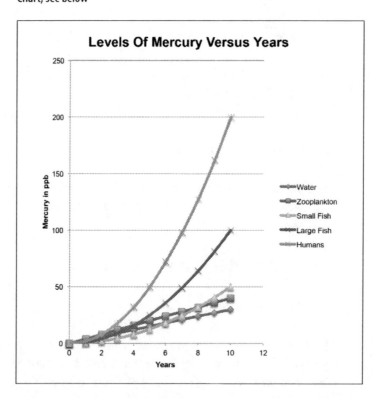

2. Exponential, because the organisms in each successive trophic level are eating many of the organisms in the trophic level below them, concentrating the lead at each step.

3. $y = \frac{1}{2}x^2$
   $18 = \frac{1}{2}x^2$
   $36 = x^2$ so $x = 6$

4. $y = x^2$
     $49 = x^2$ so $x = 7$

5. $y = 2x^2$
     $162 = 2x^2$
     $81 = x^2$ so $x = 9$

6.   Those with smaller bodies or weaker immune systems, or pregnant women, might be more susceptible to lead poisoning. Kids put more lead in their mouths (with hand-to-mouth behaviour). Lead build-up in bones can re-enter the blood during pregnancy, which then puts the fetus at risk. People who live in poverty and who do not have as much calcium in the body will absorb lead at greater rates.[2]

     $50 = 2x^2$
     $25 = x^2$ so $x = 5$

7.a. $y = 5{,}000x + 5{,}000$ where x is the number of years and y is the total compensation.

7.b. $y = 4{,}000x + 15{,}000$ where x is the number of years and y is the total costs.
       $5{,}000x + 5{,}000 = 4{,}000x + 15{,}000$
       $1{,}000x = 10{,}000$ so $x = 10$ years

8. $160 \times .578 = 92$ people

9.a.   The compensation is much less (roughly 10 times less).

9.b.   Monthly payments, because they stay the same while inflation continues, become less valuable, meaning that ongoing costs to deal with the poisoning will be harder to pay.

1. https://en.wikipedia.org/wiki/Environmental_racism
2. http://www.who.int/mediacentre/factsheets/fs379/en/

301

Lesson 41

Pillaging the Public Purse (P3s) – Answers

Opening question:

Empirical data is evidence that supports a decision and is created by observation and research. If governments are trying to justify the use of private corporations, they must assess the value of the risks that are being assumed by the corporations and compare them with the financial risks that public institutions would have to take to complete the same task. If the risks are assessed high, then it might justify offloading them, but the Auditor General of Ontario finds no evidence to support the risk assessment made by the government.

Understanding using math:

1.a.   Both the Conservative Party and the Liberal Party are friendly to the idea of privatizing public services. Infrastructure Ontario is composed of bankers, lawyers and "Bay Street types".[1]

1.b.   Upfront capital expenses (say, to build a hospital) make a government's spending large: if a government is trying to 'balance its books' (to look good for re-election,for example) it can use the P3 system and only have to log lease payments to the private interests doing the work. When those annual lease payments are spread over a repayment of (usually) 30 years, the spending is pushed into the future, long past the election date.[2]

1.c.   8,000,000,000 ÷ 60 s/min ÷ 60 min/hr ÷ 24 hr/day ÷ 365 days/year = 254 years, assuming it takes a second to say each number.

2.a.   500 staff × 40 hours/week × $8.82 savings/hour = $176,400 per week

2.b.   50 weeks × $176,400/ week = $8,820,000 per year

3. $732,000 × 0.78 = $570,960 which means both that the employer has to pay less and the employee has to pay more, or do without particular benefits that used to be covered.

4.a.   160 ÷ 493 × 100 = 32.5%

4.b.   The health care sector stands out in P3 projects in Ontario.

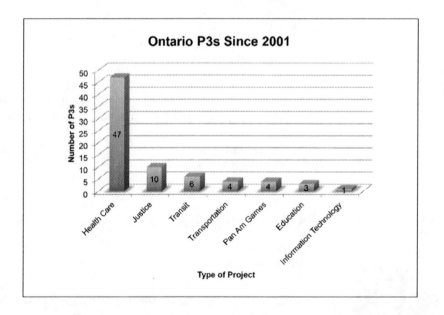

4.c.   The government would say that the value of the risks that they avoided ($18.6 billion) outweighed the added costs to the private sector (8 billion). The Auditor General's report maintained that if the government could manage and enforce cost and deadline overruns, public delivery would be far more cost effective. The Auditor General also noted that two risks included in the overall cost-comparison were 'inappropriate' and would have tipped the scales in favour of public delivery of 18 of 74 projects.[3]

5.a.　$y = 3/2x$ where x is the number of schools you build with a P3 model and y is the number of schools you could've built with the public sector.

5.b.　The coefficient is a fraction and the constant is zero.

5.c.　$y = 3/2x$　$x = 10$　　so $y = 15$

5.d.　$y = 3/2x$　$x = 20$　　so $y = 30$

5.e.　$y = 3/2x$　$x = 45$　　so $y = 67.5$

6.a.　$y = 7/5x$ where x is the number of hospitals you build with a P3 model and y is the number of hospitals you could've built with the public sector.

6.b.　The coefficient is a fraction and the constant is zero.

6.c.　7/5 is the slope and the y − intercept is zero.

6.d.　$y = 7/5x$　$x = 30$　　so $y = 42$

6.e.　$y = 7/5x$　$x = 40$　　so $y = 56$

7.　$\$75,000,000 \times 0.0382 = \$2,865,000$ interest paid annually by the municipal government.
$\$75,000,000 \times 0.062 = \$4,650,000$ interest paid annually by private business.
The difference is $\$1,785,000$.

8.　$\$400,000,000 \times 0.0382 = \$15,280,000$ interest paid annually by the municipal government.
$\$400,000,000 \times 0.062 = \$24,800,000$ interest paid annually by private business.
The difference is $\$9,520,000$.

9.　Public institutions have large amounts of money and are seen as a safe place to lend money to, so the interest that they pay is lower.

10.　Consider talking about local community centres that have added a user fee for the services that they provide.

1. http://www.who.int/mediacentre/factsheets/fs379/en/
2. http://opseu.org/blogs/peek-inside-world-privatization-and-p3s
3. https://books.google.ca/books?id=rfFTCgAAQBAJ&pg=PT50&lpg=PT50&dq=p3s+using+operating+leases+versus+capital+expenses+in+accounting&source=bl&ots=B3hD3NMs-v&sig=0Zcec_-I7YTfj-PJxvyBBH6ePKo&hl=en&sa=X&ved=0CDIQ6AEwA2oVChMI776r1LKxyAIVRj4-Ch3LlwAJ#v=onepage&q=p3s%20using%20operating%20leases%20versus%20capital%20expenses%20in%20accounting&f=false

Damned – Answers

Opening question:

Sometimes while trying to avoid one problem (coal-burning power plants, or the burning of fossil fuels to generate electricity) you create another, as described in the introduction.

Understanding using math:

1.

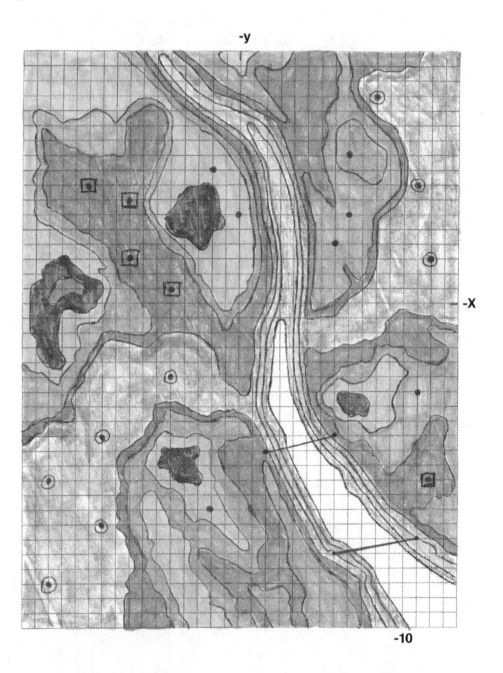

2. 60 feet above sea level at (-13, 1) and the surrounding area.

3. $(+60) - (-10) = 70$ feet

4. See contour map, last page.

5. See contour map, last page. Eight communities are put at risk.

6. Five more communities are put at risk.

7. 10 feet.

8. There are many possible answers, but one could be (13, -17) and (8, -17). The lower the dam is built means that the amount of water that will be behind the dam will be less, which will generate less power.

Pad-dling Upstream – Answers

Opening question:

If people are ashamed or embarrassed about menstrual blood, selling tampons and menstrual pads as a solution will be easier.

Understanding using math:

1. 365 days/year ÷ 28 days/cycle × 40 years × 20 menstrual pads a cycle × 0.25 per pad = $2,607

2. 365 days/year ÷ 28 days/cycle × 40 years × 20 menstrual pads a cycle × 0.30 per pad = $3,129

3.

Lifetime cost of disposable pads	Lifetime cost of tampons	Lifetime cost of reusable pads	Lifetime cost of menstrual cups
$2,607	$3,129	$1,170	$333 *6 yr avg.
		Pads: Resuables 2.2:1 Tampons: Reusables 2.7:1	Pads: Cups 7.8:1 Tampons: Cups 9.4:1

4. 20 cm × 8 cm × 0.5 cm = 80 cm³   80 cm³ × 20,000,000,000 = 1,600,000,000,000 cm³ which is the same as 1,600,000 m³
An Olympic swimming pool is 2,500 cubic metres, so the volume of discarded pads in one year is equivalent to 640 Olympic swimming pools.

5. 20,000 ÷ 4,000,000 × 100 = 0.5 %

6. 25 years.

Number of half lives	Kilograms of plastic
0	3000
1	1500
2	750
3	375
4	187.5
5	93.75
6	46.875
7	23.4375
8	11.71875
9	5.859375
10	2.9296875

7. Students should find up to date CEOs. Alex Gorsky, Alan Lafley and Thomas Falk were, at the time of publication, the CEOs, and all men.

8.a. $y = 120x$ where x is the number of reusable pads and y is the number of disposable pads that are saved.

8.b. $y = 120 \times 500 = 60,000$

8.c. $1,500,000 = 120x$ so $x = 12,500$

9.a. $y = 17,000x$ where x is the number of packages of 16 regular absorbency tampons and y is the pounds of pesticides diverted from waterways if those 16 regular absorbency tampons are replaced with organic cotton tampons.

9.b. $5,000,000 = 17,000x$ so $x = 294$ packages.

10.a. Acutely hazardous: 0.3 and moderately to highly hazardous: 0.6.

10.b. One chance in 10, or 0.1.

11.a. $\$519,976,963 \times 0.05 = \$25,998,848.15$.

11.b. The data looks exponential until after day 11.

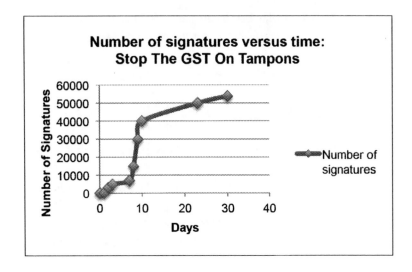

Number of signatures versus time: Stop The GST On Tampons

Lesson 44

Vice Grip – Answers

Opening question:

Answers will vary. For some people the highest priority is profit. Some investors may be ignorant of the impacts of their investments.

Lesson 45

The Drone of War – Answers

Opening question:

Notice some of the different ways that data can be conveyed. For example, the bar graph at the beginning of the lesson with the different categories, and the drone strike lines on the timeline.

Understanding using math:

1.a. Surgically precise seems like there are no fatalities besides the intended target. One calls to mind a surgeon acting with extreme accuracy.

1.b. $d = 2r$ so the blast diameter is 40 metres.

1.c. $A = \pi r^2$ $A = \pi (20)^2 = 1{,}257 \text{ m}^2$

1.e. $A = \pi r^2$ $A = \pi (30)^2 = 2{,}827 \text{ m}^2$

2.a. $39 \div 44 \times 100 = 88.6\%$

2.b.   If you only release those opposed (66%), one might assume that the others are in favour (34%). But if 3% are actually in favour, the remaining 31% are either indifferent, or unwilling to say.

3.a. $3 \div 85 \times 100 = 3.5\%$

3.b. $11,400,000,000 \div 6,600,000,000 = 1.727$ or a 73% increase.

3.c.   According to the IMF, 38 countries out of 187 have a GDP below $4.6 billion.

3.d.   According to the IMF, 60 countries out of 187 have a GDP below $11.4 billion.

4.a.   Partly it depends on the definition of each category. Partly it depends on the interests of the source (for example, the U.S. will want to minimize the number of civilian deaths).

4.b.   The United States keeps its fatality list classified.

4.c.   If civilian deaths are publicized, the U.S. opens itself to criticism and possible legal prosecution.

4.d.   Taliban sources might inflate the number of people killed, in order to discredit the United States.

4.e.   Injuries have devastating short and long term economic and social impacts.

5.a.

Total "militants" killed since 2008	High level "militants"	Mid to high level "militants"	Low level fighters
500	14	25	300

5.b. $49 \times 50 = 2,450$ drone-related deaths.

6.a. $20,240 (Canadian dollars).

6.b. $101.20 (Canadian dollars).

6.c.   Almost surely not.

7.a. $1,516 (Canadian dollars) is the per capita income, so if medical fees were $3,000 it would be extremely difficult to pay for health care.

7.b.   The emotional impact of surviving a traumatic event must be considered. The psychological impact on the family and the community and the high levels of anxiety and depression all are important.

Layers – Answers

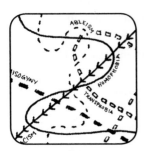

Opening question:

Answers will vary.

Understanding using math:

1. & 2.

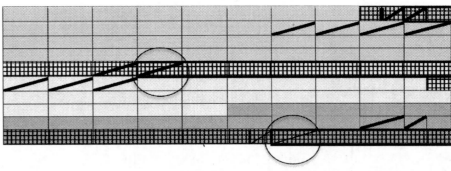

Legend

Ethnic group	
Poverty	
Depression	
LGBT	

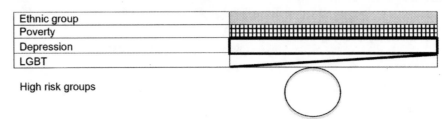

High risk groups

3. $40 \times 0.05 = 2$ for group A

4. $35 \times 0.3 = 10.5$ for group B

5. $25 \times 0.4 = 10$ for group C

6. 30% of a bigger number amounts to more than 40% of a smaller number. In this case, 10.5 is bigger than 10.

7. 50% of $2 = 1$

8. 66.6% of $10.5 = 7$

9. 40% of $10 = 4$

10. One in 8 amounts to 5%, with 20% in poverty (1), with 0.5 of those people having depression.

11. One in 7 amounts to 5%, with 40% in poverty (2), with one of those having depression.

12. One in 8 amounts to roughly 3%, with 50% in poverty (1.5), with 0.75 of those having depression.

13. Groups experiencing multiple barriers or oppressions are within the oval shapes in the diagram.

14. Ability, religion, sex, and language are other factors that could be considered.

15. The interaction between categories may create barriers that are greater than the sum of their individual impacts.

Lesson 47

The Threat of a Good Example – Answers

Opening question:

If one country is successful at fighting off colonial powers or resisting injustice broadly, it has the potential to cause a ripple effect, where other countries will be inspired to do the same.

Understanding using math:

1. $150,000,000 \times \$1.30 = \$195,000,000$

2. $\$195,000,000 \times (1.025)^{210} = \$34,837,448,815$

3. $1.50. Increasing a small number by a big percentage is still a small number.

4. 5,000 workers $\times$ \$1/hour $\times$ 10 hours/day $\times$ 5 days/week = \$250,000 wages/week

   Doubling the minimum wage would mean \$500,000 per week, or \$250,000 more a week and \$13,000,000 more per year. (Gilden had a net income of \$389 million in 2014.)[1]

5. Companies can threaten to move their factories to other countries with lower wages. The phenomenon is called the race to the bottom.

6.a. Ten.

6.b. If the public was made aware of the huge increase in murders, and particularly the international community, more pressure could be applied to the people who orchestrated the coup. When those numbers disappear, the conversation is more difficult because it is impossible to quantify the problem, and that's political.

7.a. $1,100 \times 0.80 = 880$

7.b. Probably between 30 and 40 people died, and the initial numbers were reported low to minimize the public reaction.

7.c. $110 \div 10 = 11$

7.d. Independent reports are more likely to avoid conflict of interest problems.

8. $72 \div 83 \times 100 = 86.7\%$

9. $\$20,000,000 \div \$39,000,000 \times 100 = 51\%$ drop. If aid money is helping to keep communities running and 51% of it disappears, support services can fall apart.

10.a. $\$2.80 \times 5,000,000,000 = \$14,000,000,000$

10.b. If the country owns the resource, they can put the revenue into running the country. If a foreign multinational company owns the resource, they can maximize profit and pull those assets out of the country.

1. http://www.marketwatch.com/investing/stock/gil/financials

Lesson 48

Sweet And Dangerous – Answers

Opening question:

Correlation means that two things are happening together, but one may or may not cause the other. Causation means that one of the factors causes the other. People should be cautious not to assume that correlations are causative relationships.

Understanding using math:

1. Answers will vary.

2. Answers will vary.

3.a. $25 \div 6.25 = 4$ grams per teaspoon, so a can of pop may be 10 teaspoons of sugar.

3.b. $40 \div 25 \times 100 = 160\%$

3.c. $2000 \div 355 = 5.63$ cans of pop in 2 litres, meaning 56.3 teaspoons of sugar!

3.d. $56.3 \div 6.25 \times 100 = 901\%$

4. $y = 40x$ where x is the number of cans of pop and y is the total sugar intake in grams.
125 grams is 500% of the daily recommended intake, so $125 \div 40 = 3.1$ cans.

5. $y = 10x + 36$ where x is the number of cans of pop and y is the total grams of sugar consumed. $100 = 10x + 36$ so $64 = 10x$ and x is 6.4 cans of pop.

6.a. $36 \div 4 = 9$ teaspoons of sugar in a glass of juice.

6.b. $36 \div 25 \times 100 = 144\%$

6.c.   An apple has fibre in it that slows down the release of the sugar into your bloodstream.

7.

Chocolate Bar	Grams of sugar	Percentage of daily WHO guideline
Hershey's Milk Chocolate	31	124%
Kit Kat	22	88%
Reese's Peanut Butter Cups	25	100%
Snickers	30	120%
3 Musketeers	40	160%
Milky Way	35	140%
Skittles Original Fruit	47	188%
M & M's Milk Chocolate	31	124%

8. $0.75 \times 38{,}000{,}000 = 28{,}500{,}000$
These diseases are cardiovascular diseases, respiratory diseases, diabetes and cancers and lower income countries "generally have lower capacity for the prevention and control of non-communicable diseases". Without universal health care and insurance, treatment may not be as accessible as in wealthier countries.

9. $0.82 \times 38{,}000{,}000 = 31{,}160{,}000$

10.   Cavities that cannot be treated for financial reasons can cause extreme pain. There may be low (or no) fluoride in the water, and people may not have good access to health care services.

Lesson 49

Unplug – Answers

Opening question:

Students might share their experience with what is called nomophobia (no-mobile-phone-phobia). How does their mobile device, if they have one, make their life easier? How does it limit people?

Understanding using math:

1.   The people are using more than one screen at the same time.

2.   The median number is the middle number, meaning that there were participants who sent out more and less than lower and higher than 60 texts a day.

3. The mean can be thrown off by outliers, so if, for example, there were some people who had no texts, it would bring the mean down in a way that might misrepresent the whole group.

4. $4 \times 3 \times 5 = 60$ substrata

5. Finding enough people to fill the different categories gets more and more difficult.

6. $y = 7.63x$ where x is the number of days and y is the total media exposure.
    For one week: $y = 7.63 \times 7 = 53.41$ hours
    For one year: $y = 7.63 \times 365 = 2,785$ hours
    Between the ages of 8 and 18: $y = 7.63 \times 4745 = 36,204$ hours

7. $73 \div 26 \times 100 = 281\%$ increase.

8. Answers will vary.

9. Answers may vary but could take into account the intersectional barriers that limit marginalized groups from taking part in other activities.

10. Intersectionality.

Lesson 50

Paying for It – Answers

Opening question:

If you look statistically at the work that women tend to do compared to men, a growing aging population will increase the need for caregiving and will therefore impact women to a greater degree.

Understanding using math:

Country		Minutes per day of unpaid work	Women's minutes as a percentage of men's minutes	Minutes per day of paid work	Women's minutes as a percentage of men's minutes
Canada	Men	159.6		341.4	
	Women	253.6	159	267	78
Japan	Men	61.9		471.5	
	Women	299.3	484	206.4	44
Turkey	Men	11.64		360.3	
	Women	376.7	3236	123.7	34
Sweden	Men	154		321.9	
	Women	206.5	134	268.7	83
Finland	Men	159		249	
	Women	232	146	210	84
OECD Avg	Men	137.6		328.5	
	Women	271.7	197	215.3	66
India	Men	51.8		390.6	
	Women	351.9	679	184.7	47

1.b. Turkey, with women's minutes 3236% of men's minutes. There may be several suggestions about the reasons for the discrepancy, but one might be the societal and cultural construction of gender roles.

1.c. Sweden is the country in which unpaid work is done more equally between men and women. Again, the construction of gender roles may play a large part in the duties performed by men and women.

1.d. In Turkey, women's minutes per day of paid work is 34% of men's paid work minutes. Finland has the closest match, at 84%.

1.e. There will be various answers, but they could include the question of what types of work and how much men and women are paid.

2. Occupational segregation is where women and men find themselves in different job fields (due to gender-based norms) and are then paid differentially. Vertical segregation is where men are found in the higher and better paying positions within occupations.[1]

3. In any given year, white women would have to work an additional 26.5% of the year (a full year of 52 weeks would therefore amount to an additional 13.78 weeks, or more than 3 months). Women of colour would work an additional 32% of the year, or 16.64 weeks.

4.a. Notice that some country's policies around the length of maternity have not changed in the last 25 years (Canada and Japan, for example) while some have changed significantly (Sweden). Notice that the United Kingdom provides significantly more maternity leave than the OECD countries that are listed and more than double the OECD average.

4.b.   Both Japan and Turkey have the lowest life satisfaction ratings in the list but Sweden has a high life satisfaction rating with a lower number of weeks of maternity leave. Other factors must contribute to the lower life satisfaction rating.

5.a.   Notice that there are countries where there is not paid leave for fathers (for example, Canada and Turkey). Notice also that the amount of paid leave is significantly less than the maternity leave hours and that Japan's hours have changed drastically in this timespan: there are more paid weeks for fathers in Japan than mothers.

5.b.   Answers will vary.

6.a.   If x represents the amount of unpaid work performed by men and y represents the amount of unpaid work performed by women, then the algebraic equation is $y = 3x$.

       If x represents the amount of paid work performed by men and y represents the amount of paid work performed by women, then the algebraic equation is $y = 2x$.

6.b. $y = 3x$ $15,600 = 3x$ $15,600 \div 3 = 5,200$ hours

6.c.   There are many benefits to paid work, including economic self-sufficiency, connection with a broader social network, increasing skills and confidence.

7.   Answers will vary.

8.a.   From the OECD countries, Hungary has the lowest rating at 5.3, but only 3.76% of the population works more than 50 hours a week.

8.b.   Both Norway and Switzerland have life satisfaction ratings of 7.6 and have 3.05 and 6.34% respectfully of their population working more than 50 hours a week.

8.c.   The correlation coefficient is -0.277. A negative value means that when the data point from one set is high, the other is low and vice versa. The value does not indicate whether the one variable causes the other variable, only that they are occurring together. Generally any value between -0.1 and -0.3 is considered a weak correlation (-0.3 to -0.5 is considered moderate and -0.5 to -1.0 is considered strong).

1. http://women.govt.nz/work-skills/income/gender-pay-gap

315

ABOUT THE AUTHOR

David Stocker lives with his co-conspirator Rogue, and their three kids Jazz, Kio and Storm. He has been a teacher for 17 years at City View Alternative School in downtown Toronto. Its mission is to deliver a social justice curriculum with a focus on activism to students in Grade 7-8. His first book, **Maththatmatters: A teacher resource linking math and social justice** was a best-seller and winner of the Elementary Teachers' Federation of Ontario Anti-Bias Development Award.

ABOUT THE ILLUSTRATOR

Minnow Holtz-Carriere is a student and artist from Toronto, interested in exploring politics and social justice through media analysis and art. She likes coffee, comic books, and rainy days. You can reach her at minnowhc@gmail.com.

Comments, suggestions and updates to the author welcome:
davidstocker85@hotmail.com